Writing and constructing the self
in Great Britain in the long eighteenth century

Manchester University Press

XVII-XVIII

SEVENTEENTH- AND EIGHTEENTH-CENTURY STUDIES

General Editor

Anne Dunan-Page

Seventeenth- and Eighteenth-Century Studies is a collection of the Société d'Études Anglo-Américaines des XVIIe et XVIIIe siècles promoting interdisciplinary work on the period *c.*1603–1815, covering all aspects of the literature, culture and history of the British Isles, colonial and post-colonial America, and other British colonies. The series welcomes academic monographs, as well as collective volumes of essays, that combine theoretical and methodological approaches from more than one discipline to further our understanding of the period and geographical areas.

Previously published

Bellies, bowels and entrails in the eighteenth century
Edited by Rebecca Anne Barr, Sylvie Kleiman-Lafon and Sophie Vasset

Radical voices, radical ways: Articulating and disseminating radicalism in seventeenth- and eighteenth-century Britain
Edited by Laurent Curelly and Nigel Smith

Frontiers of servitude: Slavery in narratives of the early French Atlantic
Michael Harrigan

The challenge of the sublime: From Burke's Philosophical Enquiry *to British Romantic art*
Hélène Ibata

English Benedictine nuns in exile in the seventeenth century: Living spirituality
Laurence Lux-Sterritt

Writing and constructing the self in Great Britain in the long eighteenth century

edited by
John Baker, Marion Leclair and Allan Ingram

Manchester University Press

Copyright © Manchester University Press 2019

While copyright in the volume as a whole is vested in Manchester University Press, copyright in individual chapters belongs to their respective authors, and no chapter may be reproduced wholly or in part without the express permission in writing of both author and publisher.

Published by Manchester University Press
Altrincham Street, Manchester M1 7JA

www.manchesteruniversitypress.co.uk

British Library Cataloguing-in-Publication Data
A catalogue record for this book is available from the British Library

ISBN 978 1526 12336 7 hardback

First published 2019

The publisher has no responsibility for the persistence or accuracy of URLs for any external or third-party internet websites referred to in this book, and does not guarantee that any content on such websites is, or will remain, accurate or appropriate.

Typeset
by Toppan Best-set Premedia Limited
Printed in Great Britain
by TJ International Ltd, Padstow

Contents

List of contributors   *page* vii
Acknowledgements   xii

Introduction: The written self – *John Baker and Marion Leclair*   1

PART I Early modern selves and the Reason v. Passion debate

1. Anne Killigrew: a spiritual wit – *Laura Alexander*   27
2. Charitable though passionate creature: the portrait of Man in late seventeenth-century sermons – *Regina Maria Dal Santo*   44
3. Self-love in Mandeville and Hutcheson – *Jeffrey Hopes*   60
4. Fashioning fictional selves from French sources: Eliza Haywood's *Love in Excess* – *Orla Smyth*   73
5. The death of Cordelia and the economics of preference in eighteenth-century moral psychology – *William Flesch*   95

PART II Self-exploration in the Age of Reason: division and continuity

6. 'Chaos dark and deep': grotesque selves and self-fashioning in Pope's *Dunciad* – *Clark Lawlor*   117

7	In two minds: Johnson, Boswell and representations of the self – *Allan Ingram*	135
8	'The place where my present hopes began to dawn': space, limitation and the perception of female selfhood in Samuel Richardson's *Pamela* – *Barbara Puschmann-Nalenz*	151
9	The discursive construction of the self in Shaftesbury and Sterne: *Tristram Shandy* and the quest for identity – *Gioiella Bruni Roccia*	170

PART III Romantic wanderings: the self in search of (its) place

10	The anxiety of the self and the exile of the soul in Blake and Wordsworth – *Laura Quinney*	191
11	Transgressing the boundaries of reason: Burke's poetic (Miltonic) reading of the sublime – *Eva Antal*	210
12	Self and community in radical defence in the French revolutionary era: the example of *Oppression!!! The Appeal of Captain Perry to the People of England* (1795) – *Rachel Rogers*	228

Bibliography	248
Index	263

Contributors

Laura Alexander (formerly Linker) is Associate Professor of English at High Point University, North Carolina, and the author of two books: *Dangerous Women, Libertine Epicures, and the Rise of Sensibility, 1670–1730* (2011) and *Lucretian Thought in Late Stuart England: Debates about the Nature of the Soul* (2013).

Eva Antal is a Professor of English Literature and Philosophy at Eszterhazy Karoly University, Eger, Hungary. Her Ph.D. dissertation in 2001 was on the theories and conceptions of irony. Since then she has been teaching eighteenth- and nineteenth-century British literature, contemporary literary theory and aesthetics. She published her book on irony in Hungarian in 2007, and in 2008 the English version entitled *Beyond Rhetoric (Rhetorical Figures of Reading)* was published. In 2010 she was a Visiting Grant Scholar at NIAS (the Institute of the Royal Netherlands Academy of Arts and Sciences), subsequently a Professor in Philosophy, and in 2013 she was appointed as the Vice Dean of the Faculty of the Humanities at Eszterhazy Karoly University.

John Baker is a Senior Lecturer in English in the Languages Department, University Paris 1 Panthéon-Sorbonne. He has published articles and chapters on various aspects of eighteenth-century poetry, on themes such as the night, originality, theodicy and questions related to translation and reception. He contributed to the co-authored volume *Melancholy Experience in Literature of the Long Eighteenth Century* (2011). At present he is working on the notion and identity of the 'philosophical poem', its history and development, with particular reference to the early and middle decades of the eighteenth century.

Gioiella Bruni Roccia is Associate Professor of English Literature at LUMSA University (Rome). Her major research interests lie in the interrelations among narrative, scientific and philosophical discourse during the long eighteenth century. Her publications in this field include, besides numerous articles on the most important novelists of the period, the translation and critical edition of Shaftesbury's *Sensus Communis: An Essay on the Freedom of Wit and Humour* (2006) and a monograph on John Locke, *Locke e la costruzione del lettore moderno: Sulle soglie del 'Saggio sull'intelletto umano'* (2013). She has also devoted her critical attention to authors and works that marked a turning-point in English literary history, such as the first generation of Romantic poets and the experimental fiction of the major modernist writers.

Regina Maria Dal Santo is an independent researcher cooperating with University Ca' Foscari of Venice. Her 2014 Ph.D. dissertation was on John Tillotson and happiness. She researches on sermon writing in the long eighteenth century, in particular the works of John Tillotson and Laurence Sterne. She published the articles 'Sterne, Tillotson and Human Happiness' in *The Shandean*, 25 (2014) and 'John Tillotson, Self-love and the Teleology of Happiness' in *English Literature*, 2.1 (2015).

William Flesch, Professor of English and Comparative Literature, Brandeis University, Massachusetts is the author of *Comeuppance: Costly Signaling, Altruistic Punishment, and other Biological Components of Fiction* (2008). He teaches seventeenth- and eighteenth-century English literature at Brandeis. Other publications include *The Facts on File Companion to British Poetry: 19th Century* (2009) and *Generosity and the Limits of Authority: Shakespeare, Herbert, Milton* (1992) as well as articles in *Critical Inquiry, Studies in Romanticism* and *English Literary History*.

LIST OF CONTRIBUTORS

Jeffrey Hopes is Professor of English at the University of Orléans and a member of the research group POLEN (POuvoirs, LEttres, Normes) at the University of Orléans, France. He publishes on eighteenth-century literature and cultural history with a particular emphasis on the theatre. He is the author of a book in French, *'Gulliver's Travels', Jonathan Swift* (2001) and has co-edited *Discours critique sur le roman 1650–1850* with Orla Smyth (2010) and *Théâtre et nation* with Hélène Lecossois (2011).

Allan Ingram is Emeritus Professor of English at the University of Northumbria at Newcastle. He has published books on James Boswell, on Swift and Pope, and on eighteenth-century insanity and its representation (one in collaboration with Michelle Faubert), as well as edited collections of primary material on the relations between insanity and medicine in the period. He edited also *Gulliver's Travels* (2012). Between 2006 and 2009 he was Director of a Leverhulme Trust project, 'Before Depression, 1660–1800', as part of which he was co-general editor (with Leigh Wetherall-Dickson) of a four-volume collection, *Depression and Melancholy, 1660–1800* (2012) and co-author of *Melancholy Experience in Literature of the Long Eighteenth Century* (2011). He was Co-Director of a second Leverhulme Trust project, 'Fashionable Diseases: Medicine, Literature and Culture, 1660–1830' and is currently working on relations between Swift, Pope and the medical profession.

Clark Lawlor is Professor of Eighteenth-Century English Literature at the University of Northumbria and Principal Investigator of 'Fashionable Diseases: Medicine, Literature and Culture, ca. 1660–1832', a three-year project funded by the Leverhulme Trust. He has tended to research representations of disease in literature in recent years, and has published the monographs *Consumption and Literature: The Making of the Romantic Disease* (2006) and *From Melancholia to Prozac: A History of Depression* (2012).

Marion Leclair is a doctoral student at University Sorbonne Nouvelle – Paris 3. She is finishing a Ph.D. under the supervision of Isabelle Bour on the radical novel in England (1780–1805) and has published several articles on William Godwin and other 'Jacobin' novelists of the 1790s.

LIST OF CONTRIBUTORS

Barbara Puschmann-Nalenz taught English and American Literature as a Senior Lecturer in the English Department at Ruhr-Universität Bochum until 2011. She recently co-edited *Portraits of the Artist as a Young Thing in British, Irish and Canadian Fiction after 1945* (2012) with Anette Pankratz, and *Narrating Loss: Representations of Mourning, Nostalgia and Melancholia in Contemporary Anglophone Fictions* (2014) with Brigitte Glaser. A series of her articles on 'space and place' has appeared in the annual *Symbolism* between 2005 and 2014. She is co-author of the monograph *The Orphan in Fiction and Comics since the 19th Century* with Marion Gymnich, Gerold Sedlmayr and Dirk Vanderbeke (2018).

Laura Quinney teaches English and Comparative Literature at Brandeis University, Massachusetts. She is the author of *Literary Power and the Criteria of Truth* (1995), *The Poetics of Disappointment: Wordsworth to Ashberry* (1999) and *William Blake on Self and Soul* (2009). She is currently working on the theme of existential alienation.

Rachel Rogers is a Lecturer at the University of Toulouse Jean Jaurès. Her Ph.D. research on the British radical community in 1790s Paris explored the associational culture of British residents in the French capital while also addressing their contribution to the political debates taking place in France and their transcription of history as eyewitness observers. She co-organised an international symposium on the radical Thomas Spence in Toulouse in 2014 and the resulting papers were published in 2016 as 'Thomas Spence and his Legacy: Bicentennial Perspectives', *Miranda*, 13 (2016). She has recently published an article, 'The Society of the Friends of the Rights of Man, 1792–94: British and Irish Radical Conjunctions in Republican Paris' in *La Révolution française*, 11 (2016).

Orla Smyth is a Senior Lecturer at the University of Le Havre where she teaches courses on English and French eighteenth-century literature, early modern British political thought and literary theory. Her research focuses on the interstices between fictional representation and the surrounding field of discourse in the early modern period. She has published several articles on the eighteenth-century novel including 'Eliza Haywood and the Languages of the Eighteenth-Century Novel', *Modernité du XVIIIe siècle, Hommage à Alain*

Bony, XVII–XVIII (2013) and 'The Critique and Rise of the Early Modern Novel in England, 1660–1720', in *Discours Critique sur le Roman*, 1670–1850 (2010), a volume she co-edited with Jeffrey Hopes. She is currently preparing a monograph on the early history of the novel in France and Britain.

Acknowledgements

Collective volumes of this kind, associating researchers from far afield, even (or perhaps especially) if the theme is the 'self', are necessarily a mutual and shared undertaking. This particular book started out as an international one-day conference at the Institut du Monde Anglophone (Université Sorbonne Nouvelle – Paris 3) that was held in Paris on 10 December 2013. A call for further contributions followed to broaden the scope of the papers delivered at the conference. We would like to thank warmly all the contributors, both conference speakers and chapter authors, extending thanks also to John Bender who was the keynote speaker at the conference. Our gratitude also goes to Anne Dunan-Page who, as General Editor of this series, has provided valuable help and guidance, steering the volume through its early stages. Thanks also to the Société d'Études Anglo-Américaines des XVIIe et XVIIIe siècles (SEAA) for its support, and to the Languages Department of the Université Paris 1 Panthéon-Sorbonne. Isabelle Bour, head of the CREA XVIII (Research Centre for English Eighteenth-Century Studies), which organised the conference, has actively encouraged and supported the project throughout. CREA XVIII is itself part of the PRISMES research group at the Université Sorbonne Nouvelle – Paris 3, and our thanks go also to Line Cottegnies and Alexandra Poulain (past and present Directors), for their moral and financial support and backing for the conference itself and the publication of the present volume. We extend our thanks to the anonymous readers who provided insightful, constructive and critical feedback at various stages and to the painstaking and precious work of the copyeditor. Lastly, and last is certainly in no way least, our gratitude goes – as Manchester University Press is itself a collective enterprise – to everyone involved in the production of this volume in Manchester for their always prompt, helpful and friendly advice, work and patience all along the way.

Introduction

The written self

John Baker and Marion Leclair

That our modern world is obsessed with selves is self-evident. From Margaret Thatcher's claim in 1987 that 'there is no such thing as society' but only 'individual men and women' (and their families), to social network profiles replete with selfies, and the literary vogue of self-fiction (*autofiction*),[1] the individual subject seems to be the very core of economic orthodoxy and production, political institutions, social relations and artistic creation alike in this our neoliberal age. Yet even a cursory look suggests that these multiple modern selves imply very different understandings of what the individual is and means, as well as very different ways of exploring and expressing individual subjectivity.

Against (neo-)liberalism's promotion of the autonomous economic and political subject, too often at the expense of social justice, resistance movements have sought to combine (with more or less success) a commitment to individual freedom with an attempt at collective organisation,[2] or tried to do away altogether with the idea of *self* understood as bourgeois construct.[3] Social networks allow at the same time a public amplification and propagation of the self and, by recording its multifarious incarnations, arguably provide the very continuity which John Locke (1632–1704) thought essential to the sense of personal identity; while selfies, pictures of oneself taken by oneself which, more often than not, are actually group photographs, and certainly meant for public use and large-scale sharing, are both narcissistic self-contemplation and a means to relate to other, connected, selves. As to self-fiction, which turns private testimony into public narrative, one can see it as a careful exploration of individual subjectivity and a recognition of the individual's entrapment within himself or herself, the impossibility of a collective narrative.

Interestingly, this versatility of the self, hovering between individualism and collectivity, fragmentation and continuity, isolation and connection, is already quite manifest in the English literature of the long eighteenth century. The coincidence is unsurprising, since many of the ideas and institutions which developed in the late seventeenth century and contributed to the inflation of the self still hold good today: the rise, as the two revolutions of the seventeenth century helped to decrease state restrictions on freedom of enterprise and private property, of an economic doctrine (liberalism) committed to the defence of individual responsibility and ownership, of which Locke and, later, Adam Smith, were prominent theorists;[4] the political shift from absolute monarchy to a representative government pledged to the protection of individual rights; the correlated development of an ideology of 'affective individualism' and 'self-awareness' championed by the urban, especially Protestant, commercial and professional middle classes;[5] and the growth of a consumer society and market for cultural goods, which made both the practice and consumption of culture available to a greater number of people.[6]

Even allowing for the researcher's propensity to approach the past through the prism of his or her own present, eighteenth-century representations of the self are strikingly similar to our own. The attempt of Latitudinarian theologians and moral sense philosophers at vindicating the self by turning 'self-love' into a prompt to Christian charity and general benevolence; the playful exhibition or painful exploration of self-fragmentation through Augustan satire and diaries; the search through fiction for a symbolic solution to the problematic experience of inner division and discontinuity; the twin gestures, as the American and French revolutions confronted British selves with the spectacle of collective action, of Romantic retreat into nature and self, and radical effort at conjuring up a nationwide political community through public speaking and the popular press – all these are evidence of an eighteenth-century self-awareness which this volume proposes to investigate.

THE WRITTEN SELF

It is generally agreed by commentators that, as initiator of the debate on the nature of the self that ran through the century, pride of place should go to John Locke. It was he who first focused on and anatomised the theme of what he was to call 'personal identity' in *An Essay Concerning Human Understanding* first published in 1689, to which the chapter 'Of Identity and Diversity' was added in the 1694 second edition.[7] To put it another way, it was Locke who put the (philosophical) cat among the (religious) pigeons (although the *Essay* is, at first sight, and above all to modern eyes, a rather discreet and inoffensive cat). It provoked reaction from philosophers, theologians and churchmen, in part because of what were considered to be its internal inconsistencies and aporia, in part because it seemed to negate, in a sense by neglect, belief in an afterlife and thus to work counter to Christian dogma. But in his *Essay*, Locke, a self-professed Protestant, was above all a philosopher. The 'self' that Locke sought to define was very much a modern, secular, psychological entity. He sought to look at the notion from scratch, to start, as was his wont, with a clean slate, a *tabula rasa*.

This volume seeks to record some of the mutations, literary expressions and distinctive voices of the 'self' that can be observed, read and heard during the long eighteenth century, starting with Anne Killigrew, poet and artist, and the divines Isaac Barrow and John Tillotson, then moving through an array of writers and thinkers to William Blake, William Wordsworth and the English debate about the French Revolution. Together, these voices create a narrative, a patchwork chronicle, a multilogue that will illustrate the diversity, resilience and unity of the notion of the self, however elusive the object 'self' may prove to be in the long run. In assembling them, the aim has been to explore how authors in different domains, with varying objectives and from distinctive perspectives, envisage and express the notion of self. While charting the changes and variations evident across the period in approaches to, and the experiences and understanding of, the self, we have to allow that this something called the 'self' remains somehow intact or at least indispensable. It is something at once very much a part of us and yet apart from us.

However fragile and vulnerable the self may prove to be, it is ultimately a refuge, something one can return to, or hope to return to. Alternatively, it can be viewed and experienced as something that one fashions and shows to the outside world, a mask, a *persona*. This raises the question of the 'true' or authentic self that Shakespeare teasingly includes in Polonius's self-satisfied and homely advice to Laertes prior to his son's departure for France: 'This above all: to thine own self be true, / And it must follow as the night the day / Thou canst not then be false to any man.'[8] Putting a finger on exactly *what* it is, is quite another matter. 'Self' here, then, acts as a prism, exemplifying a principle of unity, through which the various novelists, poets, philosophers, churchmen and writers of the long eighteenth century foregrounded in these twelve chapters can characterise themselves and their ways of perceiving the self.

The self and the sense of self are usually, in the eyes of many, thankfully or unthinkingly, taken for granted. 'Self' has become so pervasive a term that it passes unnoticed in everyday speech and verbal exchanges. It is the sense of identity – individual, personal identity – that makes one recognisable to others, in society at large, in family, social and professional circles, and indeed familiar to oneself, that gives the impression one can have of always being the 'same' person despite all the changes that take place in a person's life. This, however, is not always the case as experience and language testify in the most banal utterances: 'I'm not feeling myself today'; 'to be beside oneself' with anger or joy, etc. (Locke provides similar examples), and more dramatically in experiences of alienation, of feeling estranged, of losing one's mind, one's identity, or memory as in amnesia. Madness and depression, for instance, can make us 'strangers to ourselves', to employ (and displace) Julia Kristeva's phrase.[9] Some torture techniques aim specifically at the depersonalisation of the victim, as though the ultimate cruelty and punishment one could inflict on someone was to make them lose their sense of identity. Locke does not dwell on such extreme psychological dramas in his seminal addition to the second edition of *An Essay concerning Human Understanding*, 'Of Identity and Diversity', but does, tellingly, acknowledge discontinuities in the sense of self, some of which occur on an everyday, recurrent basis, between 'the *Day* and the *Night-man*' for instance, and more dramatically between the '*Sober Man*' and the '*Mad Man*'.[10] Locke's arguments turn on the fundamental notions of consciousness, continuity and memory and his anatomy of personal identity and self-consciousness underpins the volume taken as a whole. It was precisely this insistence on a problematic continuity that was to be at the heart of the contestation of Locke's arguments by Bishop Butler in his addition to *The Analogy of Religion* (1736), later in the century by David Hume, and then by Thomas Reid's 'common sense' examination of the theme of personal identity.[11] However rich the debate and the objections that followed, however valid some of the latter may be seen to be, it was Locke, on his Irish friend William Molyneux's prompting, who had set the agenda.[12]

Another feature of the self, apart from its capacity to endure not only through individual lives but also across the centuries, is the fascination and attraction it exerts across a wide range of disciplines and fields of inquiry. The notion of the self is obviously central to biography and autobiography which otherwise could not and would not exist, but also to literature, to the theatre, poetry and the novel, as well as to psychology and psychoanalysis, to painting, to photography, to gender studies, to philosophy, and to the hard sciences, where the nature of the self and self-consciousness remains a mystery.[13] The number of studies devoted to the subject in these various genres and disciplines remains impressive and shows that the term has in no way lost its currency but retains its relevance, urgency and abiding interest. In a word, the 'self' has managed to preserve, down the centuries, its impressive status of conundrum.

The making of the modern self

Raymond Martin and John Barresi speculate towards the end of *The Rise and Fall of Soul and Self* (2006) – a title that allusively suggests that the territory of the self (and the soul) could be compared to an empire – that 'very early, in prehistoric times', our ancestors, the Neanderthals, or 'some group of early hominids or humans', 'seem to have originated a future-oriented concern with death' and that the first manifestations and glimmerings of the soul or the self in the course of time thus take the form of the material traces of burial.[14] Burial rites can be taken as evidence that the disappearance of a person was accompanied by a collective recognition of that person's integrity and specific identity, the sign too of a possible belief that some part of the individual would somehow survive the physical decomposition and continue its existence in an afterlife. The soul, in the sense of a spiritual self, would thus have been with us as a defining feature of humankind from the mists of time. The awareness of death, of the death of others, the apprehension of one's own demise, and the rituals that accompany it, that leave and have left visible, durable and tangible traces are, then, signs of reflexivity, of consciousness.

More readable are the signs left by pen and paper (or its ancient equivalents of stylus and tablet) and the genesis of the self becomes easier to trace from Greek philosophy onwards. Plato's injunction to control one's passions and desires through reason, his doctrine of self-mastery, is thus the starting point of Charles Taylor's masterful study of 'the making of the modern identity'.[15] But Plato's self-mastery is a move outwards, from one's individual appetites to the recognition of a pre-existing, cosmic, rational order;[16] and it is only with Augustine and the claim, central to the *Confessions*, that it is not through the external world but in one's self that God can be found, that Taylor sees the beginning of an inward turn leading on, though in a more secularised form, to Descartes and Locke.[17]

Many more stops ought to be made in this express history of the self: in the Middle Ages, at a time when, as David Aers has forcibly argued, selfhood was defined through reference to various communities – courtly, religious, national, sexual;[18] or in the Renaissance, at a time when Robert Ellrodt and Charles Taylor identify a major turning-point in Montaigne's *Essais*,[19] from the self-exploration bent on achieving a sense of unity and stability which had dominated ancient thought, to a self-exploration willing to acknowledge, if not to celebrate, fragmentation and discontinuity, the perplexing multiplicity of selves, perhaps best seen in Montaigne's often-quoted claim that 'moi à cette heure, et moi tantôt, sommes bien deux'.[20] Yet this dispersion of self in time can be redeemed, for both Descartes and Locke, through thinking and consciousness: 'I think therefore I am', declares Descartes in the *Discours de la méthode* (1637), while Locke argues in the *Essay Concerning Human Understanding* that through consciousness and sensation, and memory, a human being can come to consider 'it self as it self, the same thinking thing in different times and places':

> to find wherein *personal Identity* consists, we must consider what *Person* stands for; which, I think, is a thinking intelligent Being, that has reason and reflection, and can consider it self as it self, the same thinking thing in different times and places; which it does only by that consciousness, which is inseparable from thinking, and as it seems to me essential to it: It being impossible for any one to perceive, without perceiving, that he does perceive. When we see, hear, smell, taste, feel, meditate, or will any thing, we know

that we do so. Thus it is always as to our present Sensations and Perceptions: And by this every one is to himself, that which he calls *self* ...[21]

Locke premises continuity as an essential element of personal identity, and thus memory, which enables consciousness to persist over time, to be aware of past actions and events, to acknowledge them, to 'own' them, as it were, to reassemble and re-appropriate them, but also to be accountable to oneself and to others. Thus consciousness re-joins and encompasses the notion of conscience – the moral and ethical, personal, and social quality of consciousness – without exactly coinciding with it. This ethical element of 'self' or selfhood, the self not only as informing an individual conscience but as a social self existing and interacting within a community, is, as we shall see in several chapters in this volume, a central feature of debates on the self in the long eighteenth century.

Historically, there are many changes in the seventeenth century which can account for this new emphasis on the individual, comprehensively connected to each other in Christopher Hill's *Century of Revolution*:[22] the needs of the expanding economy and pressure of merchants and capitalist landowners to free business and investment from government restrictions and monopolies; the Puritan commitment to individual conscience and introspection, manifest in the many Puritan diaries and autobiographies; the diffusion through the Royal Society of Baconian science, which pushed forward the frontiers of learning, 'kill[ing] traditional ideas that the heart is "nobler" than the blood, the sun "nobler" than the planets, just at the same time as the political revolution killed the idea of hierarchy in law and politics';[23] the Civil War, which did away with the absolute power of the King, and patriarchal society of vertical dependence from God to King to Lord to tenant; the Glorious Revolution which completed the victory of Civil War Parliamentarians and culminated in a Bill of Rights guaranteeing individual liberties – all this favoured the development of a sense and theory of self by setting the (propertied) individual free from the iron links of the 'great chain of being'. At the same time, practical changes were favouring self-exploration too: more comfortable houses (through the use of coal, glass windows, and chairs instead of benches) which allowed for greater privacy, perhaps the mirror too, Hill suggests, helped develop self-consciousness.[24] The democratisation of the press, as Civil War pamphlets, post-Restoration coffee-houses, and the appearance and popularity of periodical newspapers in the early eighteenth century contributed to the emergence of a 'public sphere', also created the material conditions in which self could be explored and expressed.[25] Within the pale of this volume, however, such reasons for the rise of the self can only be touched upon.

A French connection

At the beginning of the period that this volume covers, the French polymath, mathematician, philosopher and religious thinker, Blaise Pascal (1623–62), was to foreground and comment on, and even, for all intents and purposes, to invent, the substantive form of a personal pronoun, and what is one French equivalent or approximation of 'the self', 'le moi'. In the unfinished and posthumously published *Pensées* (1670), he famously wrote: 'le *moi* est haïssable',[26] a phrase translated by Joseph Walker in 1688 as 'The *Me* is to be hated' and in the early eighteenth century by Basil Kennet as 'SELF is mean and scandalous.'[27] The 'me' or 'self' in question here refers more to self-love or rather self-centredness, and the desire to dominate and assert oneself, than the 'self' *per se*, as a dispassionate object of intellectual enquiry, and indeed Pascal looks at the 'moi' from various perspectives in the course of the reflections that were to become his *Pensées*. Regina Maria Dal Santo and Jeffrey Hopes in Chapter 2 on Barrow and Tillotson, and Chapter 3 on Mandeville and Hutcheson, will show that self-love can be viewed in other and more positive lights.[28] But this *invention* of the 'moi' in French as it has been called by Étienne Balibar and by Vincent Carraud,[29] is at least as much a reference to an innovation in terminology, a needful change, as it is the claim that the 'self' had suddenly come into being. The 'self' as a term does, however, seem to have come to the fore in the latter half of the seventeenth century.[30] Locke himself, who, as Balibar has argued, really created and developed the notion of 'self-consciousness', always attentive to the uses, misuses and abuses of language, was to emphasise the necessary distance between the term and what it designates, the signifier and the signified, as he writes earlier in this chapter: 'every one is to himself that which he calls *self*'.[31] Locke tends, if not to ignore, at least to put on hold, the question of the self's immateriality and above all enters into no real discussion concerning its immortality, while the soul's (and not the self's) immortality was obviously central to Pascal's thought, and a literally crucial notion in his or, one may suppose, any apology of the Christian faith.

Locke, like Alexander Pope after him, sought to clarify the objectives of the fledgling science of man, what Pascal called 'l'étude de l'homme',[32] by establishing the limits of our knowledge, and identifying how far human inquiry could extend and be considered as valid. Pope is prudent in the formulation of his own ambition in the first Epistle of *An Essay on Man* (1733–34):

> The bliss of Man (could Pride that blessing find)
> Is not to act or think beyond mankind;
> No pow'rs of body or of soul to share,
> But what his nature and his state can bear. (I. 189–92)[33]

After Pascal, both chronologically and in terms of influence and restraint, Pope was to begin Epistle II of his *Essay* with a no-nonsense assertion of the object of man's quest for knowledge. Pope seems to be on the verge of providing a roadmap for self-knowledge as he neatly edges God out of the picture and places Man centre stage (as Locke himself does). He appears (albeit briefly, as briefly as the couplet lasts) to make things sound clear and full of promise: 'Know then thyself, presume not God to scan; / The proper study of Mankind is Man.' All well and good. A vast programme but one that is immediately compromised and knowingly self-sabotaged by the poet as he goes on to list a whole series of paradoxes, oxymorons and antitheses that combined make up a portrait of the chaotic moral identity of man, aiming to establish less his potential powers, than his pretensions, contradictions and shortcomings:

> Know then thyself, presume not God to scan;
> The proper study of Mankind is Man.
> Plac'd on this isthmus of a middle state,
> A being darkly wise, and rudely great:
> With too much knowledge for the Sceptic side,
> With too much weakness for the Stoic's pride,
> He hangs between; in doubt to act, or rest,
> In doubt to deem himself a God, or Beast;
> In doubt his Mind or Body to prefer,
> Born but to die, and reas'ning but to err;
> Alike in ignorance, his reason such,
> Whether he thinks too little, or too much:

> Chaos of Thought and Passion, all confus'd;
> Still by himself abus'd, or disabus'd;
> Created half to rise, and half to fall;
> Great lord of all things, yet a prey to all;
> Sole judge of Truth, in endless Error hurl'd:
> The glory, jest, and riddle of the world! (II. 1–18)[34]

At the same time Pope, throughout the passage, but at the end in particular, is condensing and versifying elements of Pascal's *Pensées* which he was acquainted with both in the original and through Kennet's translation:[35]

> What a Chimæra then is Man! What a surprising Novelty! What a confused Chaos! What a Subject of Contradiction! A profess'd Judge of all Things, and yet a feeble Worm of the Earth; the great Depository and Guardian of Truth, and yet a meer Huddle of Uncertainty; the Glory and the Scandal of the Universe.[36]

The self, a universal not an individual self, the identity of Man, as it emerges in Pope's heroic couplets, is presented as the quarry to be pursued, but the lines are the simultaneous acknowledgement of the inevitable failure of the enterprise of 'knowing' such a being who is at once 'The glory, jest, and riddle of the world!'. But beyond that lie the questions: who exactly is doing the pursuing and to what end? Pascal, Locke and Pope approach the self as the object of their study, rather than expressing and examining it through recording personal, subjective experience. Pope's more extrospective approach to the question of self is light years from Wordsworth's poetic quest. We appear to move progressively, not in leaps and bounds, from Pope's contained study of man, through the emotionally heightened literary age of sensibility, with the rehabilitation of emotion (though the word 'rehabilitation' is inexact and too strong as emotion was, of course, never absent) to the intensity and subjectivity of the romantic era and the expressive self. This again sounds rather too neat.

The modern self, however, did truly come into its own in the eighteenth century, albeit less as a given object than as a work in progress. Several modern commentators argue that the self came to displace the notion of the soul at that time. In M. H. Abrams's discussion of the secularisation of religious terms inherited from the past, the soul, though far from disappearing, came to occupy a rather different and uneasy, more secondary and indefinite space, and the self, a more secular, then, but also psychologically oriented and 'neutral' notion, was to become an object of study *per se*. It is possible to see in the rise of the self (and the preoccupation with 'personal identity') an example of what Abrams refers to as 'the secularization of inherited theological ideas and ways of thinking'.[37] The self, as we will see in the following chapters, is also the theatre of anguish and doubt (in Samuel Johnson, for example) as much as a source of joy or positive sentiments. Here too, Abrams, with a generous smattering of compounds featuring the 'self', was to chart the progression from the universal and religious theodicy, to the experience of personal redemption:

> the Wordsworthian theodicy of the private life (if we want to coin a term, we can call it a 'biodicy'), belongs to the distinctive Romantic genre of the *Bildungsgeschicte*, which translates the painful process of Christian conversion and redemption into a painful process of self-formation, crisis, and self-recognition, which culminates in a stage of self-coherence, self-awareness, and assured power that is its own reward.[38]

The change is a sea change, and Wordsworth's quest establishes a new sort of personal, individual soteriology. This 'biodicy' can be read as a culmination of sorts, one of the later manifestations of what Charles Taylor, quoted in Jeffrey Hopes's Chapter 3, refers to as the Augustinian 'inward turn'.[39]

The circular self

At the heart of the question of the self, and including notions that can be considered as approximately related terms – the soul, the person, the mind, subjectivity, etc. – lies the quest for a stable, discernible, describable human identity, and indeed the supposed bedrock of each individual, the personal and singular 'self'. This personal identity (identity being derived from the Latin 'idem', i.e. same), this sense of 'sameness', has come to be accepted and prized, at least in the Western world, as, one is tempted to say, the 'inalienable' essence of an individual. This is the progression mapped out by Martin and Barresi who see an evolution from the spiritual soul, to the philosophical and psychological self and, finally, to the scientific mind.[40] Much overlap remains, however, between these terms and changes, and there are many grey areas.

INTRODUCTION

The focus in this volume is on writing the self, putting it into words, as a theoretical, an ethical, and a religious or spiritual notion, a way of construing, conducting and constructing oneself, as the expression of doubt and moral and mental distress, when the self and the sense of one's identity is felt to be in jeopardy, but also as the assertion of a necessary and reassuring social identity and recognition. But 'self' is also a fertile source of linguistic innovation. Prior to the end of the seventeenth century, 'self' was mostly used as an adjective or a pronoun, but for a lone substantive use in Spenser's *Amoretti* in 1595 ('but in my selfe, my inward selfe I mean') where it is implicitly pitted against an antithetic sinful self and is roughly synonymous with 'better self'.[41] As to the Shakespearian 'to thine own self be true', it is, arguably, more an emphatic form of the personal pronoun (thyself) than a genuine substantive use of the word 'self'.[42]

The term 'self' is now used in what can appear to be an unending series of compounds.[43] If it does seem in the seventeenth and eighteenth centuries to have superseded the term 'soul', the two have, of course, continued to exist side by side. It is perhaps not totally frivolous to note that the various forms of both words behave differently. Thus 'selfless' is a positive term whereas 'soulless' is not. 'Selfish' has negative connotations whereas 'soulful' is positive. We can enjoy 'soul' music but not (as yet!) 'self' music.

'Self' has, then, proved to be a term capable of linking up with any number of other words to form compounds. The second edition of the *Oxford English Dictionary* (1989) devotes some twenty-nine pages to entries and examples either specifically related to 'self' or to its very numerous compound progeny. As a substantive, and in the general understanding and use of the term, two definitions categorise the 'self', in turn, as a succession of states, and then as an accumulation, an ensemble of disparate dispositions:

> 4a. What one is at a particular time or in a particular aspect or relation; one's nature, character, or (sometimes) physical constitution or appearance, considered as different at different times. Chiefly with qualifying adj., (*one's*) *old, former, later self.*

> 4b. An assemblage of characteristics and dispositions which may be conceived as constituting one of various conflicting personalities within a human being.[44]

A definition concerned with the philosophical use of the word insists, however, on the idea of the self as a unity, something perceived as single and unified despite its fluctuating nature:

> 3. That which in a person is really and intrinsically *he* [sic] (in contradistinction to what is adventitious); the ego (often identified with the soul or mind as opposed to the body); a permanent subject of successive and varying states of consciousness.[45]

This last definition draws attention to <u>the inescapable circularity of dictionaries, words dutifully referring to, and calling on, the help of other words to elucidate their meaning</u>. It introduces several related terms – soul, mind, subject, ego, consciousness – which are closely related to the notion of self. It also brings to mind David Hume's description of the mind's functioning where he unequivocally disowns this 'permanent subject'. Of the self-affirmer, the defender of the notion of the self, Hume notes: 'He may, perhaps, perceive something simple and continu'd, which he calls *himself*; tho' I am certain there is no such principle in me.' He continues:

> But setting aside some metaphysicians of this kind, I may venture to affirm of the rest of mankind, that they are nothing but a bundle or collection of different perceptions, which succeed each other with an inconceivable rapidity, and are in a perpetual flux and movement.[46]

Continuing his spirited defence of the rigours of philosophical inquiry against common sense and 'natural propension', Hume deploys the metaphor of drama and role-playing:

> The mind is a kind of theatre, where several perceptions successively make their appearance; pass, re-pass, glide away, and mingle in an infinite variety of postures and situations. There is properly no *simplicity* in it at one time, nor *identity* in different; whatever natural propension we may have to imagine that simplicity and identity. The comparison of the theatre must not mislead us. They are the successive perceptions only, that constitute the mind; nor have we the most distant notion of the place, where these scenes are represented, or of the materials, of which it is compos'd.[47]

There is no stasis or stability in Hume's account and perception, but a constant flux, a disorderly stream of consciousness *avant la lettre*; the self appears to dissolve before our very eyes, or rather it becomes at best a mirage, a figment of our thought and imagination.

INTRODUCTION

The author of *A Treatise of Human Nature* (1739–40) draws attention to the artifices, ruses and unceasing mobility of the mind that seeks to maintain the notion of its own identity. This identity, the very self, would be a fiction: 'The identity, which we ascribe to the mind of man, is only a fictitious one…'.[48] Perhaps, but the 'I' that does the analysing and debunking here (as Hume was well aware) continues its own assertions and finishes its elegant sentences. The same 'I' has come down to us as the philosopher, historian and essayist David Hume, author also of 'My Own Life', 'The Life of David Hume, Esq. Written by Himself' which he wrote a few months before his death in 1776.[49]

The self has always remained problematic and plural in nature. At the end of the timespan we are concerned with here, what John Keats, in his letter to Richard Woodhouse dated 27 October 1818, referring to William Wordsworth, was to dub the 'egotistical sublime', if not relevant to all writers of the time, did at least highlight the perception of the exalted self, a valorisation of individual feeling and thought as a way of being in, and expressing, the world. Keats was to valorise in his letter what looks on paper to be the exact opposite, an absence of self, a merging of subject and object, Keatsian empathy:

> As to the poetical Character itself (I mean that sort of which, if I am any thing, I am a Member; that sort distinguished from the wordsworthian or egotistical sublime; which is a thing per se and stands alone) it is not itself—it has no self—it is every thing and nothing—It has no character— … A Poet is the most unpoetical of any thing in existence; because he has no Identity—he is continually in for—and filling some other Body—.[50]

Keats presents two antagonistic selves, at least in poetic terms, the self-centred and the self-less. He is paradoxically affirming his own identity as a writer (his 'poetical character') as one of non-identity, or of total identification with the perceived and contemplated external object. But the exaltation of the self is arguably another way of merging with the outside world not totally different from Keatsian fusion through the non-self.

To return to the present, the 'self' in all its apparent complexity can be eloquently illustrated by a contemporary piece of self-writing, a text entitled 'L'autographe', where the psychoanalyst and writer Jean-Bertrand Pontalis summons up glimpses and fragments from his own past, again seeking out and querying those notions of continuity, logical and chronological progression we take for granted – which paradoxically include a sense of 'otherness' and discontinuity – the progress of a life, a 'self' (or, here, *'le moi'*) that apparently survives across time, through the different phases in a human life, and which, despite its trials, tribulations and transformations, somehow remains recognisably the same. Here is Pontalis's reflection on the passing of time and the nature of the inner self:

> When looking at a photograph of yourself taken in the distant past – your childhood or youth –, sometimes you are happy to discover the same features as those you have today. But this is rarely the case: you have difficulty imagining that you were once this laughing child with a fringe hiding his forehead, this boy with plastered-down hair celebrating his First Communion, this somewhat melancholy young man walking along the banks of the Seine, this thirty-year-old pretending to be sure of himself when in fact he really wasn't at all … You hesitate between a reassuring impression of continuity (I may have changed but, all things considered, I'm still the same person) and a sense of radical discontinuity, as if your life was just a succession of losses, of separations, the impression that each stage of your life separated you from the preceding one, that you had no stable identity and were nothing but a series of characters in search of an author.[51]

These photographs that Pontalis evokes and verbally holds up before the reader's gaze, these snapshots of the self (taken in a pre-selfie era) serve to remind us that there is indeed a past self that the present self can again 'reflect' on and seek to connect with and relate to. The 'self' as unity here becomes the self as process or series. Behind this apparently simple strategy lies the vast question of what words, paintings and photographs really reflect of the initial 'object' or 'subject'.

That Pontalis concludes the passage with an allusion to a work of literature, Luigi Pirandello's *Six Characters in Search of an Author* (1921), and that the work in question is a play, is a telling final detail. It implies that the whole question of 'person' and 'character' and 'self' is a *mise en scène*, even a *mise en abyme*, not a single reflection but a hall of mirrors, but also a construction, a creation. Where does the notion of 'person' (in life), or indeed 'character' (in a novel), come from? Who is its 'author', who brought it into being and fashioned it? These questions can quickly appear unsolvable and discouraging, perhaps even perfectly futile, and yet going back to the apparently firm ground of the self-assured couplet of Alexander Pope quoted above, the self, however elusive and protean its nature and identity, seems to be that 'something' which reflectively governs (in the nautical sense) and oversees personal identity in spite of the sense of contradiction, fragmentation, dispersal and estrangement that a person can at times experience. If the self is indeed a fiction, it is no doubt a necessary (and, in a sense, salutary) fiction, a shared and social one – a historical one too as this volume seeks to show – and an ultimate refuge, in constant search of an author (and reader).

The twelve chapters presented here all look at the way the idea of the 'self' is constructed in the writings of the time. Philosophers and theologians explicitly discuss the question of the self, contending for a 'good' or a 'bad' self, while novels, poems or diaries allow writers to explore the riddle of the self as experienced by the subject, and particularly its problematic fragmentation. As such, they complement and further the construction of the 'self' that goes on in sermons and treatises; but they are also, as some of the essays point out, nourished and shaped to a great extent by such theoretical writings on the self. The chapters look at this construction of the self through writings during a century in which, from Locke's claim that personal identity is founded on memory, to Romantic portrayals of the isolated self, something like the modern self can be said to have emerged. Rather than sketching out a Whig history of the self, in the sense of a progressive movement, with regular staging posts on the way to some final apogee and fulfilment of the self, and while acknowledging that the perception and rise to prominence of the self as a notion are in part necessarily historically determined, these chapters bear witness to the existence of different, competing ways of thinking and representing the self in the long eighteenth century. If they help to identify three distinctive paradigms in the representation of the self through the century, each yielding something like its own dominant idea of the self, it is decidedly no three-act Self's Progress from foul to fair.

In the late seventeenth- and early eighteenth-century writings this volume begins with, the self comes across as an essentially moral question. Poets, preachers, novelists and philosophers alike are engaged in a similar attempt at vindicating the self and purging it from its negative implication of selfishness by reconciling it with Christian virtue and sympathy for others. Anne Killigrew, a painter, poet and unmarried woman at the court of Charles II, tones down her self-assertion as an artist by carefully fashioning herself as a deeply religious woman: if she is to be a wit, as Laura Alexander points out, she must be a 'spiritual wit', as if the self had to be excused away.

There is no sense of excuse, however, in the writings of clergymen like John Tillotson or Isaac Barrow, who, as argued by Regina Maria Dal Santo in Chapter 2, distinguish in their sermons between a bad, 'inordinate' self-love and a good self-love which prompts Christian obedience and charity. Thus from being an (unruly) associate of Christian virtue, the self becomes its very foundation, and self-love, more than obedience to an external rule, the motivation for virtuous actions. This internalisation of virtue, relocated within the self, is continued by the moral sense philosophers of the Scottish Enlightenment. In Chapter 3 Jeffrey Hopes shows that in his answer to Bernard Mandeville's *Fable of the Bees*, Francis Hutcheson also distinguishes bad self-interest from good 'self-approbation', which is the pleasure one feels in doing right: no longer an evil passion, the self is now integral to one's 'moral sense' and altruism. Interestingly, even if in the novels of Eliza Haywood a similar conciliation of self-love (as distinct from destructive self-interest) and love of others and virtue is usually reached, the alloy is imported, Orla Smyth claims in Chapter 4, from the seventeenth-century French novelists and philosophers on which Haywood draws, rather than on contemporary British responses to the self-love/benevolence dilemma.

William Flesch in Chapter 5 underlines the debt of evolutionary biology and modern theories of cooperation to this eighteenth-century probing of self-approbation and the paradoxical pleasure it yields, because it is a pleasure based on self-sacrifice rather than self-indulgence. From Hutcheson's (and Hume's and Smith's) recognition that going against one's self-interest can be ultimately more rewarding because it secures one's own, and other people's, approval, is derived the modern understanding of selflessness as a 'costly signal': it implies a sacrifice of one's self-interest, but ends up working for one's self-interest, as selflessness is socially valued and rewarded.

In the course of the century, however, a new paradigm seems to have taken the place of the self-as-self-love. The self no longer presents itself as a moral question, but rather as a psychological question of personal identity. Diaries, novels by letters or narrated in the first person singular, stage individuals grappling with the inconsistencies of a self they experience as discontinuous or divided, while writers devise original ways to represent such fragmentation. In Pope's *Dunciad*, claims Clark Lawlor in Chapter 6, the poet conjures up a series of grotesque alternative selves, embodying various threats to his identity (as writer, as male, etc.), against which he is finally able to establish his own 'epic self'. In Samuel Richardson's *Pamela*, Barbara Puschmann-Nalenz's Chapter 8 shows that it is the alternation of interior and exterior scenes which conveys a sense of Pamela's inner division between obedience and rebelliousness to the master's law; after the marriage, the two spaces symbolically merge, as the once dangerous garden becomes the *locus amoenus* where Pamela and Mr B. enjoy pleasant 'airings'.

All divisions of self, however, do not necessarily result in a final restoration of the self's lost unity. As Allan Ingram points out in Chapter 7, both Samuel Johnson and James Boswell emerge from their various writings as profoundly divided selves; but, while Johnson urges self-coherence in spite of inner conflicts, Boswell is less reluctant to expose his own self in its helpless division. *Tristram Shandy*, on the other hand, as Gioiella Bruni Roccia argues in Chapter 9, is no mere (gleefully parodic) testimony to the self's discontinuity: it is also an account of the way in which the self constructs itself and reaches some kind of poise dialogically through its conversing and interacting with other selves.

At the dawn of the nineteenth century, as the country is shaken by the revolutions in America and France and the violent counter-revolution it provoked in England, Romantic poets and radical politicians alike reflect on the individual's place in the world and its relation to the community as a whole: the self is no longer (or less so) internally divided, but rather is at pains to find its place in relation to others and the external world. Wordsworth's poetry, argues Laura Quinney in Chapter 10, is permeated with a Neoplatonic sense of the alienation of the self on earth from the transcendental realm of ideas, which it can now but glimpse at. But in the experience of the sublime, as shown by Eva Antal's Chapter 11, the forlorn romantic self can escape its earthly prison, and be united for a time, out of itself, with something greater than itself.

But this reaching out of the Romantic self beyond the world to abstract Nature and God can be seen as a conservative shying away from reform. Radical activists, at the same time, were trying hard to keep up a sense of national community in the face of governmental repression. They used the written or oral form of the 'self-defence', as Rachel Rogers cogently argues in Chapter 12, not only to suggest, through their personal case, the general necessity of reform, but also, by addressing directly the people at large, to bring into existence as they wrote the all-inclusive political community without which there could be no reform.

Such a tidy narrative of the self's protean progress through the long eighteenth century is bound to over-simplify things, as narratives do. There is clearly room for more work and bulkier studies, foregrounding other perspectives – economic, political and legal ones, for instance – as the editors are well aware, but the volume as it is will, they hope, contribute to a better understanding of the way in which literature (in its broad sense), at a time when many of the foundations of the world as we still know it were being laid, helped eighteenth-century men and women, philosophers, churchmen, politicians and poets alike, to articulate, probe, and devise solutions to many of the riddles (the self's identity through discontinuity, the conciliation of self and other, self and community, self and world) which still daily confront our brave new selves.

Notes

1 See François Cusset, 'Contretemps: l'expérience de la revue de littérature générale', in François Cusset (ed.), *Une Histoire Critique des Années 1990* (Paris: La Découverte, 2014), p. 141.
2 See for example David Harvey's analysis of May 1968 in his *A Brief History of Neoliberalism* (Oxford: Oxford University Press, 2005), pp. 41–3.
3 See Thomas Frank's account of the Occupy Wall Street Movement: 'To the Precinct Station', *The Baffler*, 21 (November 2012).
4 See J. G. A. Pocock (ed.), *Three British Revolutions: 1641, 1688, 1776* (Princeton, NJ: Princeton University Press, 1980). See also Alan Ryan, *The Making of Modern Liberalism* (Princeton, NJ: Princeton University Press, 2012).
5 In his seminal work on *The Family, Sex and Marriage in England 1500–1800* (London: Weidenfeld and Nicolson, 1977), Lawrence Stone distinguishes between the 'restricted patriarchal nuclear family' of the late sixteenth and seventeenth centuries and the 'closed domesticated nuclear family' of the late seventeenth and eighteenth centuries. While Stone points out that in early modern England there was a decline of

INTRODUCTION

the 'open lineage family' based on kinship among the landed classes (which did not preclude a reinforcement of patriarchy within the family), it is only after the mid-seventeenth-century Civil War that the *bourgeois* ideal of 'affective individualism' and domesticity spreads from the commercial and professional middle class to the upper landed classes. See pp. 222–69.

6 See John Brewer, *The Pleasures of the Imagination: English Culture in the Eighteenth Century* (London: Harper Collins, 1997).

7 Christopher Fox's *Locke and the Scriblerian: Identity and Consciousness in Early Eighteenth-Century Britain* (Berkeley, CA and London: University of California Press, 1988) remains the most precious and succinct discussion of the questions arising from, and provoked by, Locke's added chapter. Udo Thiel provides a comprehensive study of the philosophical background to the question in his *The Early Modern Subject: Self-Consciousness and Personal Identity from Descartes to Hume* (Oxford: Oxford University Press, 2011).

8 William Shakespeare, *Hamlet*, ed. Harold Jenkins, Arden Shakespeare (London and New York: Routledge, 1990), I, iii, lines 78–80. See Ulrike Tancke's commentary on the nature of Polonius's advice in *'Bethinke Thy Selfe' in Early England: Writing Women's Identities* (Amsterdam and New York: Rodopi, 2010), p. 131. For a study on the 'rise' of the self in the Renaissance period see Robert Ellrodt, *Montaigne and Shakespeare: The Emergence of Modern Self-Consciousness* (Manchester: Manchester University Press, 2015). Ellrodt sees in Montaigne and Shakespeare 'the fountainhead of an evolution beginning in early modern times and culminating in our own age', p. vii.

9 Julia Kristeva, *Strangers to Ourselves*, trans. Leon S. Roudiez (New York: Columbia University Press, 1991).

10 John Locke, *An Essay Concerning Human Understanding*, ed. Peter H. Nidditch (Oxford: Clarendon Press, 1979). Locke's *Essay* was originally published in December 1689; the chapter 'Of Identity and Diversity' was added in the second edition in 1694. For the discussion of the night self and day self, and of the sober and the mad man, see pp. 342–5. Original emphasis.

11 Joseph Butler, *The Analogy of Religion Natural and Revealed to the Constitution and Course of Nature*, ed. W. E. Gladstone (Oxford: Clarendon Press, 1896). Facsimile edition, *The Works of Joseph Butler*, vol. 1 (Bristol: Thoemmes Press, 1995). Butler discusses the theme of personal identity in the first of two dissertations added to *The Analogy of Religion*: 'Dissertation I, Of Personal Identity', pp. 388–96; David Hume, *A Treatise of Human Nature*, ed. L. A. Selby-Bigge, 2nd edn ed. P. H. Nidditch (Oxford: Clarendon Press, 1978), 'Of personal

identity', bk I, pt 4, sect. 6, pp. 251–63; Thomas Reid, Essay III, 'Of Memory', Chapters 4–6, *Essays on the Intellectual Powers of Man*, ed. Derek R. Brookes, intro. Knud Haakonssen (Edinburgh: Edinburgh University Press, 2002), pp. 262–79.
12 See Thiel, *The Early Modern Subject*, p. 97.
13 A *New Scientist*, Special Issue was entitled 'The Self. The Greatest Trick Your Mind Ever Played', 23 February 2013, pp. 32–43. It starts with the statement that the 'intuitive sense of self is an effortless and fundamental human experience. But it is nothing more than an elaborate illusion. Under scrutiny, many common-sense beliefs about selfhood begin to unravel. Some thinkers even go as far as claiming that there is no such thing as the self.' However it also acknowledges that 'Our whole way of living relies on the notion that we are unchanging, coherent and autonomous individuals', p. 37.
14 Raymond Martin and John Barresi, *The Rise and Fall of Soul and Self: An Intellectual History of Personal Identity* (New York: Columbia University Press, 2006), pp. 290–1.
15 Charles Taylor, *Sources of the Self: The Making of the Modern Identity* (Cambridge, MA: Harvard University Press, 1989).
16 *Ibid.*, p. 115.
17 *Ibid.*, pp. 129–30.
18 David Aers (ed.), *Culture and History 1350–1600* (New York, London and Toronto: Harvester Wheatsheaf, 1992).
19 See Ellrodt, *Montaigne and Shakespeare* and Taylor, *Sources of the Self*, pp. 177–84.
20 Michel de Montaigne, *Essais*, ed. Pierre Villey (Paris: Presses Universitaires de France, 1992), III, 9, p. 964. 'My selfe now, and my selfe anon, are indeede two', *The Essayes of Michael, Lord of Montaigne*, trans. John Florio, vol. 3, ch. 9, 'Of vanitie' (London: J. M. Dent & Sons, n.d.), p. 206.
21 Locke, *An Essay*, bk II, ch. 27, §9, p. 335. Gioiella Bruni Roccia quotes this passage from Locke in Chapter 9 of this volume, note 2.
22 Christopher Hill, *The Century of Revolution* (Walton-on-Thames: Nelson, 1961; 1980).
23 *Ibid.*, p. 155.
24 *Ibid.*, p. 217. See, on the question of the mirror, subjectivity and reflexivity, Deborah Shuger, 'The "I" of the Beholder: Renaissance Mirrors and the Reflexive Mind', in Patricia Fumerton and Simon Hunt (eds), *Renaissance Culture and the Everyday* (Philadelphia: University of Philadelphia Press, 1999).
25 The idea of the emergence in the late seventeenth century of an oppositional public sphere, rooted in coffee-houses and periodicals, in which the rising middle class could articulate its grievances against

the state, dates back to Jürgen Habermas's classic thesis, *The Structural Transformation of the Public Sphere: An Inquiry into a Category of Bourgeois Society* (1962). Habermas's model has since been contested, reviewed and refined by historians. While Edward P. Thompson and Terry Eagleton, Leonore Davidoff and Catherine Hall, have drawn attention to those, women and the working class in the 'making', left aside by the Habermasian model, Joad Raymond and Sharon Achinstein have emphasised the role played by Civil War pamphlets and newsbooks in the development of public discussion, thus pushing back the birth of the public sphere to the mid-seventeenth century. Recently, Peter Lake and Stephen Pincus have argued for an even earlier birth date, tracing the development of a European public sphere, to the aftermath of the Protestant Reformation. Yet, even Pincus and Lake acknowledge a quantitative and qualitative shift between the Elizabethan period and the Interregnum on the one hand, and the 1680s on the other hand: they describe the first two as a 'prerequisite' and a 'transitional period' to the 'fully fledged post-Revolutionary public sphere' which they locate, as Habermas did, at the turn of the eighteenth century. See Peter Lake and Steven Pincus, 'Rethinking the Public Sphere in Early Modern England', in Lake and Pincus (eds), *The Politics of the Public Sphere in Early Modern England* (Manchester: Manchester University Press, 2007). See also E. P. Thompson, *The Making of the English Working Class* (London: Victor Gollancz, 1963); Terry Eagleton, *The Function of Criticism* (London: Verso Books, 1984), p. 36; Leonore Davidoff and Catherine Hall, *Family Fortunes: Men and Women of the English Middle-Class, 1780–1850* (London, Melbourne and Sydney: Hutchinson, 1987). On Civil War pamphlets and newsbooks, see Joad Raymond, *The Invention of the Newspaper: English Newsbooks, 1641–1649* (Oxford: Clarendon Press, 1996) and Sharon Achinstein, *Milton and the Revolutionary Reader* (Princeton, NJ: Princeton University Press, 1994).

26 Blaise Pascal, *Pensées*, text of the Brunschvicg edition, introduction and notes by Ch.-M. des Granges (Paris: Garnier, 1964), p. 190.

27 *Monsieur Pascall's Thoughts, Meditations, and Prayers, Touching Matters Moral and Divine as they were found in his Papers after his Death*, Done into English by Joseph Walker (London: Printed by Jacob Tonson, 1688), p. 214. *Thoughts on Religion, and other Curious Subjects*, trans. Basil Kennet, 2nd edn (London, 1727), p. 246. Kennet's translation was first published in 1704, and editions followed in 1727, 1731 and 1739/1741.

28 Alexander Pope subscribes to this benevolent and measured view of self-love in Epistle II of *An Essay on Man*, according self-love a central role in Man's moral identity: 'Two Principles in human nature reign;

/ Self-love, to urge, and Reason to restrain;' (II. 53–4) and reaffirms this interdependent system of checks and balances a few lines further down: 'Self-love, the spring of motion, acts the soul; / Reason's comparing balance rules the whole. / Man, but for that, no action could attend, / And, but for this, were active to no end;' (II. 59–62). In the following Epistle he claims that self-love reconciles private and public good, the two no longer being viewed as antagonistic but complementary, each aiding and sustaining the other (III. 269–82). Alexander Pope, *An Essay on Man*, ed. Maynard Mack, vol. III i (London and New York: Routledge, 1993). First published in 1950 by Methuen & Co. Ltd. See also a recent edition of the poem, with a substantial introduction and textual commentary, Alexander Pope, *An Essay on Man*, ed. Tom Jones (Princeton, NJ: Princeton University Press, 2016).

29 See Étienne Balibar's *John Locke: Identité et différence. L'invention de la conscience* (Paris: Éditions du Seuil 1998), p. 250, and Vincent Carraud, *L'invention du moi* (Paris: Presses Universitaires de France, 2010).
30 See below, note 43.
31 Pierre Coste, the French translator of Locke's *Essay* (1700), chose to translate Locke's 'self' as the 'le soi' rather than Pascal's 'le moi'. See Balibar, *John Locke: Identité et différence*, p. 14.
32 Pascal, *Pensées*, p. 115.
33 Pope, *Essay on Man*, ed. Maynard Mack.
34 *Ibid.*
35 See the section Émile Audra devotes to the influence of Pascal on Pope in *L'Influence française dans l'œuvre de Pope* (Paris: Honoré Champion, 1931), pp. 480–504.
36 *Thoughts on Religion, and other Curious Subjects*, trans. Kennet (1727), p. 162. The original French is as follows: 'Quelle chimère est-ce donc que l'homme? Quelle nouveauté, quel monstre, quel chaos, quel sujet de contradiction, quel prodige! Juge de toutes choses, imbécile vers de terre; dépositaire du vrai, cloaque d'incertitude et d'erreur; gloire et rebut de l'univers.' Pascal, *Pensées*, p. 184.
37 M. H. Abrams, *Natural Supernaturalism: Tradition and Revolution in Romantic Literature* (New York and London: W. W. Norton & Company and Oxford University Press, 1971), p. 12.
38 Abrams, *Natural Supernaturalism*, p. 96.
39 Taylor, *Sources of the Self*, p. 177.
40 See Raymond Martin and John Barresi, *Naturalization of the Soul: Self and Personal Identity in the Eighteenth Century* (London and New York: Routledge, 2000), Chapters 3–5.
41 41 C.I.4.b., *Oxford English Dictionary*, second edition, vol. XIV (Oxford: Clarendon Press, 1989/1991), p. 907.

42 *Ibid.*, C.I.1.a
43 The *OED* notes: 'The number of *self-* compounds was greatly augmented towards the middle of the 17th cent., when many new words appeared in theological and philosophical writing, some of which had apparently a restricted currency of about 50 years (e.g. 1645–1690), while a large proportion became established and have a continuous history down to the present time.' *Ibid.*, p. 907.
44 *Ibid.*, C.I.4.a., C.I.4.b.
45 *Ibid.*, C.I.3., pp. 906–7.
46 Hume, *A Treatise of Human Nature*, p. 252.
47 *Ibid.*, p. 253.
48 *Ibid.*, p. 259.
49 David Hume, 'My Own Life', in *An Enquiry Concerning Human Understanding*, ed. Peter Millican (Oxford: Oxford University Press, 2007), pp. 169–75.
50 *The Letters of John Keats, 1814–1821*, ed. Hyder Edward Rollins, vol. 1, 1814–18 (Cambridge, MA: Harvard University Press, 1958), letter no. 118 to Richard Woodhouse dated 27 October 1818, pp. 386–7.
51 'Quand vous avez sous les yeux une photographie de vous prise dans des temps lointains – enfance, jeunesse –, parfois vous êtes heureux d'y retrouver vos traits d'aujourd'hui. Mais c'est rarement le cas: vous avez du mal à imaginer que vous avez été cet enfant rieur avec une frange lui couvrant le front, ce premier communiant aux cheveux gominés, ce jeune homme quelque peu mélancolique se promenant le long de la Seine, ce trentenaire feignant d'être sûr de lui alors qu'il l'était si peu ... Vous oscillez entre un sentiment rassurant de continuité (j'ai beau avoir changé, tout compte fait je suis toujours le même) et celui d'une discontinuité radicale, comme si votre vie n'était qu'une succession de pertes, de séparations, que chacune de ses étapes vous séparait de la précédente, que vous n'aviez aucune identité stable et n'étiez qu'une série de personnages en quête d'auteur.' J.-B. Pontalis, *Avant* (Paris: Gallimard, 2013), p. 125. English translation by John Baker.

PART I

Early modern selves and the Reason v. Passion debate

1

Anne Killigrew: a spiritual wit

Laura Alexander

The Restoration poet and painter, Anne Killigrew (1660–85), remembered mainly for John Dryden's famous elegy, 'To the Pious Memory Of the Accomplisht Young Lady Mrs. Anne Killigrew, Excellent in the two Sister-Arts of Poesie, and Painting. An Ode' (1686), has recently received greater critical attention from scholars, including Margaret J. M. Ezell, Carol Barash, Jennifer Keith, Harriette Andreadis, and Robert C. Evans, who have examined Killigrew's poems in the tradition of seventeenth-century poet Katherine Philips, called the 'Matchless Orinda' for her well-known virtue and poetic talents. As Barash notes, Killigrew was distinctive among seventeenth-century poets because she was also skilled in painting and often drew attention to her visual artistry in her poems.[1] Her religious paintings depict two biblical scenes: *St John the Baptist in the Wilderness* and *Herodias's Daughter Presenting to her Mother St John the Baptist's Head in a Charger*. As is sometimes the case in her posthumously published *Poems* (1686),[2] Killigrew features several written works explaining her visual artistry in relation to Christian spirituality, and these poems helped Killigrew to re-define her expressions of poetical wit in relation to her spirituality, which she privileges over secularism. Her poems, 'St. John Baptist Painted by herself in the Wilderness, with Angels appearing to him, and with a Lamb by him' and 'Herodias's Daughter presenting to her Mother St. John's

Head in a Charger, also Painted by herself', accompany the John the Baptist paintings, both currently lost. Anxious to separate her writings from courtly libertine texts, Killigrew looked to religious narratives for inspiration in articulating a self that was both witty and sacred, a unique artistic position in an age when wit became synonymous with irreligious expressions and outrageous libertinism. This chapter examines that 'self' – a spiritual wit – in Killigrew's verse and the larger implications for the gendered boundaries that women writing in the period negotiated.

Killigrew's interest in religious subjects was not uncommon for women artists of the time. A maid of honour to Mary of Modena, Killigrew self-fashions a virtuous identity at court in an age where there was overall a 'gradual shift from religious to secular control of sexuality',[3] particularly for women. While we do not know exactly what the paintings depict, Killigrew's language in her poems idealises John the Baptist and attacks the darkly erotic Salome, the speaker of 'Herodias's Daughter'. Critics have rightly read Killigrew's poems in relation to the proto-feminist texts that began to emerge in the period and acknowledge that Killigrew has a distinct and often angry voice in her works. Killigrew's self-fashioned identity as a 'spiritual' wit sharply contrasted the more secular 'court wits', and the vivid poetic imagery of her religious works communicates this identity.

In her recent edition of Killigrew's works, Margaret J. M. Ezell reminds readers that Killigrew distanced herself from licentious women and the court libertines in her verse, often employing historical or biblical figures to do so. Killigrew especially sought to distinguish herself from subversive figures at court in the 1680s, including the Restoration court mistresses, and establish herself as a 'spiritual wit' in contrast to the circle of libertine court wits.[4] Edmund Wodehouse's 'Anagram on Mistress Anne Killigrew' indicates how Killigrew perceived her court identity: 'My rare wit killing sin.'[5]

Killigrew's poems about the John the Baptist paintings indicate a self-styled spiritual affinity with the saint. Like her paintings, the companion poems, 'St. John Baptist Painted by herself in the Wilderness, with Angels appearing to him, and with a Lamb by him' and 'Herodias's Daughter presenting to her Mother St. John's Head in a Charger, also Painted by herself',[6] appear to be in dialogue, providing two different perspectives on the saint to show a distinct contrast between good and evil. The language of the poem 'St. John Baptist' suggests that the saint represents eternity and light, with the speaker inhabiting a light-filled natural setting, often a virtuous space in Killigrew's art. The second poem and its accompanying painting, 'Herodias's Daughter', is more disturbing, with the queen's daughter, the infamous Salome, boasting to her mother that she has had John the Baptist decapitated to protect them both from his righteous condemnation of their lewd influence. Salome's sexual identity is associated in the poem with excesses at court, directly referenced in the poem's last line, and Killigrew collapses Salome's eroticism with her evil murder of St. John the Baptist, whom she plots against with her mother, Herodias.

Killigrew's depiction of Salome and her mother is not uncommon for the time. Similar artistic representations of promiscuous female figures frequently appear in Restoration works by court writers depicting them onstage, in verse, and in erotic fiction. Killigrew's contemporary, Aphra Behn, herself attacked as a 'loose' woman writer, wrote some of the first published erotic fiction in England in the 1680s and also features many heroines whose dark sexuality is tied to murderous ambitions or actions. There was a wide spectrum of artistic attitudes towards women's sexuality in the period, and women writers often struggled to articulate a self in their works. Marilyn L. Williamson describes the heroines and perspectives on sexuality appearing in works by women writers, 'from the pious Mary Astell, who wrote as if the body and desire hardly exist, to Aphra Behn whose central theme was sexuality or Delariviere Manley whose gospel was sexual love'.[7] Aphra Behn, and later Eliza Haywood, frequently look at the complex negotiation between the body and mind in defining what 'self' means in their works. Though Killigrew depicts the salacious Salome in 'Herodias's Daughter', she sought to distinguish herself from amatory writers and notorious women writers like Behn and often drew on biblical authority to establish her credibility and express a 'self'. Killigrew wanted to separate her artistic identity from women perceived as immoral, including women writers, and probably never intended for her verse to be published. Killigrew's father collected, edited and published her papers, originally circulated among friends. Killigrew may have chosen to depict Salome and Herodias as a prudent way to show her distance as an artist from immodest women selected from an infallible source, the Bible.

Killigrew had to take particular care with her reputation as an unmarried woman at court, though she thrived in a family that valued the arts and clearly held proto-feminist views about women's participation in the 'sister arts', poetry and painting. While we know almost nothing about Killigrew's formal training as a painter, we do know she was both talented and well regarded in her own time; she may have studied under several well-known painters, including Sir Peter Lely or Mary Beale, a contemporary commercial artist possibly known to Killigrew, who could also have frequented Lely's studio.[8] She also took care with her art, both written and visual, and painted members of the royal family.[9] Her portrait of James II, then Duke of York, was hung in the Royal Collection. It was falsely attributed to the most famous of the Restoration portrait artists, Lely, until the twentieth century, when a cleaning of the portrait actually revealed Killigrew as the painter.[10] Reflecting a desire to express a self within acceptable social, moral and religious boundaries, Killigrew usually confined her painting to 'safe' subjects, with at least one exception on a classical subject, *Venus Attired by the Graces*. The painting (reproduced in Ezell's edition of her works) features women with naked and covered bodies.[11] The nude figure of Venus, likely modelled after Mary of Modena, appears half-turned from the viewer and hiding her bare chest. Barash explains that Killigrew could not paint nudes, even for classical studies, and she wanted also to distinguish herself from another well-known seventeenth-century female painter, Artemisia Gentileschi, considered as talented but also immoral.[12] In Killigrew's poem, 'On a Picture Painted by herself, representing two Nymphs of Diana's, one in a posture to Hunt, the other Bathing', which accompanies the lost painting, *Two Nymphs of Diana, one in a posture to hunt, the other bathing*, Killigrew is anxious to establish her own virginity. The nymphs are likely not bathing nude in the painting. They chant in the poem, 'We are *Diana's* Virgin-Train, / Descended of no Mortal Strain' (1–2).[13] Though Killigrew does not overtly connect the pagan goddess Diana or the poem to Christianity, she does emphasise the purity of the women, a group the poet joins in the last line:

> Though *Venus* we transcend in Form,
> No wanton Flames our Bosoms warm!
> If you ask where such Wights do dwell,
> In what Bless't Clime, that so excel?
> The Poets only that can tell. (19–23)

They appear as a hidden race of women, depicted as powerful hunters and beings connected to natural spirituality. Known only to poets, they appear free in the poem. Nature has not oppressed these virgins, defiant in their virtue, a curious position of power in an age when profligate women in real life drew on their sexual power to influence the king and manipulate spy networks, brokerage alliances and even political negotiations between France and England. The court mistresses frequently appeared in art, even as 'chaste' religious figures. Killigrew's depiction of defiant virgins is a reaction to their influence in art and court life; it also helped her to distinguish herself as a spiritual wit.

Though *'Diana's* Virgin Train' demonstrates Killigrew's separation from the more secular women at court, it does not indicate that Killigrew sought attention. Like other women poets, including Killigrew's contemporary Anne Finch (1661–1720), Killigrew frequently chooses the retirement mode for several poems and the painting, *Self-Portrait*. The kind of spiritual self that she imagines in her works lacks any desire for worldliness. She paints natural settings as safe retreats that she distinguishes from the public eye of the court. Killigrew at times expresses anger and other times avoidance, like Finch, and looks for an 'absolute retreat' from the constant scrutiny women endured at court. Killigrew paints herself in her *Self-Portrait* without formal court attire and in a woodland, making an important statement about her lack of artifice and self-identification with the natural world, like the 'Virgin Train' accompanying Diana. Her articulation of 'self' is both natural and spiritual, setting a pattern for Finch, who also drew on nature and biblical stories to present a witty self, consciously set apart from court life. Considering that Killigrew grew up in a family of courtiers and personally held an important and visible place at court in the 1680s, the choice to depict herself without the symbols and sartorial representations of power and court life is significant to understanding Killigrew's self-perception and values. Her rejection of the licentiousness at court and its appetites, both for sensual and material luxuries, shows remarkable restraint and self-awareness at a young age. It also left an artistic legacy to Mary, Lady Chudleigh, another 'spiritual wit' invested in defining a self that was strongly spiritual and looked to biblical wisdom.

Killigrew's more stylised paintings communicate the idea of her desires for a higher spirituality and affinity with nature. The virginal figures in *Two Nymphs of Diana, one in a posture to hunt, the other bathing* 'shine like glittering Beams' (17) and 'Bathe in Springs, to cleanse the Soil' (15), which sounds also like 'soul', holding both spiritual and physical meanings. Killigrew references biblical allusions to the spiritually cleansing power of Christ and baptismal images, which recur in Killigrew's poetic depictions of St. John the Baptist, more directly associated with the ritual of baptism, wilderness and the spiritually renewing power of resurrection in the Christian faith.

In her poem 'St. John Baptist', Killigrew idealises the saint who eats only simple meat and wine symbolising communion, a spiritual feast to nourish the soul:

> The Sun's my Fire, when it does shine,
> The hollow Spring's my Cave of Wine,
> The Rocks and Woods afford me Meat;
> This Lamb and I on one Dish eat:
> The neighboring Herds my Garments send,
> My Pallet the kind Earth doth lend:
> Excess and Grandeur I decline,
> M'Associates only are Divine.[14]

The poem again draws on the natural world, which Killigrew clearly associates with virtue, in John the Baptist's pure and gentle spirit; he is likened to Christ, the Lamb, and does not indulge in materialism. His simplicity contrasts with the excesses Killigrew would have witnessed at court in the early 1680s. Noticeably, in the last line, the speaker emphasises not only the purity of the speaker but also the virtue of his 'Associates'. Not only was Killigrew very much aware that associating with libertine courtiers could be dangerous for her reputation, but it was also compromising to her soul. It was a value Killigrew must have learned early in life. Ezell explains that Killigrew's branch of the family was the more spiritually minded: 'The Killigrew family remained solidly within the Anglican Church and its hierarchy, although Anne's father Henry and her brothers-in-law were the family's only ministers, the other Killigrews apparently adhering to the pragmatic religion of the times and of the court.'[15] Besides concerns for her soul, Anne Killigrew also had to stake out a more conservative position to avoid critics casting slurs on her reputation, a concern most women writers faced. She consciously follows her predecessor Philips in 'Upon the saying that my Verses were made by another', where she argues for her rights as an artist, with 'Soul and Body pay' (10) for her poetry, which she defends against attacks of plagiarism.

Philips founded a community of women writers in the 1640s and inspired them long after her death from smallpox in 1664 at the age of thirty-two. Like Killigrew, who was twenty-five when she died in 1685, Philips was both aware of her reputation and the risks as a woman writer. Philips's poetry gave women permission to write verse, and like Philips, women often drew on the Bible or biblical narratives or imagery to establish their authority and form an artistic self.[16] Killigrew aligned herself with real-life virtuous queens and other chaste women at court. In Killigrew's 'On the Birthday of Queen Catherine', also included in her *Poems*, she praises Charles II's wife, Catherine of Braganza, a figure likened to Christ in the poem. Catherine was well known for her patience, particularly as she was frequently attacked for her foreign manners, dress, and Catholic religion by detractors, including Charles II's court mistresses, several of whom saw themselves as rivals and wanted Charles to divorce her. Famous for decadence and sexual and material excess, Charles II's court gained a reputation for being risqué and libertine. Such an influence spread out from the court. As Roy Porter explains, during the late seventeenth century, the 'public domain was growing increasingly secular. The Church's once overwhelming place in communal life was being eroded.'[17] Instead, following Charles II's court, 'Pursuit of pleasure became more respectable. Calvinist taboos against indulgence were sloughed (Cromwellian Puritans became the killjoy stormtroopers of caricature).'[18] A more secular court, of course, did not have to mean a more licentious one, but it did in the 1680s, when Killigrew arrived as a young maid of honour. It was not until after the Glorious Revolution in 1688, three years after Killigrew's death, that a backlash against the libertinism that had dominated the late Stuart court began in earnest, ultimately changing tastes and values over the next decade.

In the 1680s, Killigrew entered a vicious court still controlled by court mistresses. Some of them, including the chief mistress in the first decade of the Restoration, Barbara Palmer, Countess of Castlemaine (later Duchess of Cleveland), not only flouted their adulterous relationship with the king, but also openly mocked religious figures and institutions. Sharon Kettering, Sonya Wynne, Susan Shifrin and Nancy Klein Macguire argue for the court mistresses' powerful perceptions and positions as brokers at court. They were frequently seen as dark, erotic and evil. Known both as courtesans and spies, these women were considered politically dangerous. Louise de Keroualle, Duchess of Portsmouth, a spy for Louis XIV, was still Charles II's chief court mistress in the 1680s, and she was known, like several predecessors, including Cleveland, for passionate fits that could lead to violent outcomes for her enemies. Portsmouth had Dryden beaten in the 'Rose Street Affair' in 1679, for example, when she believed he targeted her in satire.[19]

Notorious throughout the Restoration, even after she fell from Charles II's good graces, Cleveland appears in paintings from the period as various female religious figures. This no doubt made it difficult for Killigrew and other women anxious to distance themselves from dissolute attitudes and behaviour to present an authentic self. One of a select group of women painted in Sir Peter Lely's famous *Windsor Beauties* of the 1660s, Cleveland also had herself painted as well-known biblical or religious women, including the Virgin Mary, Mary Magdalene and St Barbara, alongside other classical figures.[20] Reputed to have fathered a number of illegitimate children by various mistresses, including several by Cleveland, visually depicted with one of them as the Magdalene in art, Charles II prominently featured Cleveland and the royal mistresses following her, including Nell Gwyn, the infamous (and self-dubbed) '*Protestant Whore*'. Charles II had them painted frequently throughout his reign and gave them and their children titles, wealth, prestige and power that lasted even after his death in 1685. Likely owing to the power granted to the royal mistresses, all women at court were as susceptible as men were to accusations of libertinism. Artists at court found it nearly impossible to define and present a self separate from court life, a struggle Dryden frequently lamented, especially in his post-conversion works and letters. It is no wonder that Killigrew, who was genuinely spiritually minded, would have expressed anger in her poetry at what she perceived as their destructive influence and deleterious power.

We find that anger most stringently expressed in Killigrew's poetic depiction of Salome, the female libertine she attacks in the poem 'Herodias's Daughter'. Salome is the speaker, but she does not compel sympathy. Rather, Salome details a murderous description of St John the Baptist's death:

> Behold, dear Mother, who was late our Fear,
> Disarm'd and Harmless, I present you here;
> The Tongue ty'd up, that made all *Jury* quake,
> And which so often did our Greatness shake;
> No Terror sits upon his Awful Brow,
> Where Fierceness reign'd, there Calmness triumphs now;
> As Lovers use, he gazes on my Face,
> With Eyes that languish, as they sued for Grace;
> Wholly subdu'd by my Victorious Charms,
> See how his Head reposes in my Arms.
> Come, join then with me in my just Transport,
> Who thus have brought the Hermit to the Court.[21]

In the biblical narrative recounted in the Gospels of Mark (6:14–29), Luke (9:7–9) and Matthew (14:1–12), King Herod Antipas of Judea divorces his wife Phasaelis and marries Herodias, the divorced wife of his half brother, Herod Philip I, in defiance of Mosaic Law. John the Baptist speaks out against this marriage, but Herod does not have him killed due to his popularity with the people. Herodias's beautiful daughter, Salome, and her mother both hate John the Baptist, whom Herod imprisons. After Salome dances at a festival honouring Herod's birthday, the king promises to give her anything she wishes. Outraged on behalf of her mother, Salome requests the head of John the Baptist. Though reluctant, Herod has John beheaded to satisfy his promise to Salome. Salome gives the head to her mother.[22] The story, particularly the scene of Salome with the head of John the Baptist, was a frequent narrative depicted in paintings in the period. Historically regarded as an erotic figure of evil, Salome appears like other biblical temptresses, including the violent Jezebel and Delilah, also frequently imagined as cradling the head of the sleeping Samson before his tresses and source of divine, masculine power are cut. As an Anglican and an artist, Killigrew would have been familiar with artistic representations of Salome and John the Baptist, whose feast day she likely celebrated with her family at church. The feast day is one of the oldest in the Christian tradition, occurring on 29 August in both the Catholic and Anglican calendars.

'Herodias's Daughter' is a chilling poem that features a disturbed speaker. Salome describes the experience in the religious language of sublime 'Transport' (11). The image of the cradled head appears in her arms like a child, but instead of a maternal image of mother and child, also a frequent artistic trope, the poem inverts the tradition of Mary, Mother of God holding the infant or small Christ-child. Salome instead 'cradles' the head of a man she has murdered, an indication of her madness. After death, she treats the head with maternal and erotic care, lovingly attending to it as she might do either for an infant or a lover. John the Baptist appears as though asleep and 'repos[ing] in [her] Arms'. He 'gazes' at her in death, a macabre image that Salome interprets as 'lover-like'. Part of Salome's boast to her mother suggests that John the Baptist wanted her sexually before his death, looking on her 'Victorious Charms' as he 'sued for Grace'. Salome casts him as a forlorn lover; his eyes 'languish', though he is dead, incapable of longing now for any woman. The interpretation of the saint is meant to show her sexual pride and profanation of John the Baptist's holiness. She treats him as a lustful man rather than a prophet of God. Her triumph is that her evil has drawn out 'the Hermit to the Court' compelling him away from the wilderness, even if it is to condemn her. The attention is heady for her, and she sounds unbalanced in her delusion of sexual power.

Though we cannot see what Killigrew actually painted in the accompanying visual image, the title indicates that the artist has represented St John the Baptist as a decapitated figure. The horrific image cannot also be erotic, though Salome treats the head as a sexual trophy, her mind demented in its murderous triumph. Though the painting is lost, it seems doubtful that Killigrew would have painted languishing eyes, at least in the way that Salome describes them in the poem, because the image does not cohere with Killigrew's other, idealised representation of St John the Baptist, described as Christ-like in the poem 'St. John Baptist'. The language suggests instead that Salome has misinterpreted the compassion in his eyes in her madness, which Killigrew emphasises in the poem's movement through the speaker's triumphant and horrific tones.

Salome's dark sexuality forms her troubled mental state in the poem. This kind of character would have been familiar to Killigrew. Such women frequently emerge in popular plays in the Restoration by leading dramatists. Main characters in two popular plays in the period, Nathaniel Lee's Statira in *The Rival Queens* (1677) and Dryden's Cleopatra in *All for Love* (1677), for example, appear as highly erotic and mentally disturbed queens sure of sexual triumph even as their actions lead to violent deaths for themselves and others. Behn's erotic narrative of the murderous escaped nun, Isabella, in *The History of the Nun* (1689) likewise seems to lose her reason entirely after committing the murder of her first husband, and this leads her to murder her second husband. Behn's narrator connects her body's nervous condition and madness to various transports of emotion she experiences before and after killing her two husbands. In the poem, Killigrew's Salome, then, also experiences a dark 'Transport' (11) and seems similarly poised in a tradition of sexualised female figures appearing in Restoration works that feature women who lose some or all rational capacity as they embrace real or imagined fantasies about their sexual power over men.

Women writers' responses to such figures varied. Behn wanted to create some understanding, even sympathy, for her disturbed heroines, including one of her most famous would-be murderers, Angellica Bianca, Willmore's cast-off mistress in *The Rover* (1677). Angellica Bianca threatens her ex-lover with a gun when he pursues Hellena, her rival, but Behn clearly wants the audience to side with Angellica, a maligned figure bought and sold and desirous of love outside of the marketplace. Behn is more ambiguous with heroines like the fictitious Miranda, the heroine of her novella, *The Fair Jilt* (1688). Miranda destroys a priest after he rejects her advances. Killigrew is more conclusive in her treatment of Salome. She shows the sexually subversive *femme fatale* as a cunning and unrepentant figure, totally lacking in the capacity for redemption or sympathy from the reader. Killigrew's poem 'Herodias's Daughter' argues for a genealogy for such women. Salome speaks directly to her mother, Herod's queen, in the poem, and like Salome, Herodias emerges as another dangerous, sexual woman whose wish for John the Baptist's death is made into a gruesome reality by her avenging daughter. There is no mercy shown to her victim, and we are not called by Killigrew to feel anything but disgust for her intentions and actions, an effort to help distinguish her spirituality and self from this depravity.

Like Lee, Dryden and Behn, Killigrew most likely turned to the powerful court mistresses for real-life models for Salome.[23] While Cleveland dominated the first half of Charles II's reign, the two most prominent mistresses during the last decade of Charles II's reign were foreigners, Portsmouth and Hortense Mancini, Duchess of Mazarin, both artistically significant in their literary influence during James II's reign, when Killigrew was writing and painting at court. Both Portsmouth and Mazarin appeared frequently as sexualised figures in art and drama. Mazarin, the dedicatee of Behn's *The History of the Nun*, was a well-known gamester living apart from her husband. She held salons in her home in Chelsea after her liaison with Charles II ended. As James E. Evans suggests: 'For most authors Mazarin epitomised the corruption of the Carolean court ... For all, whatever their point of view, Mazarin embodied the kinds of dangerous or attractive manifestations of philosophical and "real life" voluptuousness that were associated with Epicurean tranquillity and libertine frenzy.'[24]

The famous diarists Samuel Pepys and John Evelyn both recounted in their diaries that all of these women wielded power over the king, who granted their wishes, however disastrous to his image in England or abroad.[25] Even after Charles II died, many of the mistresses continued to prosper and wield significant social and literary influence. Even the more virtuous Mary Astell based her proto-feminist text, *Some Reflections on Marriage*, on the plight of Mazarin's disastrous marriage to her mad husband, who cut her off from funds and her children. Delarivere Manley partially wrote her scandal fiction *The New Atalantis* in response to gossip about Cleveland, still influential in 1700. Even after their deaths, these mistresses inspire similar figures in Daniel Defoe's novels, most notably *Roxana* (1724), which directly references Nell Gwyn.

It may be that Killigrew had none of these women in particular in mind – she does not give us enough clues to indicate any clear historical representations in her poems – but Williamson argues that 'the stereotypes that define all women according to their sexual behaviour dominate the reputations of Philips and Behn as well as the writers who use them for models', including Killigrew, seen as one of the 'politically, socially, and artistically conservative' women writers of the era.[26] Whatever interest Killigrew had in the mistresses was buried in literary and biblical allusion, as in the case with Salome. To communicate a spiritual self, she needed to condemn the public images of 'loose' women. Charles II's court was filled with visible female bodies, as paintings of the time show. Several of his mistresses were painted bare-chested or nude, and he physically fondled Nell Gwyn in public spaces like the theatre, a space all courtiers frequented. Pepys owned posters of several of the mistresses, including a nude engraving of Gwyn, which he hung prominently in his office in the Admiralty.[27] James Grantham Turner argues that such popular conceptions of the king's 'whores' tainted the entire court culture.[28] No one could escape gossip about them; no woman writer could avoid comparisons because they were perceived to expose the mind as other women did the body. Exposure formed a part of all women writers' concepts and presentations of a self. It had to be dealt with, either through acceptance, even sympathy, as in Behn's works, or with judgement and harsh condemnation, as in Anne Killigrew's art.

Men, even the king, were not exempt. Despite his own fascination with women's bodies, Pepys calls Charles's public concern for his mistresses a 'horrid effeminacy'.[29] John Spurr argues that Charles's libertine courtiers saw the king as weak, a 'slave to lust'[30] and ruled by dominant women. Sexually uninhibited women were seen to be weakening both to the king, perceived to be manipulated by them, and the nation.[31] Like Dryden, Killigrew must have seen obvious parallels between Charles II and classical or biblical kings succumbing to beautiful, erotic women, symbols of luxurious excess in the Restoration.[32] It was not difficult for women to acquire reputations for wantonness and experience frequent attacks from satirists. Killigrew responded by creating a separate identity as an artist, a self with a 'natural' identity imbued with spiritual wit.

Killigrew's best known poem defending her art, 'Upon the saying that my Verses were made by another', describes difficulties for women writers in articulating a self because they were often lumped together with promiscuous women or regarded as deranged for wishing to write. The mind-body association fuels Killigrew's anger since her poetry is appreciated by critics of her gender: 'My Numbers they Admir'd, but Me they scorn'd' (40). It is her 'self' that is at stake. She says she'll 'pay' (10) for the privilege of writing and describes the writing process and her reception, including the false accusations of plagiarism, in terms likened to rape for women writers: 'Rifl'd like her, each one my Feathers tore' (37). The experience left her feeling 'swallow'd up' (45), a violation of self. Killigrew wrote a number of bitter, melancholy poems that feature jaded speakers with a self disillusioned by life, as in 'The Miseries of Man', where she describes the 'truly wretched Human Race!' (19) in some detail. Her poem, 'An Invective against Gold', describes the worst of the 'Poisons' of a 'fruitful Earth' and 'Monsters she gave Birth' (1–2).

The speaker laments 'the Heavenly Fair despis'd' (15) and features 'A Hag like Hell, with Gold, more highly priz'd; / Men's Faith betray'd, their Prince and Country Sold, / Their God deny'd, all for the Idol Gold' (16–18). The hag is a figure like Salome and a similar character to the infamous 'Whore of Babylon' depicted in Revelation 17 and 18. The speaker of 'An Invective against Gold' alludes to an apocalyptic vision of divine retribution in the 'severe Reward at the last Day' when 'Some strange unheard-of Judgment thou wilt find, / Who thus hast caus'd to Sin all Human Kind' (22–4). In several poems, including 'An Invective', Killigrew's speakers offer little hope in this life for the virtuous Christian, and death recurs in Killigrew's poetry as the final resting place for the soul, an eerie foreshadowing of Killigrew's own early demise. In this life, betrayal and political intrigue consume the human race, mired in evil. It is a common theme running throughout Killigrew's poems and offers some evidence of the difficulties Killigrew found in defining a self.

In 'The Miseries of Man', Killigrew echoes the most infamous libertine during the Restoration, John Wilmot, the Earl of Rochester, in his *Satyr Against Reason and Mankind*. Like Rochester's speaker, Killigrew describes mankind as lower than the animals, which do not prey on their own kind as man does:

> As Man does Man, more skilful to annoy,
> Both Mischievous and Witty to destroy.
> The bloody Wolf, the Wolf does not pursue;
> The Boar, though fierce, his Tusk will not imbrue
> In his own Kind, Bears, not on Bears do prey:
> Then art thou, Man, more savage far than they. (95–100)

Only death releases the speaker from a 'wretched' (19) state, where '*Men* their own Kind with hostile Arms pursue' (90). It is a similar condition to the 'Brink of black Despair' (15) imagined in Killigrew's 'The Discontent', where the Muse, often despairing or depressed herself in Killigrew's verse, proclaims 'there's nothing Good' (24). But of course there was 'good', at least in the way that Killigrew values virtue and spirituality in the poetical language of 'St. John Baptist' and 'On the Birth-Day of Queen Catherine'. Charles II's court may have been an 'eroticised institution'[33] and a dangerous place for women, especially women artists and poets, but Killigrew helped to uphold Philips's Society of Friendship, an alternative artistic community for women who rejected the prominent libertine culture of the 1680s. As Killigrew's speaker makes clear to her muse in 'Upon the saying that my Verses were made by another',

> No Love of Gold shall share with thee my Heart,
> Or yet Ambition in my Breast have Part,
> More Rich, more Noble I will ever hold
> The *Muses's* Laurel, than a Crown of Gold. (5–8)

Killigrew's subversion can be found here, in these lines, which stake out her position as an artist untainted by worldly concerns. Her art did not make use of the visible body, as Behn's did, but demonstrated the exercise of the intellect attuned more to spiritual rather than secular worlds. The age's best poet, Dryden, wrote a moving elegy to her after she died; the poem praises Killigrew's art and her virtue, but in a meaningful way that connected the two writers and their common interest in spirituality. Unlike her contemporaries, Killigrew sought no patron, fame, riches, or preferment; instead, she wanted to express a different artistic identity. Just so with Dryden, whose conversion to Catholicism marked a turning away from secular concerns in his works. In this way, the two writers were not so different, as perhaps Dryden saw even in 1686. Both lived among the court but ultimately turned away from it to express a wholly different articulation of the 'self' – a spiritual wit.

Notes

1. Carol Barash, *English Women's Poetry, 1649–1714: Politics, Community, and Linguistic Authority* (Oxford: Clarendon Press, 1996), pp. 156–7.
2. Killigrew's father, Dr Henry Killigrew, edited her *Poems* and had them published the year after she died.
3. Marilyn L. Williamson, *Raising Their Voices: British Women Writers, 1650–1750* (Detroit: Wayne State University Press, 1990), p. 30.
4. See Anne Killigrew, *'My Rare Wit Killing Sin': Poems of a Restoration Courtier*, ed. Margaret J. M. Ezell (Toronto: Iter and Centre for Reformation and Renaissance Studies, 2013), pp. 1–2.
5. The anagram is taken from Ezell's title of her 2013 edition of Killigrew's poetry cited in the previous note. The source appears on p. 1. I am grateful for the information contained in this edition of Killigrew's works. As Ezell herself makes clear, 'Prior to 2009, no manuscripts of Killigrew's poetry were known to exist' (p. 31), but more information about the poet is being uncovered each year.

6 The poems will hereafter be referred to by a shortened title, 'St. John Baptist' and 'Herodias's Daughter'.
7 Williamson, *Raising Their Voices*, pp. 30–1.
8 Killigrew, 'My Rare Wit Killing Sin', pp. 29–30.
9 *Ibid.*, p. 33.
10 *Ibid.*, p. 29.
11 The painting was acquired by Falmouth Art Gallery, Cornwall, in 2012. Killigrew's other existing paintings include *Portrait of James II as Duke of York* (Royal Collection, Windsor Castle), *Self-Portrait* (Private Collection), and *Venus and Adonis* (engraving by Lens, Yale Center for British Art). Barash's *English Women's Poetry* lists a number of other paintings referred to in her poems and in Dryden's ode to her (Appendix C).
12 Barash, *English Women's Poetry*, p. 156.
13 Line references to the poems by Anne Killigrew are here and hereafter included in the text and placed in parentheses following the quotation, when the poem title is mentioned. The edition used is '*My Rare Wit Killing Sin': Poems of a Restoration Courtier*, ed. Margaret J. M. Ezell (Toronto: Iter and Centre for Reformation and Renaissance Studies, 2013).
14 Ezell, '*My Rare Wit Killing Sin*', pp. 59–60.
15 *Ibid.*, p. 5.
16 Williamson, *Raising Their Voices*, pp. 78–83.
17 Roy Porter, *English Society in the Eighteenth Century*, rev. edn (London and New York: Penguin Books, 1990), p. 226.
18 *Ibid.*, p. 227.
19 Laura Linker, *Dangerous Women, Libertine Epicures, and the Rise of Sensibility, 1670–1730* (Burlington, VT: Ashgate, 2011), p. 19.
20 Ezell, '*My Rare Wit Killing Sin*', p. 9.
21 *Ibid.*, p. 60.
22 Flavius Josephus also recounts John the Baptist's death in his historical account, *Jewish Antiquities*, bk XVIII, ch. 5. Killigrew may or may not have been familiar with this account. Richard Morton's introductory notes indicate that her father was very learned, and Killigrew obviously consulted a number of classical texts, evident in her poetic allusions and structures.
23 See Laura Linker's *Dangerous Women, Libertine Epicures, and the Rise of Sensibility, 1670–1730* for extended examinations of the historical models writers employed in discussions of the female libertine.
24 James E. Evans, '"The Splendour of Our Golden Age": The Duchess of Mazarin and Epicurean Voluptuousness in Late Stuart England', *1650–1850 Ideas, Aesthetics, and Inquiries in the Early Modern Era*, 19 (2012), 46.

25 See Susan Shifrin, '"At the end of the Walk by Madam Mazarines Lodgings": Si(gh)ting the Transgressive Woman in Accounts of the Restoration Court', in Susan Shifrin (ed.), *Women as Sites of Culture: Women's Roles in Cultural Formation from the Renaissance to the Twentieth Century* (Burlington, VT: Ashgate, 2002), pp. 195–205.
26 Williamson, *Raising Their Voices*, pp. 20 and 21.
27 Charles Beauclerk, *Nell Gwyn: Mistress to a King* (New York: Grove Press, 2006), p. 62.
28 James Grantham Turner, *Libertines and Radicals in Early Modern London: Sexuality, Politics, and Literary Culture, 1630–1685* (Cambridge: Cambridge University Press, 2002), p. 245.
29 R. Latham and W. Matthews (eds), *The Diary of Samuel Pepys* (Oxford: Oxford University Press, 2000), vol. 7, p. 288.
30 John Spurr, *England in the 1670s: 'This Masquerading Age'* (Oxford: Blackwell, 2000), p. 209.
31 Evans, 'The Splendour of Our Golden Age', p. 48.
32 Ros Ballaster, 'Performing *Roxane*: The Oriental Woman as the Sign of Luxury in Eighteenth-Century Fictions', in Maxine Berg and Elizabeth Eger (eds), *Luxury in the Eighteenth Century: Debates, Desires and Delectable Goods* (Basingstoke: Palgrave, 2003), p. 165.
33 Spurr, *England in the 1670s*, p. 197.

2

Charitable though passionate creature: the portrait of Man in late seventeenth-century sermons

Regina Maria Dal Santo

In preaching before King Charles II at Whitehall on 2 April 1680, John Tillotson, the future Archbishop of Canterbury, gave the portrayal of the passionate individual thus: if a man 'be subject ... to his own lusts and passions ... the tyrant is at home, and always ready at hand to domineer over him; he is got within him, and so much the harder to be vanquished and overcome'.[1] Tillotson was playing on recent memories of the Civil War and on the palpable menace of having a possible Catholic 'tyranny' in the near future with the Duke of York inheriting his brother's throne. Passionate, like political, disorders could only be fought with absolute control, a firm hand and divine assistance. Tillotson encourages his congregation to study the passions, to attentively reflect on which of them determine or 'rule' their own character, and to taste the sweetness of freedom and happiness in the name of religion: 'The pleasure of commanding our appetites, and governing our passions, by the rules of reason (which are the laws of GOD) ... gives us the satisfaction of having done that which is the best and fittest ...'.[2] John Tillotson became Archbishop of Canterbury in 1691, but his role as one of the most influential preachers of the seventeenth and eighteenth centuries began earlier, in the 1660s, when he was appointed to instruct the fashionable London congregations at Lincoln's Inn and at St Lawrence Jewry. His sermons show us how the Restoration Church was trying to dialogue with the growing interest in literature and philosophy, in the human passions.[3] Both philosophical essays and sermons analysed passions under two categories: they are positive, they are a clear sign of God's benevolence,[4] they help human beings to find their place and direction in the world, and to take decisions as they stimulate inclination or aversion. On the other hand, they might become inordinate appetites, and have disruptive consequences on society. Hence the obsession with control and the possibility of taming them through proper Christian education while developing correct habits. Indeed, Tillotson claims that 'custom will reconcile men almost to any thing' and that 'true pleasure, and perfect freedom are no-where to be found but in the practice of virtue'.[5] Reason and the passions were investigated to build a new anthropological system in which the search for happiness was prominent. Being among the most widely read publications of the age, sermons had to combine human interests and interrogations, an increasing desire for independence from Providence and the necessity of divine law in order to maintain the status quo, while proving that religion alone can provide happiness and pleasure.

The re-evaluation of passions in an age that had witnessed their disruptive power in the enthusiastic Puritan trends during the Civil War was a demanding task to undertake, especially for the Church of England, which was trying to distance itself from the Calvinist hard line while attempting to restore its supremacy in the Christian instruction of people. Nonetheless, sermons on passions were centred on man as a human being in his relationship both with himself and with God, and therefore they could be more viable for publication, especially if used for the purpose of self-improvement or for family readings at home. In engaging the congregation more in the sermon's topic, they could also revive attendance at church services, which was waning. The rational and well-defined structure of the sermon and its rather scientific prose best suited the instructive purpose of the clergymen who had to touch the hearts of both literate and illiterate congregations. Sermons investigated those passions which were particularly highlighted by examples in the Bible, such as pride, envy and covetousness. These all served clergymen to provide the congregations with wrong models to study, and to rebuke them for their behaviour. However, while the discussion of these inclinations did increase obedience to God by insisting on fear of eternal punishment, it did not provide a positive counterpart to exploit to strengthen an obedience invigorated by the pleasures of religion. On the contrary, the passion of love, understood both as self-love and neighbourly love, allowed clergymen ample occasions to prove to the public that it was not only possible but in their interest to exercise these passions. Drawing from the Stoic philosophy[6] which asserted that happiness was to be found in the complete control of the passions resulting in an *aequus animus,* a balanced mind, clergymen insisted on the uniqueness of religion to furnish people with this type of control, as they encouraged each member of the congregation 'to live to himself alone (*sibi vivere*), or, in Christian fashion, to God alone, scorning the entanglements of the world'.[7] The good Christian could therefore aspire to perfection only in his union with, and dependence on, God, appreciating his limits and understanding the power that passions have on him.[8] Being a passion, self-love was not classified as virtuous or vicious. St Thomas Aquinas considered the passion *amor* as 'an expression of the teleological dynamism that underlies human actions',[9] as every individual feels an appetite for a particular object according to the good, i.e. the love, that he or she can derive from it. If people employ love to assess their choices and actions, they become the primary object of human natural love, as 'to seek for one's own good and perfection is to love self'.[10] Nevertheless, taking frail human nature into consideration, a distinction between 'ordinate' and 'inordinate' self-love must be drawn. The former, virtuous passion consists in determining one's best interest and happiness, i.e. choosing God to be the chief love of the good Christian's life, especially in the exercise of virtue and charity. Inordinate self-love instead places the love for God 'as a secondary good',[11] thus leaving the soul unguarded and prey to multiple sins which lead to damnation. Therefore, self-love becomes an epistemological source, unavoidably necessary to realise eternal salvation, as long as it is combined with reason and obligation through the imitation of divine perfection.[12]

The Latitudinarian idea of self-love could be best exemplified by the works of Isaac Barrow (1630–77), mathematician and dear friend of Tillotson. His sermons, written mainly for university congregations, became popular for the manner in which Barrow thoroughly covered the topics he meant to analyse.[13] Barrow describes self-love as 'the most common [passion], so deeply eradicated [rooted] in our nature, and so generally overspread in the world, that no man thoroughly is exempted from it, most men are greatly tainted with it, some are wholly possessed and acted by it'.[14] Resuming Aquinas's distinction between innocent and culpable self-love,[15] Barrow demonstrates how this passion can be exploited 'to the preservation and enjoyment of our being' and how the guidance of reason leads us to 'have a sober regard to our true good and welfare; to our best interest and solid content'.[16] In his love and bounty, God framed the human being as a creature 'capable of tasting comfort',[17] providing the promise of future rewards and punishments, the use of wisdom and virtue which are both in accordance with self-love and the obedience to his law, whose purpose is both temporal – the improvement of one's life – and spiritual – the contentment of mind and peace of the soul. This is, according to Barrow, proof that God desires his creatures to pursue those pleasures that they are capable of, 'most ample riches, most sublime honours, most sweet pleasures, most complete felicity'.[18] In contrast, culpable self-love – which first caused original sin – is described as 'foolish and vicious, ... false and equivocal love, usurping that goodly name'.[19] Its consequences are the spreading of pride, arrogance, envy, jealousy, injustice and avarice, which all affect the relationship between human beings, because 'being blinded or transported with fond dotage on ourselves, we cannot discern or will not regard what is due to others; hence we are apt upon occasion to do them wrong'.[20] As culpable self-love can easily assume its worst form, self-conceit, Barrow advises his congregation to 'very carefully and impartially examine and study' themselves daily:[21] this virtuous practice of questioning one's conscience to check the flows of the passions allows the individual a better knowledge of him- or herself, to ensure control over vicious inclinations. The portrait of humankind that comes to light from Barrow's sermons is that of inherently benevolent but frail creatures who, though easily corrupted, preserve their dualistic nature in their tendency towards happiness and preservation.[22] He therefore encourages the congregation to master their self-love through sincere charity, describing the latter as the propulsive spur towards everlasting happiness.

In their campaign for the moral reformation of manners to rehabilitate English society's moral standards, Tillotson and the Latitudinarians questioned the reconciliation of duty towards God and the human quest for happiness: gaining control over one's passionate side grants enjoyment of present happiness and provides reassuring peace of mind at the hour of death and everlasting beatitude in the afterlife. Present and future bliss entirely revolve on the imperative *nosce te ipsum*, the only means which generates a proper, hopefully objective, perception of one's evil inclinations and virtues while promoting acquaintance with the divine residue in the soul. Tillotson demonstrates to his congregation that, in conforming to divine law and the covenant of leniency, which requires obedience and a measure of self-denial, they achieve a certain degree of 'true pleasure and perfect freedom'[23] because they are able to control the passions by using reason. He advocates eudæmonism because 'religion enlightens the minds of men, and directs them in the way wherein they should go; it seasons the spirits and manners of men, and preserves them from being putrefied and corrupted'.[24] Indeed, moral precepts are reasonable and profitable as they command 'nothing that is unnecessary and burthensom ... but what is reasonable, and useful, and substantial'.[25] God is therefore portrayed as a just, compassionate judge who does not charge his creatures with anything but what rational religion already tells them to do for the improvement of both temporal and eternal benefit:

> So that taking all things into consideration, the interest of our bodies and souls, *of the present and the future, of this world and the other*, religion is the most reasonable and wise, the most comfortable and compendious course that any man can take in order to his own happiness.[26]

The process of knowing and controlling oneself contributes to human satisfaction and to 'the pleasure of wisdom and discretion':[27] the happiness that comes from 'a clear conscience, and a mind fully satisfied with it's [sic] own actions'[28] is incomparable to any sensual pleasure. Every faculty of the human mind, from its quickness to its judgement, is modified and amplified by the power that religion can exercise on passions and lusts. Only religion can improve human health, 'the life of life', as it is 'pure, and even, and lasting, and hath no guilt or regret, no sorrow and trouble in it, or after it'.[29] The link between obedient self-love on the one hand, and pleasure on the other is therefore cemented. Pleasure can be experienced 'within the limits of virtue':[30] each individual must have 'a competency of the things of this world' and might enjoy them according to his or her capacity: 'he must eat and drink within the bounds of temperance and health, and must wear no more clothes than are for his convenience'.[31]

The Latitudinarians had to prove to their congregations that they believed their whole nature, both physical and spiritual, having being moulded by God, could be 'improved by observing the manifest footsteps of divine power, wisdom, and goodness, which occur in the works of nature and providence'.[32] Tillotson maintained that, though degenerate sinners, human beings still have 'something which the blindest passion cannot deny to be good and amiable'[33] and this humanity emerges when they confront their fellow creatures. Advising them to 'reintroduce themselves to a form of humanity',[34] Latitudinarian sermons encouraged the doctrine of work, ensuring the active participation of laymen in the life of the community.[35] Believing in the power of reason aided by Grace, Barrow claims that each individual should act 'according to the good rules of humanity':[36] these imply being upright, a sincere friend and working for the comfort and peace of society. If people are disrespectful of their nature, they lose their independence and the benefits deriving from charity, as love turns into a 'vile and pitiful slavery'.[37] In Tillotson, self-love and the moral active role of people in reforming society are interdependent, as both are induced by 'the self-seeking motives of human action'[38] and are concerned with morality. Morality therefore appears unavoidably linked to self-interest 'spurred on by the powerful incentives of eternal reward and punishment'.[39] Tillotson's concession to self-love is directed by his willingness to instruct people and to obtain the maximum result from his preaching. He exhorts his audience to improve in love even though it is a passion because once the passion is 'under the government of our reason, [it] is the most natural, and easy, and delightful of all the affections which GOD planted in human nature'.[40] He knows that, before acting, natural reason judges the profit that might be derived from the exercise of piety, temperance, wisdom and mercy, as people are mainly persuaded by 'the prospect of advantage, the apprehension of danger, and the sense of honour'.[41] The desire for profit in turn steers an increase in charitable works, as 'GOD values this [mercy, and alms to the poor] above all our external devotion'.[42] Coupled with prudence, a 'self-conscious ethical principle among English divines',[43] self-love therefore acquires a new ethical light, becoming a form of 'ennobled self-interest'.

Charity sermons in the late seventeenth century analyse self-love in relationship with charitable activities, somehow rehabilitating the image of humankind as totally depraved creatures.[44] When people do good, Tillotson affirmed, they are 'in the easiest posture'[45] which is the most congenial to their nature. Anyone can profit from the increase of charitable activities, from the single executioner to the whole society, as societal relations are 'founded in that which no man can divest himself of, in human nature'.[46] The image that modern philosophy gave of humankind did not satisfy the purpose of Tillotson's moral campaign which, on the contrary, had to draw from ancient philosophy to support human benevolence and friendship:

> the contrary principle, laid down by a much deeper and wiser man, I mean Aristotle, is most certainly true, 'that men are naturally akin and friends to each other'. Some unhappy accidents and occasions may make men enemies, but naturally every man is a friend to another.[47]

These sermons therefore reconcile human benevolence with a capacity to perfection: their aim is to incentivise not only individual, but public happiness, though the fulfilment of this beneficial project is possible only if the dependence on both God and on the fellow creatures for temporal and everlasting welfare is taken into consideration. Barrow believes that it is the innate desire for happiness that encourages people to promote their own welfare, taking charity and the profit of doing good into consideration:[48]

> He therefore hath made the love of ourselves to be the rule and standard, the pattern, the argument of our love to others; imposing on us those great commands of loving our neighbours as ourselves, and doing as we would be done unto; which imply not only a necessity, but an obligation of loving ourselves.[49]

His sermons for the poor unite passions with interest and rewards in discussing mankind's charitable disposition: charity is described as 'the fulfilling of God's law, the best expression of all our duty toward God, of faith in him, love and reverence of him'[50] and its commandments contain 'great reasonableness and equity'.[51] He states that, as human beings are attracted by 'a love of society and aversation from solitude, inclinations to pity and humanity, pleasant complacencies in obliging and doing courtesies to others',[52] their affections can easily be transferred to other objects, i.e. their more unfortunate neighbours. In so doing, their souls are engaged in virtuous activities, which help keep them away from sloth and inactivity. Reason and experience provide assistance in distinguishing between true self-love and 'a corrupt fondness toward an idol of our fancy mistaken for ourselves'.[53] Barrow therefore exhorts his audience to reflect on 'the motion of our own heart, and observing the course of our demeanour toward ourselves'.[54] This is the measure by which someone can be conscious of what he wishes for himself and of his partiality in judging his actions:

> Do we not sincerely and earnestly desire our own welfare and advantage in every kind? Do we not heartily wish good success to our own designs and undertakings? Are we unconcerned or coldly affected in any case touching our own safety, our estate, our credit, our satisfaction or pleasure? ... this doth inform us, what we should wish and covet for our neighbour.[55]

Where 'ill education and custom' give rise to inordinate self-love, self-will and self-interest,[56] charity and proper Christian instruction rectify these passionate alterations and lead human beings to become aware of the humanity which naturally 'flows from [their] good-nature'.[57] By making the happiness of one's neighbour one's own, the individual is able to create the perfect balance between self-love and charity, while also adding to the happiness of both donors and recipients:

> We cannot be happy without good-nature, and good-humour, and that good-nature cannot behold any sad object without pity and dolorous resentment, good-humour cannot subsist in prospect of such objects; considering that charity is an instrument, whereby we may apply all our neighbour's good to ourselves, it being ours, if we can find complacence therein.[58]

Once more, the covenant of leniency dictates the rule: people cannot be happy if they do not consider their infirmities, bend down their pride and self-conceit and do not look at others with a humble eye:[59] 'we do either bring down our self-love to such a moderation, or raise up our charity to such fervency, that both come to be adjusted in the same even level'.[60] Both the knowledge of oneself and the prescription to divine law furnish a rule of charity, as Barrow claims that 'thus reflecting on ourselves, and making our practice toward ourselves the pattern of our dealing with others, we shall not fail to discharge what is prescribed to us in this law: and so we have here a rule of charity'.[61]

The delicate balance between self-love and charity rests on temporal and eternal welfare: the truly charitable Protestant satisfies his neighbour's basic physical needs but also instructs him in religion, changing his ignorance into profitable Christian knowledge. In so doing, equity should always predominate because 'all charity beneath self-love is defective, and all self-love above charity is excessive'.[62] Hence Barrow asserts the idea that charity can improve human nature only if coupled with religion which allows human beings the possibility of putting their compassionate impulse into action. It shows the vanity of worldly things and their inconvenience for the attainment of eternal happiness while it presents humankind as it really is, weak and vile, unable to act but with the assistance of divine providence. Though religion 'condemneth self-love, self-pleasing, self-seeking, as great faults', these passions 'do not seem absolutely bad; or otherwise culpable, than as including partiality, or detracting from that equal measure of charity which we owe to others'.[63] The most encouraging example that proves the force of charity and control of the passions is the one given by Jesus, as in Him 'virtue conquer[ed] nature, and charity triumph[ed] over self-love'.[64]

In *A Sermon preach'd at the Morning-Exercise at Cripplegate*, Tillotson discusses human adaptability, comprehension and tolerance on a broad level. He justifies the fact that charity is based on self-love[65] by claiming that self-love makes all human beings equal: this passion is not influenced by education and custom, but is driven by self-preservation and thirst for happiness. In Tillotson, charity is both an obligation to the law of God and an innate part of human nature. The exhortation to do good is coupled with the importance given to self-love and self-interest. A human being is evaluated from a double perspective, as a creature shifting from innate benevolence to self-love. Even if divine law was set for the benefit of mankind and the Creator requires human obedience, Tillotson underlines the fact that the social attitude of human nature has predominance in a person when he or she feels disposed to charitable acts:

> The frame of our nature disposeth us to it, and our inclination to society, in which there can be no pleasure, no advantage, without mutual love and kindness. And equity also calls for it, for that which we ourselves wish and expect kindness from others is conviction enough to us that we owe it to others.[66]

As with eighteenth-century charity sermons, Tillotson evokes the donor's ability to 'hear the voice of his own instincts'.[67] He explores the social function of compassion, and the key-words that we often hear in his sermons are interest and happiness. When people experience, for example, the pleasure of giving instead of receiving, they feel they have 'a more happy spirit and temper'.[68] Moreover, someone who is 'beneficial and [does] good to others, hath the happiness of a great reward'.[69] To do good is the proper way of acting 'of a noble, and generous, and large heart' which is free and open, 'ready to do good, and willing to communicate, and thinks it's [sic] own happiness increased, by making others happy'.[70] Individuals with these characteristics therefore lay aside those forms of inordinate self-love which are a hazard for the benefit of society at large. Charity offers the opportunity to improve human perfectibility, because 'to be good and to do good, is the excellency of virtue, because it is to resemble GOD in that which is the most amiable and glorious of all his other perfections'.[71] Donating to others is a symbol of magnitude and an efficient way to stimulate people to 'approach towards divinity',[72] as 'by goodness and kindness, by mutual compassion and helpfulness, men become gods to one another'.[73]

The picture of humankind that Tillotson elaborates starts out as the sketch of a group of selfish individuals seeking only their happiness, but it evolves into the portrait of social animals who live to increase the benefit of their country. The thirst for happiness, 'one of the first principles that is planted in the nature of man',[74] influences human beings at such a high rate that they are only 'led by interest', and 'love or hate, chuse or refuse things, according as [they apprehend] them to conduce to this end'.[75] Human self-interest is based on the principle of self-preservation. God implanted in humankind the necessity of laws and a natural inclination to religion, which is 'the strongest band of humane society, and so necessary to the welfare and happiness of mankind, as it could not have been more, if we could suppose the Being of GOD himself to have been purposely designed and contrived for the benefit and advantage of men'.[76] Charity provides a clear picture of human frailty and the need of sociability for survival; it gives us 'a just sense and acknowledgement of our state, that we are insufficient for our own happiness, and must depend upon the kindness, and good-will, and friendship of other men'.[77] The good Christian therefore becomes a profitable citizen, and religion stimulates the extirpation of all those passions, i.e. pride, covetousness and peevishness, that limit and endanger one's relationship with others, promoting at the same time love and trust. Religion 'is the greatest friend to our temporal interests'[78] as it leads Christians to do good while working on their beneficial peace of mind: 'though our charity should fall upon stony and barren ground, ... yet there is a pleasure in being conscious to ourselves, that we have done well'.[79] It only imposes profitable obligations on people, so that they can follow their consciences in 'all civil offices and moral duties' to increase mutual love and strengthen 'good-will and confidence among men, which are the great bands of peace'.[80]

Tillotson assures his audience that if they know they are living a holy life, following divine dictates, they will be freed from 'anxieties of guilt, and the fear of divine wrath and displeasure'.[81] The prospect seems, indeed, a very enjoyable one. Following the path indicated by his friend Barrow, Tillotson's charity sermons therefore combine interest, both individual and collective, with morality and good works. They remind the audience of the benefits and advantages of such a practice, as 'the laws of Christianity do likewise secure both the private interests of men and the publick peace'.[82] Hence Tillotson reasonably answers the contradictory assumption that passions and obedience can coexist. If charity equals self-love, the fulfilment of one's supreme interest under the control of religion is pleasure and happiness. Charity and genuine self-love are therefore as inseparable as religion and morality and can ensure the moral reformation the Latitudinarians aspired to.

Notes

1 John Tillotson, Lord Archbishop of Canterbury, *The Works of the Most Reverend John Tillotson ... In Twelve Volumes. Containing Two Hundred And Fifty Four Sermons And Discourses On Several Occasions*, etc. (London: Printed for R. Ware, A. Ward, J. and P. Knapton et al., 1743). Sermon 28, vol. 2, p. 285.
2 *Ibid.*, p. 282.
3 Susan James, *Passion and Action: The Emotions in Seventeenth-Century Philosophy* (Oxford: Oxford University Press, 2003), p. 2.
4 Patrick Müller, *Latitudinarianism and Didacticism in Eighteenth-Century Literature: Moral Theology in Fielding, Sterne, and Goldsmith* (Frankfurt: Peter Lang, 2009), pp. 131–2.

5 Tillotson, *The Works of the Most Reverend John Tillotson*, Sermon 28, vol. 2, pp. 281–2.
6 For a discussion on the influence of Stoicism on Latitudinarian ideas see Chapter 5, 'The Latitudinarians' Conception of Reason', in Martin I. J. Griffin, *Latitudinarianism in the Seventeenth-Century Church of England* (Leiden; New York; Köln: Brill, 1992). For further discussion see also Philip A. Smith, 'Bishop Hall, "Our English Seneca"', *PMLA*, 63:4 (Dec. 1948), 1191–3. According to Smith, Stoicism appealed to Anglican divines in the seventeenth century due to its encouragement to follow 'right reason', which in Christian terms corresponded to following nature, i.e. natural religion. Other reasons are the Stoic appeal to a system of moral values proposed for the benefit of individuals, the perception of the existence of superior entities who govern the universe and desire human good, the belief in providence and in the afterlife and the insistence on self-reflection.
7 Maren-Sofie Røstvig, *The Happy Man: 1700–1760* (Oslo: Norwegian University Press, 1962), pp. 49–51.
8 James, *Passion and Action*, p. 252.
9 Stephen Pope, 'Expressive Individualism and True Self-Love: A Thomistic Perspective', *The Journal of Religion*, 71:3 (July 1991), 387.
10 *Ibid*.
11 For clergymen in the seventeenth century, self-love was defined also as an intellectual evil, not just a moral one. On self-love see Dirk F. Passmann and Hermann J. Real, 'The Intellectual History of "Self-Love" and *Verses on the Death of Dr. Swift, D.S.P.D*', in Hermann J. Real (ed.), *Reading Swift: Papers from the Fifth Münster Symposium on Jonathan Swift* (Munich: Wilheim Fink, 2008), pp. 343–62 and 351–6. See also Tillotson, *The Works of the Most Reverend John Tillotson*, Sermon 142, vol. 8, pp. 3513–14.
12 Müller, *Latitudinarianism and Didacticism*, pp. 192–3.
13 Tillotson affirmed that the sermon *The Duty and Reward of Bounty to the Poor* was 'received with universal approbation' as Barrow 'seems to have exhausted the whole argument, and to have left no consideration belonging to it untouched'. Isaac Barrow, *The Theological Works of Isaac Barrow, D.D., Master of Trinity College, Cambridge*, In Nine Volumes, edited by the Rev. Alexander Napier, M.A., Trinity College, Cambridge, Vicar of Holkham, Norfolk (Cambridge: at the University Press, 1859), p. lxxxiv.
14 *Ibid.*, Sermon 51, vol. 4, p. 80.
15 Tillotson also describes 'culpable self-love' in *A Sermon preach'd at the Morning-Exercise at Cripplegate*, p. 444: 'In judging of your present condition and circumstances, always abate something for the presence of them, and for self-love, and self-interest, and other passions. He,

that doth not consider, how apt every man is unequally to favour himself, doth not know the littleness and narrowness of human nature.' Thomas Birch, *The Life of the Most Reverend Dr. John Tillotson, Lord Archbishop of Canterbury. Compiled chiefly from his original papers and letters. The Second Edition* (London: Printed for J. and R. Tonson *et al.*, 1753), pp. 437–69.
16 Barrow, *The Theological Works of Isaac Barrow*, Sermon 51, vol. 4, pp. 83–4.
17 *Ibid.*, p. 85.
18 *Ibid.*, p. 87.
19 *Ibid.*, pp. 87–8.
20 *Ibid.*, p. 82.
21 *Ibid.*, p. 94.
22 *Ibid.* See p. 109: 'Every man is in some kind and degree bad, sinful, vile; it is as natural for us to be so, as to be frail, to be sickly, to be mortal: there are some bad dispositions common to all, and which no man can put off without his flesh'.
23 Tillotson, *The Works of the Most Reverend John Tillotson*, Sermon 28, vol. 2, p. 282.
24 *Ibid.*, Sermon 83, vol. 5, p. 1319.
25 *Ibid.*, Sermon 5, p. 133.
26 Added emphasis. *Ibid.*, Sermon 28, vol. 2, p. 286.
27 *Ibid.*, p. 282.
28 *Ibid.*, Sermon 6, vol. 1, p. 162.
29 *Ibid.*, Sermon 28, vol. 2, p. 284. See also Sermon 119, vol. 7, p. 2011: 'The Christian religion is a great happiness to the world in general, though some are so unhappy as to be the worse for it; not because religion is bad, but because they are so.' Sermon 158, vol. 9, p. 3792: 'We shall reap the pleasure and satisfaction of it in our own minds, and all the other mighty advantages of it in the world, and the vast and unspeakable reward of it in the other.' See Sermon 4, vol. 1, p. 115: 'Religion does likewise tend to the happiness of the outward man. Now the blessings of this kind are such as either respect our health, or estate, or reputation, or relations; and in respect of all these religion is highly advantageous to us.'
30 *Ibid.*, Sermon 28, vol. 2, p. 293. See also Sermon 27, vol. 2, pp. 250–1: 'The temporal felicity of man, and the ends of government can very hardly, if at all, be attained without religion.'
31 *Ibid.*, Sermon 92, vol. 6, p. 1469.
32 Barrow, *The Theological Works Of Isaac Barrow*, Sermon 2, vol. 5, p. 56.
33 Tillotson, *The Works of the Most Reverend John Tillotson*, Sermon 33, vol. 2, p. 403.

34 W. M. Spellman, 'The Latitudinarians and the Church of England, 1660–1700' (Athens, GA and London: University of Georgia Press, 1993), p. 116.
35 Cf. Tillotson, *The Works of the Most Reverend John Tillotson*, Sermon 3, vol. 1, p. 108: 'It concerns every one to live in the practice of religion and virtue, because the publick happiness and prosperity depends upon it. It is most apparent that of late years religion is very sensibly declined among us. The manners of men have almost been universally corrupted by a civil war. We should therefore jointly endeavour to retrieve the ancient virtue of the nation, and to bring into fashion again that solid and substantial, that plain and unaffected piety, ... which flourished in the age of our immediate forefathers.'
36 Barrow, *The Theological Works Of Isaac Barrow*, Sermon 51, vol. 4, p. 92.
37 *Ibid*.
38 Henry W. Sams, 'Self-Love and the Doctrine of Work', *Journal of the History of Ideas*, 4:3 (June 1943), 321.
39 Gregory F. Scholtz, 'Anglicanism in the Age of Johnson: The Doctrine of Conditional Salvation', *Eighteenth-Century Studies*, 22:2 (1988–89), 204.
40 Tillotson, *The Works of the Most Reverend John Tillotson*, Sermon 33, vol. 2, p. 400.
41 *Ibid.*, Sermon 102, vol. 6, p. 1667.
42 *Ibid.*, p. 1671.
43 Sams, 'Self-Love and the Doctrine of Work', p. 322.
44 R. S. Crane, 'Suggestions Toward A Genealogy of the "Man of Feeling"', *Journal of English Literary History*, 1:3 (Dec. 1934), 207–8.
45 Tillotson, *The Works of the Most Reverend John Tillotson*, Sermon 33, vol. 2, p. 402.
46 *Ibid.*, p. 403.
47 *Ibid.*, pp. 403–4.
48 See *ibid.*, Sermons 207, 208 and 209, *Of the necessity of good works*, vols 10–11. See also Sermons 106, 107, 108, 109 and 110, *Of the nature of regeneration, and its necessity, in order to justification and salvation*, vol. 6, in which Tillotson develops the idea of regeneration of the self through faith supported by charity. Tillotson insists on the active role the individual plays in the process, assisted by God's grace. See vol. 6, p. 1758: 'The grace of GOD is necessary to the conversion of a sinner, but it is not necessary that he should be only passive in this work. Experience tells us the contrary, that we can do something, that we can co-operate with the grace of GOD.' On the role of grace see W. M. Spellman, 'Archbishop John Tillotson and the Meaning of Moralism', *Anglican and Episcopal History*, 56 (1987), 418.

49 Barrow, *The Theological Works Of Isaac Barrow*, Sermon 51, vol. 4, pp. 85–6.
50 *Ibid.*, Sermon 1, vol. 1, p. 19.
51 *Ibid.*, p. 28.
52 *Ibid.*, p. 126.
53 *Ibid.*, Sermon 28, vol. 2, p. 327.
54 *Ibid.*, Sermon 27, vol. 2, p. 301.
55 *Ibid.*, pp. 302–3.
56 Barrow is mainly concerned with inordinate self-love and its consequences, self-will and self-interest, as these encourage people to act against the public good and ruin social intercourse. A self-willed individual indulges in 'pleasing one's self in [his or her] choice, and proceeding without or against reason' to the point of sacrificing 'the greatest benefits of society (public order and peace, mutual love and friendship, common safety and prosperity) to [his or her] private will and humour'. (*Ibid.*, Sermon 52, vol. 4, pp. 118 and 120). Self-interest instead makes people believe that 'the good state of things is to be measured by their condition; that all is well if they prosper and thrive'. These people 'do nothing *gratis*, or for love' and reverse the natural order in society, disobeying their governors. See *ibid.*, Sermon 52, vol. 4, pp. 122–3.
57 *Ibid.*, Sermon 28, vol. 2, p. 327.
58 *Ibid.*, p. 334.
59 Tillotson makes much the same point in *The Works of the Most Reverend John Tillotson*, Sermon 20, vol. 2, p. 14: 'It is a very considerable part of our duty, and almost equall'd by our SAVIOUR with the first and great commandment of the law. It is highly acceptable to GOD, most beneficial to other, and very comfortable to ourselves. It is the easiest of all duties, and it makes all others easy; the pleasure of it makes the pains to signify nothing, and the delightful reflexion upon it afterwards is a most ample reward of it.'
60 Barrow, *The Theological Works Of Isaac Barrow*, Sermon 27, vol. 2, p. 306.
61 *Ibid.*
62 *Ibid.*, p. 310.
63 *Ibid.*, p. 313.
64 *Ibid.*, p. 317.
65 Tillotson, *A Sermon preach'd at the Morning-Exercise at Cripplegate*, pp. 438–9.
66 Tillotson, *The Works of the Most Reverend John Tillotson*, Sermon 20, vol. 2, p. 13.
67 Rita Goldberg, 'Charity Sermons and The Poor: A Rhetoric of Compassion', *The Age of Johnson*, 4 (1991), p. 203.

68 Tillotson, *The Works of the Most Reverend John Tillotson*, Sermon 213, vol. 11, p. 81.
69 *Ibid.*, p. 87.
70 *Ibid.*, p. 81.
71 *Ibid.*, p. 82.
72 *Ibid.*, p. 86.
73 *Ibid.*
74 *Ibid.*, Sermon 3, vol. 1, p. 94.
75 *Ibid.*
76 *Ibid.*, Sermon 27, vol. 2, p. 251.
77 *Ibid.*, Sermon 213, vol. 11, p. 83.
78 *Ibid.*, Sermon 3, vol. 1, p. 95.
79 *Ibid.*, Sermon 213, vol. 11, p. 84.
80 *Ibid.*, Sermon 3, vol. 1, p. 99.
81 *Ibid.*, Sermon 4, vol. 1, p. 114.
82 *Ibid.*, Sermon 5, vol. 1, p. 139.

3

Self-love in Mandeville and Hutcheson

Jeffrey Hopes

Let us begin with two quotations from Locke's *Essay Concerning Human Understanding*: 'For it is by the consciousness it has of its present Thoughts and Actions, that it is *self* to it *self* now, and so will be the same *self* as far as the same consciousness can extend to Actions past or to come.'[1] '*Self* is that conscious thinking thing (whatever Substance, made up of whether Spiritual, or Material, Simple, or Compounded, it matters not) which is sensible, or conscious of Pleasure and Pain, capable of Happiness or Misery, and so is concern'd for it *self*, as far as that consciousness extends.'[2] Locke's argument that *self* results from consciousness of self, while it seeks to establish *self*'s unicity, in time and space, demonstrates, by the very terms in which he presents this argument, that it is indelibly reflexive.[3] It is a reflexivity that is evident in the reflexive pronouns (here 'itself') and in the numerous compound nouns in which 'self' figures: self-denial, self-belief, self-interest, self-esteem, self-confidence and, of course, self-love. The question of *self* in early eighteenth-century moral philosophy cannot be reduced to matters of grammar or semantics, but it is important to re-establish those reflexive links which such pronouns and compound nouns suggest and which always accompany and vastly outnumber the use of the word 'self' in isolation. The tentative hypothesis underlying what follows is that in the late seventeenth and early eighteenth centuries, the isolation of *self*, its elevation to the status of a thing 'in itself', emerges from such reflexive usages in the course of what Charles Taylor calls 'the inward turn', the rejection of the rationalist 'extrinsic' thinking of which Hobbes and Locke are exemplars.[4] Rather than examine, as Taylor and others have done, the lineage of this new moral philosophy from the Cambridge Platonists through Shaftesbury to Hutcheson and, in some respects at least, to Hume, Rousseau and the Romantics, I will here focus on a particular confrontation between the philosophy of moral sentiment and the 'extrinsic' thinking it was attacking, that which saw Francis Hutcheson oppose Bernard Mandeville over the issue of self-love.

Before turning to Mandeville's *Fable of the Bees*, a brief chronology is in order. The Earl of Shaftesbury published the first versions of two of the most important essays of his *Characteristicks* (1711) in 1699 (*An Inquiry concerning Virtue or Merit*) and 1709 (*Communis Sensus*). Mandeville's poem *The Grumbling Hive* appeared in 1705 before being similarly incorporated into the first edition of *The Fable of the Bees* in 1714. Mandeville does not refer explicitly to Shaftesbury in the 1714 edition, but it seems clear that his attack on the notions of natural virtue and sociability and on the Stoic philosophy which underpinned them, had Shaftesbury in mind. It was, however, the publication of the third edition of the *Characteristicks* in 1723 which elicited a specific response from Mandeville in his much expanded 1723 edition of the *Fable of the Bees*, most fully in the essay *A Search into the Nature of Society*. It is this edition that Francis Hutcheson refers to in his *Inquiry into the Original of our Ideas of Beauty and Virtue* which appeared in 1725. On one imprint of this first edition (but not on the other and subsequent editions and imprints) the title bears the inscription: 'In which The Principles of the late Earl of SHAFTESBURY are Explain'd and Defended, against the Author of the *Fable of the Bees*: and the Ideas of *Moral Good* and *Evil* are establish'd, according to the Sentiments of the Antient *Moralists*. With an Attempt to introduce a *Mathematical Calculation* in Subjects of *Morality*.' This may have been a printer's addition, but it is an accurate description of the polemical dimension of Hutcheson's work. Contrary to Charles Taylor's assertion that 'Hutcheson doesn't spend that much time on Mandeville',[5] not only does he refer explicitly to the *Fable of the Bees*, he engages with some of the central tenets of

Mandeville's work, in particular with the additions to the 1723 edition.

Mandeville's paradox of private vices and public benefits is well known, but the *Fable of the Bees* is also a treatise on the passions. The question of the passions was one which had troubled theologians and philosophers throughout the seventeenth century. Even before Descartes's *Les Passions de l'âme* (1649), Nicolas Coeffeteau (1620) and Marin Cureau de La Chambre (1640) had sought to classify the passions and to identify their causes and effects.[6] But it was Descartes's seminal work which initiated a whole series of French treatises on the subject in the second half of the century, a genre that continued through to the end of the eighteenth century, culminating in Condillac's *Essai sur les appétits et les passions* published during the French Revolution.[7] Although these French treatises were generally translated into English, there was no similar production by English or British writers until the works of Mandeville and Hutcheson. It is clear that they were consciously participating in a European debate of which many of their readers would have been ignorant. For most English writers, the passions were there to be tamed and so approached from a religious and didactic standpoint.[8] In theological terms, sin was explained by the transgression of Adam and Eve whereas the positive elements of human nature were attributed to mankind's being created in God's image. But the origin and the purpose of the passions, not to mention the way they operated, were the subject of constant theological debate. According to Nicolas Malebranche, an important influence on Hutcheson, the passions predated the Fall as it was the desire to taste the fruit of the tree of knowledge which led Adam and Eve into transgression.[9] Desire could be seen either as the premise of the passions, or as a passion in itself (as it was for Descartes). The passions, in their widest sense, could not be purely negative; love, for Malebranche, was what drew man to God, the consequence of the love God has for himself and the proof of man's need for, indeed his dependence on, his fellow humans.

Coping with the dual nature of the passions, the way they pull both ways, to virtue and to vice, proved a major theological challenge; a distinction between religious and worldly passions could be drawn, but only in terms of their effects and their direction. Passion itself seemed to require more fundamental explanation. Similarly, bodily and spiritual concerns might be separated, but the most obvious characteristic of the passions was the link they demonstrated between the soul and the body. Appetites (sometimes defined as passions, sometimes not) began in the body but could generate desires seated in the mind. Passions such as love or hate, happiness and sadness, originated in the mind or the soul and generated physical effects such as blushing or tears. It was the physiological nature of the passions which induced Descartes to write his *Passions de l'âme*, and which much later was to inspire so much of the sentimental literature of the eighteenth century. The passions were, then, a problem to philosophers and theologians of all hues, the source of desire and so of action (as Locke and later Hume pointed out), but also an obstacle to rational thought, so that the mastering of the passions seemed a necessary step to equanimity, clear-sightedness and good judgement.

The idea that the passions were to be, if not conquered, at least tamed and put to constructive use, could be applied to radically different conceptions of human nature. For some, the passions were the proof of man's original sin or of his fundamentally selfish nature. For others, they clouded and perverted man's rationality or, as for Shaftesbury, his virtuous nature. In both cases, if happiness through proximity with God is seen as the ultimate end of human existence, and vice and enslavement to the corporeal are construed as misery, then the passions should be judged by the degree of happiness or misery they procure. Here happiness could also be defined as pleasure and misery as pain, though they might have both corporeal and spiritual dimensions. This happiness or misery could be individual or collective; indeed the two might not coincide, so that the pleasure of one individual could be detrimental to the happiness of others or the well-being of the whole imply the misery of some. The question of happiness and misery, pleasure and pain, in their individual and social dimensions, is basic to the debate on the passions, though of course the idea that we should seek to be happy could itself be contested if it was thought, as was the case with Calvinists, that we had no cause to be happy at all.

The debate on the passions is essential to a full understanding of *The Fable of the Bees* and to Mandeville's treatment of the question of self-love in particular. As he states in the *Vindication of the Book*, published in August 1723 in response to its presentment by the Grand Jury of Middlesex, 'It describes the Nature and Symptoms of human Passions, detects their Force, and disguises and traces Self-Love in its darkest Recesses'.[10] At times, Mandeville seems to equate self-love with pride or vanity, but the distinction between them is in fact important. Embroidering on Hobbes, Mandeville declares that:

> There is nothing so universally sincere upon Earth, as the Love which all Creatures, that are capable of any, bear to themselves; and as there is no Love but what implies a Care to preserve the Thing beloved, so there is nothing more sincere in any Creature than his Will, Wishes and Endeavours to preserve himself. This is the Law of Nature, by which no Creature is endued with any Appetite or Passion but what directly or indirectly tends to the Preservation of himself or his Species.[11]

The essential sincerity of the passions is contrasted with the hypocrisy which derives from the effects of custom, manners and education. Referring explicitly to Shaftesbury, Mandeville denounces the 'Specious Cloak of Sociableness',[12] a cloak which hides self-love under the hypocrisy of disinterested benevolence. This is the source of those moral virtues which, in his celebrated formula, 'are the Political Offspring which Flattery begot upon Pride'.[13] So glory 'consists in a superlative Felicity which a Man, who is conscious of having perform'd a noble Action, enjoys in Self love, whilst he is thinking on the Applause he expects of others',[14] while gratitude is always self-interested and our shame at the vice of envy 'is owing to that strong Habit of Hypocrisy, by the Help of which, we have learned from our Cradle to hide even from ourselves the vast Extent of Self-love, and all its different Branches'.[15] In a brilliantly caustic passage in which he discusses the motivations of the man who, at table, leaves the choicest pieces of food to others, Mandeville explains that such apparently disinterested behaviour is in fact motivated by the desire to be esteemed by others, 'and if he gets nothing else by it, the Pleasure he receives in reflecting on the Applause which he knows is secretly given him, is to a Proud Man more than an Equivalent for his former Self-denial, and over-pays to Self-love with Interest, the loss it sustain'd in his Complaisance to others'.[16] Even that sympathy for the misfortunes of others, which for Shaftesbury and later sentimentalists represented the defining characteristic of the 'Man of Feeling', is described as rooted in the pleasure that derives from self-love: 'when we are sincere in sharing with another in his Misfortunes, Self-Love makes us believe that the Sufferings we feel must alleviate and lessen those of our Friend, and whilst this fond Reflection is soothing our Pain, a secret Pleasure arises from our grieving for the Person we love'.[17] Self-love is thus not just the source of all the passions; it fuels the very hypocrisy with which we seek to hide and deny its influence.

For Mandeville, these passions, and the self-love that engenders them, are the driving force of society (a word which Mandeville uses in its modern sense), the source of wealth and prosperity. It is reasoned hypocrisy (rooted nonetheless in self-love) which condemns the inhabitants of the grumbling hive to a life of miserable frugality and saps the foundations of pleasure and happiness. As for Hutcheson, he was no more concerned with the theological arguments about the origin of the passions than were Mandeville or Shaftesbury; what they all address is their social impact and utility. The language of the *Inquiry into the Original of our Ideas of Beauty and Virtue* suggests that it was John Locke who, along with Shaftesbury, constituted the most immediate philosophical influence on Hutcheson's work, yet their concerns and objectives could hardly be more different. In the *Essay Concerning Human Understanding*, Locke had focused almost exclusively on the senses, impressions and ideas, relegating the passions to near anecdotal status. In postulating the existence of a moral sense in the *Inquiry*, Hutcheson was neither seeking to contradict Locke's rejection of the existence of innate ideas nor to simply provide a convenient and diplomatic label for an innate sense of right and wrong. Hutcheson sees the moral sense as operating in the same way as the other senses, all of which seek pleasure rather than pain. In the *Inquiry* he justifies the use of the term 'moral sense', arguing that it corresponds to the way we receive perceptions from our other, external, senses, 'a Determination of the Mind, to receive any Idea from the Presence of an Object, which occurs to us, independently on our Will'.[18] Similarly virtue, according to Hutcheson, is desirable because it is lovely. This is why he also postulates the existence of a sense of beauty which draws us to the aesthetic ideal of 'Uniformity amidst Variety'.[19] Because moral and aesthetic judgements will necessarily differ from one person to another, he acknowledges that many will deny the existence of these internal senses, even though the same variety of impressions can be seen to derive from the external ones. The reason for this is '"That we have got distinct Names for the *external Senses*, and none, or very few for the *Internal*;" and by this are led, as in many other Cases, to look upon the former as some way more *fix'd*, and *real*, and *natural*, than the latter.'[20] It is hardly surprising then that Hutcheson frequently reformulates his definition of these internal senses, calling them in the *Essay on the Nature and Conduct of the Passions and Affections* which appeared in 1728, 'Determinations of our Nature',[21] and the moral sense a natural state of 'Goodwill, Humanity, Compassion, mutual Aid, propagating and supporting Offspring, Love of a Community or Country, Devotion, or Love and Gratitude to some governing Mind'.[22] The terminological difficulty that Hutcheson faces demonstrates that our ability to formulate ideas of our senses depends on the imperfect vocabulary at our disposal.

In both the *Inquiry* and the *Essay*, this concept of the moral and aesthetic senses, and the shifting terminology Hutcheson uses to describe them, rub up against the language of the passions. Two different philosophical traditions come together in Hutcheson's work, each with its own frames of reference, the one derived from Shaftesbury and the Latitudinarians, the other rooted in the seventeenth-century debate on the passions. In the *Inquiry*, Hutcheson stresses the importance of the passions and the power of self-love. In the first treatise of the *Inquiry*, where he asserts that we are endowed with a sense of beauty and order, Hutcheson argues that the pleasure which beautiful objects inspire is of a different order from the pleasure we feel at the gratification of our own self-interest. Even if we might pursue beautiful objects from motives of self-love, the sense of their beauty must necessarily precede our desire for them. Hutcheson does not deny the existence of self-love, but he refuses to recognise the status of prime-mover of the passions which Mandeville accords it. Indeed, he refuses to reduce all the passions and all human behaviour to one single cause. Following Gershom Carmichael,[23] he criticises Pufendorf for deriving all the duties of man from the sole principle of sociability. To Hutcheson, religion, self-love and sociability are distinct and need to be addressed separately in order to assess their respective importance. It is the concordance of self-interest, reason and the internal sense of beauty which produces the greatest pleasure, while the contemplation of the conflict between them, as for example in theatrical tragedies, affects us deeply.

In the second treatise of the *Inquiry*, on 'Virtue or Moral Good', Hutcheson extends this reasoning to the area of morals. Some objects induce pleasure on the basis of the natural good or happiness they procure, whereas 'Those Objects which may procure others equally pleasant, are call'd *Advantageous*: and we pursue both Kinds from a View of *Interest*, or from *Self-Love*.'[24] But here again, 'Our Sense of Pleasure is antecedent to *Advantage* and *Interest*, and is the Foundation of them. We do not perceive Pleasure in Objects, because it is our *Interest* to do so; but Objects and Actions are *Advantageous*, and are pursu'd or undertaken from *Interest*, because we receive Pleasure from them.'[25] Hutcheson goes on, however, to differentiate the pleasure derived from actions pursued out of self-love from the pleasure that comes from our moral sense, a pleasure that mirrors the aesthetic sense described in the first treatise: 'It is plain we have some *secret Sense* which determines our Approbation without regard to *Self-Interest*; otherwise we should always favour the fortunate Side without regard to *Virtue*.'[26] Virtue, an almost aesthetic quality, might be counterbalanced by self-interest, but 'our Sentiment of Perception of its *Beauty* cannot'.[27]

Turning to Mandeville, Hutcheson states that the virtuous affections which spring from the exercise of the moral sense cannot come from self-interest. It follows then 'That *Virtue* is not pursu'd from the *Interest* of *Self-Love* of the *Pursuer*, or any Motives of his own Advantage'.[28] The two forces behind benevolence, the public-spirited pursuit of virtue and self-love, are sometimes opposed and sometimes concur. The degree of benevolence achieved can thus be calculated by comparing the relative strength of both. This conclusion then forms the basis for Hutcheson's reply to Mandeville, one in which he deals with those same passions which his opponent defined as based on self-love. Crucially, to Hutcheson, passions procure a sense of unease and as such cannot be indulged out of self-interest. It is these passions, or rather an excess of them, that pose a threat to benevolence: 'The ordinary Springs of *Vice* among Men, must then be suppos'd to be a *mistaken Self-Love*, made too violent, so as to overcome *Benevolence*.'[29] The notion of 'mistaken self-love', like the association of self-love with the violent passions, indicates that in order to counter Mandeville, Hutcheson alters his conception of self-love so that it becomes in itself morally neutral. It is only when it is exacerbated by the violent passions that it is opposed to benevolence. Here, as later on in the *Essay*, Hutcheson argues against the idea that reason is ultimately the only judge of virtue. The passions are symptomatic of the exercise of the moral sense which precedes and founds rational judgement.

Unlike Mandeville, Hutcheson sees the congruence of private and public interests not as a paradoxical or perverse advancement of a public benefit which is ultimately nothing but the sum of private interests, but as the natural result of the presence of a moral sense which informs both actions inspired by self-interest and those which are benevolent, altruistic or public-spirited: 'So far is *Virtue* from being (in the Language of a late Author) the *Offspring of Flattery, begot upon Pride*', he writes, 'that *Pride*, in the bad meaning of that Word, is *the spurious Brood of Ignorance by our Moral Sense*; and *Flattery* only an *Engine, which the Cunning may use to turn this moral Sense in others, to the Purposes of Self-love in the Flatterer*.'[30] Pride and flattery can no more negate the existence of the moral sense than the operations of the violent or self-interested passions.

The publication, three years later, of the *Essay* is a recognition, both of the importance of the issues raised in the *Inquiry* concerning the emotional complexity of the working of the moral sense and of the need to expand on the *Inquiry*'s analysis and to elucidate its difficulties. In the Preface, Hutcheson remarks on the way in which 'the Perfection of Virtue consists in "having the *universal calm Benevolence*, the prevalent Affection of the Mind, so as to limit and counteract not only the *selfish Passions*, but even the *particular kind Affections*"'.[31] He makes clear in the first section of the *Essay* that both affections and passions originate in the working of the moral sense, defining them as 'those *Modifications, or Actions of the Mind consequent upon the Apprehension of certain Objects or Events, in which the Mind generally conceives Good or Evil*'.[32] He then proposes a classification of the senses which expands the category of internal senses to include not just the moral sense and the sense of beauty (here called 'the *Pleasant Perceptions*'),[33] but the public sense and the sense of honour, defined as the pleasure felt in the approbation or gratitude of others (something Mandeville would have simply defined as pride).

By acknowledging the way in which self-love and benevolence interconnect through the passions, while at the same time defining virtue in terms of pleasure rather than rationality, Hutcheson renders himself vulnerable to Mandeville's argument that pleasure derives from self-love. Without the crutch of the existence of the moral sense, which sometimes seems to be proved tautologically, Hutcheson's argument would collapse. Ultimately however, he bases his whole argument on the utility of benevolence, as had Shaftesbury. And it is here, when he ceases to try to out-argue Mandeville and opposes his own moral generosity to the misanthropy which Mandeville struggled to deny, that Hutcheson wins out:

> What is that which we feel in our own Hearts, determining as it were our Fate as to Happiness or Misery? What sort of Sensations are the most lively and delightful? In what sort of Possessions does the highest Joy and Self-Satisfaction consist? Who has ever felt the Pleasure of a generous friendly *Temper*, of *mutual Love*, of *compassionate Relief and Succour* to the distressed; of having *served a Community*, and render'd Multitudes happy; of a strict *Integrity*, and *thorow Honesty*, even under external Disadvantages, and amidst Dangers; of Congratulation and publick Rejoycing, in the Wisdom and Prosperity of Persons beloved, such as Friends, Children, or intimate Neighbours? Who would not, upon Reflection, prefer that *State of Mind*, these *Sensations of Pleasure*, to all the Enjoyments of the *external Senses*, and of the *Imagination* without them?[34]

The *Essay* also returns to the problematic question of the relationship between virtue, the moral sense, self-love and the passions. Hutcheson here introduces a new notion of self-approbation (and its opposite, self-condemnation) which enables him to recruit a form of self-love to the cause of the moral pleasures and which 'make[s] us delight in our own *selves*, and relish our very *Nature*'.[35] Apologising for being rather too metaphysical, Hutcheson goes on to argue that other sensations (or affections) are related,

> by the Constitution of our Nature, to something different from our *selves*; to a *Body* which we do not call *Self*, but something belonging to this *Self*. The other *Perceptions* of *Joy* or *Pleasure* carry with them Relations to *Objects*, and *Spaces* distinct from this *Self*; whereas 'the Pleasures of Virtue are the very *Perfection of this* SELF, and are immediately perceived as such, independent of external Objects.'[36]

In this passage Hutcheson quite literally, and visually, detaches *self* from self-interest and self-love. The moral sense, with the help of the crucial notion of virtuous, disinterested self-approbation, becomes constitutive of the self and so of self-love itself. It is a remarkable move, one which breaks free from the grip of Mandeville's self-love by detaching and redefining the self which can now be loved in the cause of benevolence and virtue. Yet while it enables Hutcheson to go on to write his own treatise on the passions without having constantly to situate himself in relation to Mandeville, it is not an insight that he otherwise develops, as he tends to return to the previous opposition between benevolence and self-interest. It would be left to others, notably Archibald Campbell, to develop this idea. In Campbell's *Enquiry into the Original of Moral Virtue*, published in 1733, all virtuous actions are founded in a self-love which is explicitly opposed both to Mandeville's association of self-love and private vice and to Hutcheson's initial opposition between self-love and benevolence.

Hutcheson's interrogation of the reflexivity of the notion of self-love and his often heroic attempts to counter Mandeville's reduction of the passions to pure self-interest, constitute a crucial step in the construction of a conception of human nature in which the self's search for happiness is allied to, indeed inseparable from, the same self's intrinsic sociability, benevolence and altruism. The essential link that Mandeville established between self-love and its public benefits becomes redefined so that virtue and individual self-interest are no longer incompatible but mutually beneficial, an idea that Adam Smith develops in *The Theory of Moral Sentiments* (1759) and which, up until today, informs so much of the defence of self-love as a necessary condition for the love of others. Such a reassuring and mutually acceptable philosophy can however never wholly escape the sceptical, mocking eye of Mandeville's pitiless scrutiny. The time has surely come to see Mandeville not so much as a proto-capitalist, but as the first great analyst of modern narcissism.

Notes

1 John Locke, *An Essay Concerning Human Understanding*, ed. Peter H. Nidditch (Oxford: Clarendon Press, 1979), bk II, ch. 27, §10, p. 336. All italics in quotations are in the original.
2 *Ibid.*, bk II, ch. 27, §17, p. 341.
3 Like Locke, I use *self*, in italics and without an article, whenever it is a philosophical concept. If it is the word 'self' that I am referring to, I put it in single quotation marks. 'The self' would suggest a normative acceptation of the existence of a concrete reality. Self without an article and without italics lies somewhere in between.
4 Charles Taylor, *Sources of the Self : The Making of the Modern Identity* (Cambridge, MA: Harvard University Press, 1989), pp. 177 and 253.

5 *Ibid.*, p. 259.
6 Nicolas Coeffeteau, *Tableau des passions humaines, de leurs causes et de leurs effets* (Paris, 1620); Marin Cureau de La Chambre, *Les charactères des passions*, 5 vols (Paris, 1640–62).
7 See, amongst others, Père Claude Ameline, *Traité de la volonté, de ses principales actions, de ses passions et de ses égarements* (Paris: G. Desprez, 1684); Jean Besse, *Traité des passions de l'homme, où suivant les règles de l'analyse l'on recherche leur nature, leur cause et leurs éfets* (Paris, 1699); Antoine Maubec, *Principes phisiques de la raison et des passions des hommes* (Paris: B. Girin, 1709); Charles Le Brun, *Expression des passions de l'âme: Conférences données en 1668* (Paris, 1713); Jean-Baptiste-Joseph Lallemand, *Essai sur le mécanisme des passions en général* (Paris: P.-A. Le Prieur, 1751); Jacques Valleton Candillac, *Essai sur les appétits et les passions* (Montpellier, 1801).
8 A representative example would be Isaac Watts, *The doctrine of the passions explain'd and improv'd: Or, A brief and comprehensive scheme of the natural affections of mankind, attempted in a plain and easy method; with an account of their names, nature, appearances, effects and different uses in human life: to which are subjoin'd moral and divine rules for the regulation or government of them*, 2nd edn (London, 1732). In English, as indeed in French, the most influential and far-reaching writings on the passions in this period are novels.
9 Nicolas Malebranche, *De la recherche de la vérité*, ed. Jean-Christophe Bardout, 3 vols (Paris: Vrin, 2006). See bk 1, ch. 1, bk 5, ch. 1 and the first of the *Eclaircissements*. The same problem beset the debate on the origin of evil, in particular the explanation for Satan's expulsion from heaven. If, as Milton for instance had suggested, he was guilty of the sin of pride, where did this pride come from? On this question, see in particular William King, *De Origine Mali* (London, 1702) translated later into English as *An Essay on the Origin of Evil* (London, 1731). It is also a question that preoccupies Daniel Defoe in *The History of the Devil* (London, 1727).
10 Bernard Mandeville, *The Fable of the Bees*, ed. Phillip Harth (Harmondsworth: Penguin Books, 1970), p. 404.
11 *Ibid.*, p. 214.
12 *Ibid.*, p. 244.
13 *Ibid.*, p. 88.
14 *Ibid.*, pp. 90–1.
15 *Ibid.*, p. 158.
16 *Ibid.*, p. 111.
17 *Ibid.*, p. 165.
18 Francis Hutcheson, *An Inquiry into the Original of our Ideas of Beauty and Virtue* (London: John Darby, 1725), p. 109.

19 *Ibid.*, p. 15.
20 *Ibid.*, p. 74.
21 Francis Hutcheson, *An Essay on the Nature and Conduct of the Passions and Affections* (London: John Darby and Thomas Browne, 1728), p. 91.
22 *Ibid.*, p. 199.
23 Gershom Carmichael became Professor of Moral Philosophy at Glasgow University in 1727, two years before his death. His *Supplements and Observations upon the two books of the distinguished Samuel Pufendorf's 'On the Duty of Man and Citizen'* appeared (in Latin) in 1718 and in an expanded second edition in 1724.
24 Hutcheson, *Inquiry*, p. 103.
25 *Ibid.*
26 *Ibid.*, p. 112.
27 *Ibid.*, p. 116.
28 *Ibid.*, p. 127.
29 *Ibid.*, p. 159.
30 *Ibid.*, p. 206.
31 Hutcheson, *Essay*, p. xvii.
32 *Ibid.*, p. 1.
33 *Ibid.*, p. 5.
34 *Ibid.*, pp. 136–7.
35 *Ibid.*, p. 159.
36 *Ibid.*, pp. 159–60.

4

Fashioning fictional selves from French sources: Eliza Haywood's *Love in Excess*

Orla Smyth

Even a cursory look at the English fiction market of the last three decades of the seventeenth century and the early decades of the eighteenth immediately makes plain the important place therein of French fiction. French *nouvelles galantes*, *nouvelles historiques* and *histoires* were promptly translated into English and the number of those translations, as well as the promptitude with which so many of the titles were translated, suggests that they were very avidly read.[1] This was reading-matter bought for immediate consumption. These books were not bought to adorn the bookshelves of private libraries; they were read for pleasure, handed on to friends, and then gradually, and in varying degrees of wear and tear, finally thrown out. A score of authors, many of whose names are today largely unfamiliar even to scholars of early modern fiction, were for decades very popular with English readers.

As has long been recognised, and most significantly since the pioneering work of Ros Ballaster, English women writers drew on this fiction and they were no doubt influenced in doing so by the prominence within that corpus of a considerable number of women writers. Ballaster complained about the way English historians of literature were casting this amatory fiction within an indigenous tradition of English popular culture and she emphasised the importance of recognising the French provenance of this fiction and the way it popularised, while also reworking, the 'almost exclusively aristocratic forms of French love fiction'.[2] Thanks to important revisionist work, largely undertaken by feminist scholars, this English amatory fiction has found its way back into print and, for the first time, into curricula.

Scholars working on amatory fiction have in recent times been engaging in productive exchange with research in another area of topical interest, the study of the period's evolving languages of the self.[3] Focusing on the relationship between the narrativisation of individual experience in the amatory fiction and the sources the writers drew on, these studies have been examining the conceptual and linguistic vocabulary used by narrators, and by the characters themselves, when interpreting and giving expression to human motivation, and when analysing the thought-processes of the characters. This work encourages us to think about the lexicon being deployed by authors to confer meaning on experience as both individual and social. In this key area of scholarship on the historical understanding of the self, we are finally getting around to thinking about how novels might have been providing readers with conceptual tools, turns of phrase and a lexicon that they would assimilate and draw on in accessing and making sense of their own inner experience and their experience of the social world.

Approaching these questions from a perspective firmly situated within the English historical tradition, it has been tempting to hypothesise a non-adventitious relationship between the emergence in this period of new Whig conceptions of political authority, Locke's adumbration of the self of consciousness and consent, and the new prominence, both in theatre and prose fiction, of women's writing voicing concerns about personal choice and gender inequalities. This almost intuitive supposition that there must be a link between the explorations of female subjectivity we find in the amatory fiction and the period's new discourse on the individual subject, Locke's personal identity, explains the fact that today's scholarship, exploring the relations between the period's evolving language of the self and the representation of individual and social experience in the early novels, focuses so resolutely on English-language material. So it is that in the search for concepts and a language germane to understanding the representation of fictional selves and their interaction with others in these early novels, scholarship has homed in on Locke or, because his famous *Essay Concerning Human Understanding*

(1689) generated such a flurry of interest in the questions raised by the postulates of the Lockean self, on one or more of the many competing philosophical currents that were brought into the fray, British Epicureanism, materialist and Hobbesian thought.

Considering this amatory fiction as an important conduit of a language of the self, I want to reiterate Ballaster's insistence on the importance of the French influence and in making that case I shall highlight the significance of three prime conceptual clusters that played a particularly important role in French prose fiction of the last three decades of the seventeenth century. The English writers, I suggest, would appropriate those ideas and that language and use them creatively in their own narrativisations of a self perceiving and negotiating a social world. This is to suggest that French thought had developed a rich and highly textured language of the self, and that key concepts and vocabularies of that language circulated widely in English culture both via French fiction and the amatory fiction which drew on its resources and that, in ways this chapter will examine, this fiction participated in the discursive production of identity in the early modern period.

The first of these themes, the self of self-interest, enjoyed a long history of theorisation in France. The *honnêteté* literature, revising, adapting and developing Castiglione's *Il Cortegiano* (1528), elaborated the rules of polite society and analysed in detail the subject's negotiation of the social world (of the court or the salon), and also of necessity staged an enquiry into the subject.[4] This literature was heavily indebted to reason-of-state theory and frequently endorsed the underlying postulate of man as guided by self-interest. In the final decades of the seventeenth century, *moralistes* such as François de la Rochefoucauld, Jacques Esprit and Pierre Nicole, dissected the human subject and laid bare, beneath the noble and altruistic motivations ascribed to human behaviour, the secret workings of *amour-propre*.[5] Ambition, glory-seeking, pride and vanity are in this discourse near synonyms, and in prose fiction, it is as ambition that this explanatory concept of human motivation is most generally figured. However, if *amour-propre* came to occupy pride of place in Jansenist analyses of fallen human nature, it is important to remember that *amour-propre* and the other members of that taxonomic group and most notably glory and ambition, never entirely lost the more prestigious connotations they had enjoyed in a not too distant past. In his classic study, *Morales du grand siècle*, Paul

Bénichou traced the contours of the aggrandising vision of human nature and exaltation of the self that would characterise Corneille's tragedies.[6] Cornelian tragic heroes inspired the admiring awe of spectators for their ability to sacrifice personal pleasures to the duties they owed to their own glory, a glory that was both personal and supra-personal. Bénichou's study concentrated on theatre, but his analyses could be extended to the domain of prose fiction and its exaltation of the self. The romances notably valorised love, but they also valorised deeds of glory. In *Artamène ou le grand Cyrus* (1649–53), Madeleine de Scudéry finally reunites her hero with his beloved once he has proven his military valour in the victory over the Massagettes: feats of glory and true love were the special preserve of the idealised elite celebrated in this fiction. Indeed, it is significant that in Scudéry's later short prose fiction, *Mathilde d'Aguilar* (1667), a novel which, as Nathalie Grande points out, reveals the author sacrificing many of the heroic values of her earlier production, the relationship between ambition and love is figured in oppositional terms.[7] Yet, even in that later fiction, Scudéry's hero, Alphonse, will have ample occasion to satisfy his ambition and acquire glory on the field of battle before finally sacrificing the claims of ambition to those of love. It is important to remember that the claims of love and ambition could enter into opposition, but that they could also be conceived and figured as complementary and even interdependent. Today's readers are surprised to find a passionate lover like Monsieur de Clèves making nervous enquiries into the social status of the woman whose beauty and charms have raised in his heart an extraordinary passion and esteem, but worldly ambition was considered a defining attribute of noble souls.

The second feature of the French discourse on the self that is pertinent to an understanding of the amatory fiction is its enquiry into love as passion. In the later decades of the century, with the rise of Cartesian Augustinian thought, the idealisation of love as passion, consecrated throughout a long literary and philosophical tradition, underwent decisive revision. Cartesian rationalism had reaffirmed the dualism – previously attenuated in writings drawing on Platonic, Plotinian or Thomist sources – of passion and reason. Jansenist thought retained the major premise of Descartes's *Les Passions de l'âme* (1649), but jettisoned the minor. Accepting the binary opposition that opposed in absolute terms reason and passion, they rejected his sanguine affirmation to the effect that 'even those whose souls were weakest could acquire a very absolute control over their passions'.[8] What emerged was a framework of interpretation of human experience affirming simultaneously the necessity for happiness of empire over the passions, and the human impossibility of exercising that empire. In the space of fiction, and no doubt at least partially due to the weight of the literary tradition idealising the passion of love, the capacity to experience passion was itself figured, despite its inconveniences, as the distinguishing characteristic of a particular elite. By way of an ironic inversion of Descartes's postulate that not all souls enjoyed the same strength, a mass of literature predicated the existence of superior souls who, by virtue of their superiority, were uniquely subject to the ravages of passion. The Portuguese nun's enthralment to passion made her a victim of the French chevalier, but her heights of passion also conferred on her a heroic stature unattainable to her inconstant lover, worthy only of pale loves.[9]

The third important feature of this discourse of the self bears on the presence in the soul of passions or ideas which escape the subject's mental perception. The development of this theme is, as Geneviève Rodis-Lewis insisted, not to be understood as a direct legacy of Cartesian thought but rather of the fact that it was Cartesianism that helped assure the cultural prominence of Augustinian thought. As she points out:

> The resemblances at the level of the detail, and the opposition of the whole to Aristotelianism, made starkly clear to the public of that time the internal affinities between Cartesianism and Augustinianism. Consequently, the rise of the new philosophy was linked to an ancient tradition for which the obscurities of knowledge of oneself were an essential theme.[10]

Unconscious thought, in the sense of thought or affective states which escape the perception of the perceiving subject, became, along with the self of self-interest and the governing opposition between passion and reason, a key concept in the arsenal of those who were exploring in a variety of fictional forms the self and its representation. From the confluence of these discourses, French writers of the last three decades of the seventeenth century drew on and developed a highly elaborate conceptual and lexical storehouse which lent itself admirably to the task of giving expression to individual and social experience.

The French provenance of these thematic motifs becomes most evident when one considers the way in which they interact one with the other in the narrative exploration of the adventures of a small cast of characters negotiating the problems of their interpersonal relations but also their relation to their social environment. The case will be made here by proposing a reading of Eliza Haywood's *Love in Excess* (1719). This might be considered a somewhat tendentious choice of text, as critics have long acknowledged the influence on Haywood of French novels. Ros Ballaster would even suggest that 'Haywood's entire *œuvre* could be interpreted as imitations of French fiction ...'.[11] In my reading of *Love in Excess* I will draw attention to the theory of the self that subtends its representation of human experience, that is to say, the key concepts and structuring oppositions which underlie its figuration of the subject and his or her negotiation of the love relation. Scholars familiar with early modern fiction will recognise that many of my observations have a wider import because they are pertinent to an understanding of other novelists of the period, notably the women novelists who preceded Haywood but some of the male novelists also.

The three-part structure of *Love in Excess*

Love in Excess is a three-part novel retracing the educational journey of the main character, the count D'Elmont. Throughout the first part, D'Elmont remains faithful to his credo which erects as prime and sole legitimate human motivation the pursuit of ambition. In conformity with his principles, he seduces Amena and marries Alovysa, 'one of the greatest fortunes in all France',[12] and the first part closes on an encomium to ambition and a scathing denigration of the powers of love. D'Elmont teases his brother for attaching importance to love and 'such a toy, as he argued woman was'.[13] The second part opens with D'Elmont's doctrine being undone. He discovers love as passion and, at the same time, the erroneousness of his former thinking.[14] When he meets Melliora, 'that heart which had so long been impregnable surrendered in a moment', and he feels a 'discomposure he had never felt before'.[15] The thematic focus here is the same as that which had animated the most popular and influential French prose fiction of the last three decades of the preceding century: the irresistible powers of passion. These powers of passion constitute a risk for Melliora because D'Elmont is married, but the text evinces considerable leniency in its treatment of the 'errors' both of judgement and behaviour to which its irresistible influence leads the protagonists, because such powerful passion is also the sign of their noble souls. The third and final section completes the analysis. Having renounced ambition and enrolled himself firmly in the ranks of those whose sole preoccupation is love, D'Elmont has now to prove himself the constant lover, and Haywood to illustrate, by means of oppositions, the distinction between D'Elmont's true and noble passion and its ignoble analogue. During his Italian travels, D'Elmont will be besieged by a number of women irresistibly drawn to his charms, but it is primarily by means of Ciamara, a kind of female double of the D'Elmont of the second part, that Haywood figures the difference between two kinds of passionate love. Led on by her passion, Ciamara goes to extreme lengths to obtain sexual favours from D'Elmont in a way that is reminiscent of D'Elmont's own strategies to seduce Melliora in the previous section. It is only when it has become clear that Ciamara's passion for D'Elmont is purely physical that the two characters are dissociated. 'Taken with his beauty', the narrator tells us, Ciamara 'wished no further than to possess his lovely *person*, his *mind* was the least of her thoughts.'[16] D'Elmont's passion for Melliora is of a different kind, for although her 'lovely person' certainly entered into the equation, that passion was indissociably bound to his 'just admiration for [her] real merits'.[17] This opposition between the different passionate loves of Ciamara and D'Elmont allows Haywood to delineate precisely the argument of the third and final section. It is necessary to do so because there can be no question of undermining the argument of the second part: passion cannot be 'circumscribed'.[18] Passion is not subservient to the will, it is on the contrary an 'absolute controller' and it is a logical consequence of that understanding that no one can be held accountable for what is not within human powers to avoid.[19] By refusing the pleasures of Italian society, avoiding or declining the advances of the various women who are drawn to him by the 'powerful influence' of his attractions,[20] and also by proving himself a loyal friend to Melliora's brother, D'Elmont will prove the nobility of his passionate love and invalidate that well-known tenet of the doxa on the mutability of passionate love.[21] Having made this three-stage progress over the course of the narrative, he will be rewarded at the end with a happy, conjugal marriage.

Modern readers are less familiar than Haywood's contemporaries were with the narrative practice (partially excised from this outline) of inlaying the main narrative with mirror characters and intercalated stories exemplifying variations of its themes, but Haywood takes care to foreground this educational journey by carefully indicating the thematic pertinence of each of the three stages. This outline of the narrative structure was a necessary preliminary to a more detailed examination of the way in which these key concepts of interpretation of human behaviour as they were theorised in the French tradition – self-interest, passion versus reason, and the unconscious – illuminate the way this fiction frames its analysis of the differences between the sexes. Kathleen Lubey quite rightly points out that 'Haywood's authorial logic does not espouse a binary opposition to masculinity ...'.[22] Haywood was certainly interested in the experience of women as women, but she explored that experience within the terms of an anthropological vision that shared little of the fixity her contemporaries were increasingly ascribing to identity as gendered.

From her reading of the short novels of the last three decades of the seventeenth century, Haywood is highly conscious of the complex axiological valence of self-love or ambition. When in the first part of *Love in Excess* she stages the opposition between the claims of ambition and those of love, she focuses on the pursuit of self-interest as an important explanatory concept for understanding the antagonistic relations between the sexes. Men in whom ambition is the reigning passion, as D'Elmont's behaviour will illustrate, devalue women. Women are, from this perspective, nothing more than a pleasurable 'fashionable amusement', as Amena ruefully comes to realise.[23] In *Reflections on the Various Effects of Love* (1726) Haywood drew attention to the way in which these twin motivations of the human condition introduced a form of inequality between the sexes because they exercised their influence asymmetrically:

> A Woman, where she loves, has no Reserve, she profusely gives her all, has no Regard to any Thing, but obliging the Person she affects, and lavishes her whole Soul.—But Man, more wisely, keeps a Part of his for other Views, he has still an Eye to Interest and Ambition![24]

Women's greater disposition to passion, because unalloyed by self-interest, was a kind of floating axiom of the discourse and contributes to the literature's tendency to focus on female rather than male subjectivities. It should not be forgotten, however, that the full title of this text was *Reflections on the Various Effects of Love, according to the contrary Dispositions of the Persons on whom it operates.* Thematic exploration of the rival claims of love and self-love lent itself to a reading of the relations between the sexes, but it could also be conducted in terms of the 'contrary dispositions' of persons or of characters. The D'Elmont who enters the third stage of his progress has left ambition behind him. 'Ambition', the narrator tells us, 'once his darling passion, was now wholly extinguished in him.' Thinking no longer of 'making a figure in the world', he can dedicate himself to proving the true and constant character of his love as passion.[25] We need to remember that just as D'Elmont's excess of passion will make him guilty of errors that are forgivable, the same is true also of the errors he is led into by the strong force of ambition. Ambition, like the passion of love, springs from 'an affluence of the nobler spirits', and while a number of passions are the effects of a 'base and sordid nature', both ambition and love are, as the text indicates, the effects of 'an exalted one'.[26]

As we have seen, the central section of *Love in Excess* explores, just as the French fiction had done, the difficulties encountered by noble souls as they attempt to comply with the moral injunction to exercise control over their passions. The staging of this conflict makes plain the contradictions of the discourse by simultaneously lamenting and valorising the force of uncontrollable passion. The enviable destiny the French novels willingly attributed to those whose 'cold temperaments' saved them from the torments of passionate love cut two ways.[27] Haywood is unsparing in her disdain for those 'insipids' who presumptuously cast judgement on those whose 'elegance of thought, delicacy, or tenderness of soul' make them susceptible to real love as passion.[28] D'Elmont, as one might expect, does not fall into the category of those whose 'cold temperaments' destine them to tepid love. The erstwhile disbeliever in the powers of love is soon in thrall to 'sleepless nights, and restless days' and 'countless burning agonies'.[29] The unequal contest between reason and passion is staged in the familiar framework of an illicit love. D'Elmont is married, and Melliora, who shares his passion, is the daughter of his own former guardian, and now his ward. D'Elmont's attempts to seduce his ward constitute therefore a threat to her virtue.

The three main seduction scenes in this section all testify to Haywood's perspicacious treatment of the structuring devices she has borrowed from late seventeenth-century French literature. D'Elmont knows that his love for Melliora is reciprocated, as the narrator takes care to indicate.[30] It is also important that the first two seduction scenes are preceded by testimonies to Melliora's intelligence and D'Elmont's admiration for that intelligence. Just prior to the first seduction scene, D'Elmont had discovered her reading Fontenelle's *Plurality of Worlds*, and the second is preceded by Melliora's lively participation in a discussion on the passion of love, a contribution which had made plain to all 'the force of her reason, the delicacy of her wit, and the penetration of her judgment'.[31] D'Elmont's love is based not only on the beauty but also 'the real merits of the object beloved'.[32] In all of these scenes, the narrator carefully draws attention to the fact that Melliora fears not just the acts of her seducer but also, because of the influence of her own passion, her own complicity in those acts.

In her treatment of this familiar theme, Haywood focuses, as many of her French precursors had done, on the different subject positions which, in ways that were dependent on circumstances, women and men could occupy. Her two main characters find themselves in circumstances which mean that there is between them a 'separate interest', and so there cannot be that 'congruity of love and friendship' that D'Elmont evokes in pleading his case.[33] D'Elmont's appeal to friendship is rejected because he is trying to make use of that claim to Melliora's prejudice, as she indicates. Haywood is not prepared to undermine the tenets of the French literature, and so these three trial scenes all terminate in what we might be tempted to call failures on the part of D'Elmont, because Melliora's honour is saved only thanks to the fortuitous intervention of one or other supernumerary. Except that, of course, Haywood is simply proving the truth of the postulates of her analytic framework of interpretation of human behaviour.

In the third and extended trial scene, the focus shifts from the quandaries of the male character to the same quandaries as encountered by the female character. The longest disquisition on the irresistible powers of passion is voiced this time by the narrator and with a view to creating compassion for the difficulties of the trial as faced by Melliora. If D'Elmont now has occasion to throw his 'eager arms' around the waist of Melliora, she is, we are informed, 'no less transported'.³⁴ D'Elmont is the initiator of physical contact, but the narrative focus is now on the receiver of 'burning kisses' and the 'painful pleasure' and 'racking kind of extasie' which 'might perhaps had they been now alone, proved her desires were little different from his'.³⁵ Melliora becomes the spokesperson for physical restraint but her argumentation rests on her own inability to resist both his overtures and her own desire:

> Do I not bear, at least, an equal share in all your agonies? Has thou no charms – Or have not I a heart? – A most susceptible, and tender heart? – Yes, you may feel it throb, it beats against my breast, like an imprisoned bird, and fain burst it's [sic] cage! To fly to you, the aim of all it's [sic] wishes!³⁶

Collapsing into his arms, it is again the fortuitous arrival of a secondary character that prevents the outcome the narrative's logic considers inevitable. To accept as a truth of the human condition the empire of the passions is also to accept that the individual, when under their influence, does not have the will to undertake and carry out those acts which he or she knows are right. This empire of the passions is a reality of the human condition which means that it applies not just to men (who often use it as an excuse for unscrupulous behaviour) but also to women.³⁷

The third important finding of the discourse on the self of the French tradition bore on the existence of unconscious thought or affect. In that final trial scene of *Love in Excess*, D'Elmont has stolen into Melliora's room at night and is prompted by last-minute scruples of honour and compassion to take his leave. Those efforts are jeopardised by Melliora's unknowing revelation in her sleep that she too is prey to the same sexual desires as he is. The scene is a rewriting of the famous scene in *La Princesse de Clèves* (1678) in which Nemours, who has arrived on horseback, steals by night into the garden at Coulommiers and gazes unseen on the princess, who, in a state of relative undress because of the heat, is 'gracefully and gently' decorating with ribbons the cane that belongs to him and then proceeds to contemplate *en rêverie* his portrait.³⁸ The sexual connotations of the scene are of course unlikely to have escaped Haywood, and in her rewriting of it she more or less abandons any remaining ambiguity, preferring instead to have her narrator descant on the ways in which the sleeping state gives free rein to unconscious desires which, when we are awake, are subject to the self-censorship of thought and the influence of 'honour and virtue' or, as we might say, conscience.[39]

Warm fiction: the affective experience of reading

Critics have long recognised the importance of the way in which Haywood's prose makes a strong appeal to the reader's fantasy desire. As Richard Savage phrased it, Haywood's warm descriptions 'at once ... prove the force of language, and the sweets of Love'.[40] The eroticised scenes have as effect that the difficulty of the moral challenges faced by the characters – the forlorn attempt to exercise rational control, the superior force exercised by passion – is vicariously *experienced* by the reader. As critics and readers have realised, it is difficult to extract much morally uplifting instruction from these fictions because the characters invariably succumb, regardless of whatever attempts they might make to resist. But the instructive value of these fictions had been construed very differently in France. In anglophone criticism in our time, many analyses of Haywood's 'warm prose' assume that the affective states experienced by readers pre-existed in a pretty straightforward way the arousal generated by the reading process. In France, the enquiry into the relation between prose fiction and the secret recesses of the soul, had arrived at some very different conclusions. Most particularly over the course of the *Querelle de la Princesse de Clèves*, a whole host of writers elaborated a theory of fiction which postulated its value in terms of the 'science du coeur'.[41] The Abbé de Charnes gave Mme de La Fayette credit for having discovered a new and extremely pleasant way of combining the science of the heart and that of the Belles Lettres and in analyses of the novels that most successfully promoted an absorbed empathetic reading, a whole range of discourse on the novel privileged this formula, the 'science of the heart'.[42] These testimonies to the way in which readers revelled in an absorbed reading and thereby entered into the 'hearts and minds' of individualised characters attest to the realisation that this experience involved not just the discovery of the secret recesses of the heroine's heart and mind but also the hitherto secret workings of their own interior selves. In his review of Du Plaisir's novel, *La Duchesse d'Estramène*, Etienne Pavillon gives us an idea of how these authors conceived the special learning to be derived from reading the new fiction. 'How well the heart is understood in your Duchesse d'Estramène', he wrote in the pages of the *Mercure galant*, 'I recognise at every moment my own feelings which had escaped my knowledge.' And he concludes his encomium to Du Plaisir's short novel by thanking the author for the knowledge he acquired of feelings which had, prior to the reading experience, escaped his conscious knowledge.[43]

The revived Augustinianism of the last decades of the seventeenth century is clearly related to this new theory of prose fiction as endowed with special powers as a science of the human heart. In the opening pages of *De la Recherche de la vérité* (1674), Nicolas Malebranche had famously announced that 'The most beautiful, pleasant and necessary of all our knowledge is no doubt knowledge of ourselves. Of all the human sciences, the science of man is the most worthy of man.'[44] Malebranche had insisted not only on the importance, but also the undeveloped status, of the 'science de l'homme'. 'We are not able to provide definitions which allow us to know the modifications of the soul', he wrote, 'we do not know the soul or its modifications by ideas, only by sentiments, and such sentiments, as pleasure, for example, or pain, or heat, etc. are not attached to words.'[45] Already in 1683, in his discussion of what he called the 'new novels', Du Plaisir was emphasising the importance of the new fiction in precisely those terms:

> Gaining knowledge of the movements of the heart is not less difficult than understanding the features of the mind. It requires great expertise to penetrate to the bottom of that abyss, to avoid getting lost among so many small differences, to render vividly such imperceptible subjects, and to explain things which, because of the little knowledge we have had of them up till now, still remain without words to designate them.[46]

Some three decades later, Marivaux was still exploring the implications of these secret movements of the heart for which we lack an adequate vocabulary in his periodical essays 'Sur la clarté du discours' and 'Sur la pensée sublime' (1719). Marivaux posits the great writer as an individual possessing exceptional gifts both of understanding and, most importantly, giving expression in language to the complexity of the 'movements of the heart'. Marivaux is at one level battling against too rigid an interpretation of what is meant by 'discursive clarity'. The justification he advances for what might seem like irregular prose is based on the idea that there are modifications of the soul for which we do not have terms, but that an adept use of prose can overcome that lack by expressing in a particular way a modification we do have words for. In the right hands, those of the talented writer, prose can actually communicate to the reader an idea of modifications of the soul (or sentiments) despite the fact that the language does not possess words for them.

These ideas are eminently pertinent to understanding Haywood as a writer of prose fiction. She liked to preface her novels with dithyrambic poems celebrating her powers of language and the firing force of her evocations of passion. The new short fiction was offering readers an experience that was in many ways utterly new. The long romances had remained attached to the spoken word. The reader accessed the thoughts and feelings of the characters by listening in as such to the conversations of the various *devisants*. It is perfectly telling of this feature of the romances that when Madeleine de Scudéry published compilations of extracts from her earlier fiction in the last decades of the seventeenth century, she chose to entitle them 'conversations'.[47] But what we say is very different from what we think and feel and the new short fiction, the novel we should say, found its niche when it dedicated itself to narrating in prose the inner feelings and intoxicating emotions of fictional characters in all the disorder of the unspoken word. The new fiction struggled to render in words and communicate to readers the turbulent inner world of the heart and minds of its characters, and the challenge was so significant that we find frequent reminders of the difficulty, and even the impossibility, of achieving that end.

> But how (when left alone, and abandoned to the whirlwinds of her passion,) the desperate Alovisa behaved, none but those, who like her, have burned in hopeless fires can guess, the most lively descriptions come far short of what she felt.[48]

Haywood's prose in its whirlwind periods attached itself to rendering not just the heart-throbbing throes of passionate desire but also consternation 'more easily imagined than expressed', or violent sorrow similarly 'more easily imagined than expressed', and joy 'impossible to express' and torrents of indignation 'hardly possible to imagine, much less to describe'.[49] And love, of course, of all the passions, was that which posed the greatest challenge to the descriptive powers of an author, love which:

> fills the mind with a thousand charming ideas, which those untouched by that passion, are not capable of conceiving, yet it entirely takes away the power of utterance, and the deeper impression it had made on the soul, the less we are able to express it, when willing to indulge and give a loose to thought; what language can furnish with words sufficient, all are too poor, all wanting both in sublimity, and softness, and only fancy! a lovers fancy! can reach the exalted soaring of a lovers meaning![50]

Yet all of these emotions, so 'impossible to be described', were in Haywood's hectic prose very effectively communicated to the reader and, as the encomiastic prefatory poems and the extraordinary commercial success of the publication suggest, readers revelled in this experience in which they felt and discovered, while reading, the innermost recesses of their own hearts.

To approach this fiction from this perspective is to destabilise any straightforward distinction between representation and the subject. If, in later decades, the debate was to centre on the confusion between the fictive representation and the real world as object of that representation, here the fuzziness is situated at the boundary which separates the text and the reader. Marivaux struggled with this problem in his *Réflexions sur l'esprit humain* (1749), and it is a complex one. Marivaux wanted to suggest that the great writers should be recognised for the importance of their role as scientists; scientists of the human soul. In urging the value of that science, he emphasised its fundamental necessity for every social being.

> Let us imagine a science of such immediate necessity that absolutely every man, let him be who he will, must have some mastery of it and very promptly also, failing which he cannot be admitted to that competition of interests, relations, and reciprocal needs which link us one with another.[51]

Marivaux's dilemma was that he had to predicate a social being already equipped with at least a minimal level of competence of the human heart – such knowledge was a prerequisite of social existence – while simultaneously claiming that the scientific findings of the great writers were of inestimable value to those participating in that society. In all of these analyses we find the same conviction that the reader of fiction appropriates, while reading, a language of self which conveys knowledge of that interior self, and that, in a sense, what the reader finds in the text is him- or herself as subject. Examining the fiction of the early novelists in these terms, we encounter the same problems as Marivaux in thinking through this relation between the reader and the text. We are positing a reader or a listener endowed already with at least a minimal level of linguistic material by means of which she understood her own self, but we are also suggesting that the reader who put down the book or left off listening was not identical with her earlier self because she had acquired enhanced conceptual and linguistic tools enabling an enhanced access and thus fuller understanding of that interior self.

Eliza Haywood and the findings of the French 'petit roman'

Eliza Haywood's literary imagination was profoundly influenced by her reading of the French short novels of the last three decades of the seventeenth century. In the final pages of her translation of Edmé Boursault's imitation of the *Lettres portugaises*, we find the announcement of an upcoming publication *The Danger of giving way to Passion in Five Exemplary Novels*.[52] The titles she had intended to include in a single volume were finally published in separate editions as *The British Recluse*, *The Injur'd Husband*, *Lasselia*, *The Rash Resolve* and *Idalia*. In both her projected single-volume publication as well as in the individual novels she finally published, Haywood was following the example of Mme de Villedieu who had published as a collection the four short *nouvelles* included in *Les Désordres de l'amour* (1675). In the concluding paragraphs of Mme de Villedieu's collection, the narrator explains that the stories which make up the volume were chosen with a view to inspiring in readers a horror of the malignity of love.[53] Haywood's novels were presented to readers under identical auspices. We learn in the preface to *Lasselia* that the author's only 'design in writing this little Novel, as well as those formerly publish'd', was 'to remind the unthinking Part of the World how dangerous it is to give way to passion'. However, of all the French novels which influenced Haywood, the one that very clearly exercised the strongest hold over her imagination was *La Princesse de Clèves*. The novels that were initially intended to make up the *Five Exemplary Novels* include multiple borrowings from important scenes and characters in Mme de La Fayette's novel. In *The British Recluse*, the Princess de Clèves's fears that Nemours would, with time, have other passions are realised in the experience of Cleomira who first encounters Lysander at a ball in circumstances that replicate in detail the first encounter between the princess and the duke. Like the princess who withdraws from life at the court, Cleomira finally abandons the world and she goes to live in a house seventy miles outside London. In *Lasselia*, among the many very precise echoes from Mme de La Fayette's novel, we note that the heroine actually retires not to Coulommiers, but to Collumiers! These are merely external indices of influence, whereas we are interested here in plumbing some of the more profound implications of imitating French fiction. As regards the future of the novel in England, the single most important finding which Haywood transmitted to the form can be identified in a seemingly small but actually extremely telling detail from *Love in Excess*, and it is on this point that this analysis will conclude.

At the end of the second part of Haywood's novel, D'Elmont's wife Alovysa, just like the Prince de Clèves, very opportunely dies, leaving D'Elmont free to marry Melliora. Like the princess, Melliora considers that, because of her part in the unhappy events leading to the death of the Count's wife, her guilt is sufficient obstacle to any union with D'Elmont:

> Melliora looked on herself as the most guilty person upon earth, as being the primary cause of all the misfortunes that had happened, and retired immediately to a monastery, from whence, not all the entreaties of her friends, nor the implorations of the amorous D'Elmont could bring her.[54]

Melliora's reasoning is identical to that of the princess and she considers criminal her passionate love for D'Elmont while he was married: 'She was now resolved to punish by a voluntary banishment from all she ever did, or could love, the guilt of indulging that passion, while it was a crime.'[55] What we find in Haywood's novel is an abbreviated form of what is actually, from the point of view of narrative fiction, the most important scene in La Fayette's novel.

Based on her own experience, and on the knowledge she gleans from the experience of others, the Princesse de Clèves forges her own moral code, one that is not based on the beliefs and values of her social milieu, but one that will nevertheless guide her in the decisions she will make with respect to her own conduct. The Duc de Nemours points out that her scruples about marrying him are 'fantômes': no moral code constitutes an obstacle to their marriage; and the princess accepts that analysis. 'I am sacrificing a lot', she admits, 'to an obligation which only exists in my imagination.'[56] But she will nonetheless remain faithful to that obligation as she herself sees it, for reasons that will remain enigmatic to the duke. The princess does not deduce a rule from any outer order of being, nor does she rely on doxa. She relies only on her own process of thinking, with all the uncertainty that entails. It is this moral autonomy, this analytic self, which gives her character its richness. The incorporation into the plot of the character's own self-consciously subjective analysis of events and the determination of the ensuing events by that analysis constitutes a crucial innovation of the new novel. A novelistic world becomes obsolete. Exterior obstacles, for so long the mainstay of novelistic plot, cannot rival with the analytic depth which the novel achieves by incorporating into itself this autonomous subjectivity. Haywood seized the importance of Mme de La Fayette's contribution, perhaps in ways that few others did. Her imitations of her fellow writer's most famous novel testify to that awareness as, again and again, she comes back to that text in her own fiction.

For anyone interested in charting early modern changes in the conception of the self, the short novels of this period are an obvious place to look. These novels invite analysis of the concepts and ideas subtending both the representation of character as well as the forms of interaction between characters. This chapter has attempted to show that if we are to examine the discursive production of identity in this period we cannot limit our enquiry to sources of the self emanating from the language of empiricism. These novels are steeped in a language that one might be tempted to call Cartesian rationalism except that one would have to include a wider range of material than such a term generally embraces. The late seventeenth-century French novels are key because they draw on a multiplicity of sources, notably the literature of *honnêteté*, Cartesian rationalism reconfigured in Jansenist thought, the renewed Augustinianism emphasising the obscurity of the soul and Malebranche's advancement of the 'science of man' and his theory of 'sentiments'. The language of the self the early English writers drew on was much richer than any single philosophical source could provide.

Notes

1 R. I. Le Tellier, *The English Novel, 1660–1700: An Annotated Bibliography* (Westport, CT: Greenwood Press, 1997), pp. 395–417 and *The English Novel, 1700–1740: An Annotated Bibliography* (Westport, CT: Greenwood Press, 2002), pp. 549–64. Camille Esmein-Sarrazin's critical anthology of seventeenth-century discourse on the novel is an invaluable resource for anyone interested in seventeenth-century French prose fiction, *Poétiques du roman: Scudéry, Huet, Du Plaisir et autres textes théoriques du XVIIe siècle sur le genre romanesque* (Paris: Honoré Champion, 2004), as also is her study, *L'Essor du roman: Discours théorique et constitution d'un genre littéraire au XVIIe siècle* (Paris: Honoré Champion, 2008). The work of Christian Zonza on this short fiction is also extremely valuable, *La nouvelle historique à l'âge classique (1657–1703)* (Paris: Honoré Champion, 2007). See also an important article by Emmanuel Bury, 'A la recherche d'un genre perdu: le roman et les poéticiens du XVIIe siècle', *Perspectives de la recherche sur le genre narratif français du XVIIe siècle* (Pisa/Geneva: Edizioni Ets-Editions Slatkine, 2000), pp. 9–33.
2 Ros Ballaster, *Seductive Forms: Women's Amatory Fiction from 1684 to 1740* (Oxford: Oxford University Press, 1992), p. 66.
3 J. Drury, 'Haywood's Thinking Machines', *Eighteenth Century Fiction*, 21:2 (Winter 2009), 201–8; J. B. Kramnick, 'Locke, Haywood, and Consent', *English Literary History*, 72:2 (2005), 453–70; Rebecca Tierney-Hynes, 'Fictional Mechanics: Haywood, Reading, and the Passions', *The Eighteenth Century*, 51:1–2 (Spring/Summer 2010), 153–72.
4 The long-time classic on this subject is Maurice Magendie's, *La politesse mondaine et les théories de l'honnêteté en France au XVIIe siècle de 1600 à 1660* (Paris: Presses Universitaires de France, 1925). That work has been significantly revised and supplemented by Emmanuel Bury, *Littérature et politesse: L'Invention de l'honnête homme (1580–1750)* (Paris: Presses Universitaires de France, 1996) and Jean-Pierre Dens, *L'Honnête homme et le critique du goût: esthétique et société au XVIIe siècle* (Lexington, KY: French Forum, 1981). The most important recent work in French on the importance of the discourse on 'amour propre' in terms of an evolving understanding of the self is Jean Rohou's *Le XVIIe siècle, une révolution de la condition humaine* (Paris: Éditions du Seuil, 2002).
5 François de la Rochefoucauld, *Réflexions, ou Sentences et maximes morales*, first French edition 1665, translated into English as *Epictetus Junior, or Maximes of Modern Morality* in 1670 (including 201 maxims), and then by Aphra Behn as *Seneca Unmasqued, or Moral Reflections* in 1685 (including 392 maxims); Jacques Esprit, *La Fausseté des vertus*

humaines, first French edition 1678, translated in 1691 as *The Falsehood of Human Virtues*; Pierre Nicole, *Essais de morale*, first French edition 1671, a first translation appeared in English in 1682 as *Moral Essays*. The publication history of these texts is complicated as they all appeared in various revised editions in French, and they would also appear in English translations in varied selections.

6 Paul Bénichou, *Morales du grand siècle* (Paris: Gallimard, 1948), pp. 15–67. Cartesian optimism on the subject of human powers is often associated with the idealisation to be found in the Belles Lettres of the period (1630–70). Descartes shares that literature's commitment to the idea of 'noble and strong souls'. 'It is easy to believe that all the souls which God puts in our bodies are not equally noble and strong', he observes in article 161 of the *Passions de l'âme*. While insisting that even the weakest souls could acquire absolute control over the passions (art. 50), 'good birth' was an aid to virtue because it fostered high self-esteem, and self-control and determination to exercise the will in conformity with virtue, relied on high self-esteem. Descartes was redefining Cornelian *generosity*, centring it more squarely on exercise of free will (and thus away from public recognition of that merit), but pride and generosity were closely allied in the sense that they both consisted in the good opinion one had of oneself. For Descartes, *generosity* rested on true grounds, that is the exercise of free will, whereas pride rested on unjust grounds. See René Descartes, *Œuvres philosophiques*, III (1643–1650), eds Ferdinand Alquié and Denis Moreau (Paris: Classiques Garnier, 2010), p. 996, and pp. 1067–74.

7 Madeleine de Scudéry, *Mathilde*, critical edition by Nathalie Grande (Paris: Honoré Champion, 2002), p. 50.

8 Descartes, *Œuvres philosophiques*, III, p. 996 (my translation).

9 In the second letter, Marianne expresses her disdain for the lover who was never capable of accessing the same heights of passion as she does: 'you are more to be pitied than I am, and it is better to suffer everything I suffer, than to enjoy the languishing pleasures you derive from your mistresses in France', *Lettres portugaises, suivies de Guilleragues par lui-même*, ed. Frédéric Deloffre (Paris: Editions Gallimard, 1990), p. 81. She returns to this idea frequently in the subsequent letters: 'I regret for your sake the infinite pleasures you have lost' (p. 85), 'I have experienced enough to know that you are not capable of a great passion' (p. 94); 'Do know that I realise that you are unworthy of all my feelings' (p. 100) (my translations).

10 G. Rodis-Lewis, *Le problème de l'inconscient et le cartésianisme* (Paris: Presses Universitaires de France, 1950), p. 106 (my translation).

11 Ballaster, *Seductive Forms*, note 26, p. 41.

12 Eliza Haywood, *Love in Excess, Or, The Fatal Enquiry* [1719], ed. David Oakleaf (Peterborough, ON: Broadview Press, 2000), p. 81.
13 *Ibid.*, p. 83.
14 'How often did he curse the hour in which Alovysa's fondness was discovered? And how much more his own ambition which prompted him to take advantage of it?' *Ibid.*, p. 94.
15 *Ibid.*, p. 90.
16 *Ibid.*, p. 231. Original emphasis.
17 *Ibid.*, p. 114.
18 *Ibid.*, p. 191.
19 *Ibid.*, p. 191.
20 *Ibid.*, p. 219.
21 See on this subject, N. Luhmann, *Love as Passion: The Codification of Intimacy* (Cambridge, MA: Harvard University Press, 1986). His study of the subject remains, in my view, an important one.
22 K. Lubey, 'Eliza Haywood's Amatory Aesthetic', *Eighteenth-Century Studies*, 39:3 (April 2006), 309–22.
23 Haywood, *Love in Excess*, p. 45.
24 Haywood, *Reflections on the Various Effects of Love, according to the contrary Dispositions of the Persons on whom it operates* (London: N. Dobb, 1726), p. 12.
25 Haywood, *Love in Excess*, p. 169.
26 *Ibid.*, p. 192.
27 Love is 'a desire of the soul which blindly draws it to the object which suits it. There are cold temperaments in which it settles and those people are happy', we read in a novel by Madame de Villedieu (Marie-Catherine Desjardins), *Annales galantes de Grece* (La Haye: Adrian Moetjens, 1688), pp. 388–9 (my translation). She points out that in others, the desire for glory and recognition can have the same effects as that constitutional coldness of temperament.
28 Haywood, *Love in Excess*, p. 191.
29 *Ibid.*, p. 116.
30 *Ibid.*, pp. 101 and 105.
31 *Ibid.*, p. 111.
32 *Ibid.*, p. 114.
33 *Ibid.*, p. 115.
34 *Ibid.*, p. 127.
35 *Ibid .*, p. 127.
36 *Ibid.*, p. 130.
37 See in particular on this subject, Luhmann, *Love as Passion*.
38 Madame de La Fayette (Marie-Madeleine Pioche de La Vergne), *Romans et nouvelles*, ed. Alain Niderst (Paris: Bordas, 1990), p. 386.
39 Haywood, *Love in Excess*, p. 121.

40 *Ibid.*, p. 86. David Oakleaf's edition of the novel presented panegyric poems by various authors which prefaced the second volume, one of which includes this praise of Haywood from Richard Savage.
41 See in particular, Esmein, *Poétiques du roman*, pp. 603–814.
42 *Ibid.*, pp. 671–701.
43 *Ibid.*, p. 686.
44 Nicolas Malebranche, *Œuvres*, eds Geneviève Rodis-Lewis and Germain Malbreil, vol. 1 (Paris: Gallimard, 1979), p. 13 (my translation).
45 *Ibid.*, p. 351.
46 Du Plaisir, *Sentiments sur les lettres et sur l'histoire avec des scrupules sur le style*, ed. Philippe Hourcade (Genève: Droz, 1975), p. 52 (my translation).
47 Madeleine de Scudéry, *Conversations sur divers sujets* (Paris: Claude Barbin, 1680) and *Conversations nouvelles sur divers sujets* (Paris: Claude Barbin, 1684).
48 Haywood, *Love in Excess*, p. 47.
49 *Ibid.*, pp. 52, 68 and 99.
50 *Ibid.*, p. 127.
51 This text of Marivaux's was part of a series of talks he gave to the Académie française in 1748. He had begun with 'Réflexions en forme de lettre sur l'esprit humain'; the quotation is from the second talk, entitled 'Réflexions sur Corneille et Racine', *Journaux et œuvres diverses*, eds Frédéric Deloffre and Michel Gilot (Paris: Garnier frères, 1969), p. 476 (my translation).
52 *Letters from a lady of quality to a chevalier. Translated from the French. By Mrs. Haywood* (London: printed for William Chetwood, at Cato's-Head, in Russel-Street, Covent-Garden, 1721). Boursault's *Treize Lettres amoureuses d'une Dame à un Cavalier* had first appeared in print in 1699 in the collection entitled, *Lettres nouvelles* (Paris: N. Gosselin, 1699–1700).
53 Villedieu, *Les Désordres de l'amour*, ed. Micheline Cuénin (Geneva: Droz, 1995), p. 208.
54 Haywood, *Love in Excess*, p. 165.
55 *Ibid.*, p. 165.
56 La Fayette, *Romans et nouvelles*, p. 410.

5

The death of Cordelia and the economics of preference in eighteenth-century moral psychology

William Flesch

Biology recapitulates economics: at least evolutionary biology seems to be rediscovering and analysing the same kinds of ideas that the great eighteenth-century economic psychologists (from Mandeville to Hume to Smith) had explored. Over the last few years there has been a heated debate among evolutionary theorists – scientists, mathematicians, the odd humanist – about whether altruism is possible, given the core idea that evolution is driven by the selection of winners in the cut-throat competition for reproductive success. This is often called evolution by natural selection, but not even Darwin saw natural selection as the whole story.[1] In the history of life on earth, sexual selection came to be as important to evolutionary change as natural selection was, indeed perhaps more important. But even before the evolution of sexuality there was what is now called (controversially) signal selection of which sexual selection is simply an example.

As has been well documented, perhaps most notably by Alfred O. Hirschman, eighteenth-century economic discourse was driven by an attempt to reconcile the passions and the interests.[2] Passions are selfish, but their selfishness may blind us to our own strong interests in cooperating with others. Central to evolutionary game theory is the situation called Prisoner's Dilemma, where acting selfishly leads to worse outcomes for all concerned than acting unselfishly. We are tempted to act selfishly for two reasons: 1) any player in a Prisoner's Dilemma-style game will do better acting selfishly than he or she would acting unselfishly, no matter what the other players do; and 2) even if a player recognises that it would be better for all if all acted unselfishly, she or he also recognises that (like her or himself), every other player will recognise that it will be better for him- or herself to act selfishly no matter what anyone else does. In particular, it is much better for every player to act selfishly if the other players do. Knowing that they know this is another incentive to act selfishly – as they will also know. Economic analysis not only describes motives for selfishness: it provides them. (Indeed, economists have the worst joint outcomes in competitions related to Prisoner's Dilemma, because they rightly expect each other to act selfishly – and so they do.)

Prisoner's Dilemma provides a sadly apt model for the evolutionary dynamics of natural selection (and its Smithian idea of advantage:[3] as the old joke goes, 'I don't have to outrun the bear; I only have to outrun *you*'). How could the cooperation or the unselfishness humans sometimes manifest ever have evolved to escape the non-cooperative impasse of Prisoner's Dilemma? Some recent ideas in evolutionary game theory suggest an interesting solution. Acting against one's own interests is a form of *costly signalling*. As with conspicuous consumption in anthropology (as analysed from Veblen to Mauss to Bataille), and courtship rituals in reproductive biology (for example, the peacock's tail, or the flamingo's colour, which are not only useless for survival but also costly to maintain), acting against one's own interests is a way of showing that one can *afford* to act against them, and showing that one can afford to act against one's own interests is – by a strange and natural antithesis – a way of promoting one's own interests. Its very uselessness makes the costly signal useful. This may make it sound like its uselessness is illusory, then, except that it is also costly to anyone, signaller or receiver to value costly signals. The way costly signals organise relationships involves a transmutation of the very concept of value, a transmutation deep enough that it cannot be reduced (as rational choice economists wish to reduce it) to a homogenous metric measured by 'revealed preference'.

The thinking of eighteenth-century analysts of human motivation and human psychology was far more informed by literary insights and literary questions than the thinking of biologists and economists is now, so that the eighteenth-century versions of these arguments also address literary and aesthetic concerns, even as they are affected by those concerns. Any evolutionary psychology worth its kosmotropic salt will have to accommodate literary experience, and the eighteenth-century economic psychologists are much closer to literary psychology than their social-science- and maths-minded twenty-first-century inheritors.

The literary dimensions of the issue of human motivation arise out of the question of vicarious experience which is, depending on your perspective, either a puzzle in itself or the solution to the puzzle of Prisoner's Dilemma, and therefore more generally to the puzzle of cooperation and sociality. Why do we care about how and what other people feel, think, experience, suffer, risk, undergo, need – why do we care about what *they* care about, or would care about – when their experiences do not have any other effect on our own except that we care about them? Smith raises this issue when he discusses, early on in *The Theory of Moral Sentiments*, sympathy for the dead. The fact that sympathy does not necessarily mean feeling *what* someone else is feeling, but feeling *for* them shows that sympathy is about more than orienting oneself in the shared social space we must negotiate (a feature any account of primate nature, even a straightforwardly selfish one, must include). It is about some primordial feeling on their behalf, even if they are not there, because they are dead – or fictional.[4] The solutions to Prisoner's Dilemma and to the problem of 'the emotions caused by fiction' have the same evolutionary sources.

To simplify too much, Smith is responding to the kinds of arguments Mandeville was making decades earlier in *The Fable of the Bees* and his book-length set of notes to that poem, which Jeffrey Hopes discusses in Chapter 3 of this volume. Mandeville's argument about human motivation is irrefutable on its own terms, because it is tautological. To the extent that people have a choice as to what they do, they will choose to do what they choose to do – or to be slightly more precise, they will end up choosing to do what they end up choosing to do. What is important to note about Mandeville and about those writing after him is how much they observe about the contexts of choice. Despite his cynicism, Mandeville has genuine and deep insights into moral psychology, and like all such insights they show often surprising connections between what look like different psychological states or motives. Mandeville is cynical about human nature because he is a prophet of tautology (to use a phrase of Dryden's), but it is only by an empty tautology that one can say that all motivations are reducible to a single one. Any such single motivation would have to be a purely formal or circular concept like 'preference' or 'pleasure' or 'motivation' itself, words which add no explanatory power. It is empty to say that we prefer what we prefer, that we take pleasure in what we take pleasure in, that we are motivated by what motivates us. The question (as the Humean William James will also argue over a century later),[5] is not 'What gives pleasure?' but 'What *kind* of pleasure does it give?' Pleasures are plural and heterogeneous, and there is no single entity called pleasure. In the same way, Adam Smith was clear that money functioned as a unit of account and a medium of exchange but had no value in itself, even if it made it possible to mediate the values of other things.[6] As Marx points out, even before Smith and Mandeville, Locke was distinguishing 'worth' from 'value': worth is what Marx called use-value and is heterogeneous and stable; 'value' is exchange-value; it is local ('*pro hic et nunc*') and a function of supply and demand.

Thus, much moral assessment of human motivation depends on how *we* value what people value. We cannot assume that there is only one thing we value, on pain of the tautological vagueness of saying that we value what we value, but we can still argue about whether there are a myriad of different values, in which case the panoply of human motivation starts making the idea of value itself seem unnecessary and empty (we arrive at tautology from the other direction), or (far more likely) just a reasonable number of different, sometimes competing values, in which more likely case we can predict behaviour in certain situations, especially where only one or two kinds of value are at issue. This is an argument in evolution too. There is more than one thing an organism has to do to win the self-rewarding game of reproductive success: the organism must survive, and it must reproduce, and those two supreme values will sometimes conflict. They will conflict especially often in species which engage in sexual reproduction, since a minimally successful replacement equilibrium requires such individuals to average more than one offspring (since in sexual reproduction, each member of the next generation replaces some of the genes of each of its parents with the genes of the other and so dilutes each parent's genetic legacy). The question in evolutionary biology is whether it is better to see *more* than just these two values at work, more than just these two values of survival and reproduction driving the interactions. This is a question for what we could call evolutionary economics – a question for what *is* called evolutionary game theory. Can an array of specific and mutually irreducible values evolve that could not be predicted from their evolutionary backgrounds? For example, do we find useful adaptations in a potential mate *ipso facto* sexually desirable (as many popularising views of evolution assert), or are desirable attributes in fact unpredictable from first principles, like the peacock's burdensome tail or the flamingo's toxin-derived colour – or the tragic hero or heroine's reckless and fatal courage? To repeat: eighteenth-century economists were already thinking these issues through in very pertinent ways with respect to human psychology. Game theory in general is about whether and how best moves are dictated in any situation, and while it sometimes takes what looks like a tautological view of values (we keep purely numerical score of the players' results), the scores are actually just measures of what each player values *for* him- or herself. (This should be obvious since the real world games that game theory models are rarely zero-sum. Everyone can be happy, or unhappy: there is no iron law of scarcity in the distribution of value. Everyone might be happy at a party, and each of them unhappy if the party is cancelled.) The question then is whether there is a universal measure of value (which would justify Mandeville's more cynical pronouncements about universal selfishness), or whether we can value things unselfishly and thus for themselves. Is there such a thing as unselfishness, or is unselfishness itself just a preference which, like all preference, is by definition selfish? Evolutionary game theory, just because it is predicated on the necessity for reproductive success, would provide a gold standard for measuring unselfish motivation if it could show that we sometimes choose things for reasons other than, and counter to, their immediate contributions to our well-being or survival or reproductive success.

Even in the terms we inherit from eighteenth-century economic psychology, it seems that the greater the plurality of value the less possible it is to reduce, say, generosity to selfishness, as Mandeville does when he sees generosity as merely a way to gratify one's own sense of self-worth. Maybe generosity is indeed a way of gratifying a sense of self-worth, but the interesting issue about a person then becomes the very fact that she or he values her or himself for their generosity, not the abstract idea that they are motivated by whatever will tend to an increase in gratification.

Not that Mandeville is at all reductive in his description of the dynamics of the mind. If his ideas of valuation tend to be cynically reductive, his pluralistic psychological insight has considerable power. Thus, writing about envy, he says:

> we are ever employ'd in wishing well for our selves, every one according to his Judgment and Inclinations, and when we observe something we like, and yet are destitute of, in the Possession of others; it occasions first Sorrow in us for not having the Thing we like. This Sorrow is incurable, while we continue our Esteem for the Thing we want: But as Self-Defence is restless, and never suffers us to leave any Means untried how to remove Evil from us, as far and as well as we are able; Experience teaches us, that nothing in Nature more alleviates this Sorrow than our Anger against those who are possess'd of what we esteem and want. This latter Passion therefore, we cherish and cultivate to save or relieve our selves, at least in part, from the Uneasiness we felt from the first.[7]

Notice, first, that he has to concede that what we, each of us, wish for is idiosyncratic, determined by *individual* judgement and inclinations; then, that sorrow is our reaction to not having what we see someone else possess, but also that such sorrow is itself a passion we do not wish to feel, though it is the expression of our wish to have something (or at least a reaction to the failure to satisfy that wish); but we do not wish to feel sorrow – so why do we? – which means it is a passion which gives rise to another passion – anger – which we value not so much because of its object (those possessed of what we want) as because feeling it relieves the uneasiness that our sorrow makes us feel. It would be far easier for our self-defence to counteract our sorrow by suppressing and undoing it, but instead we feel and even cherish the presumably negative affect of anger. This is very astute and accurate psychological description, but it does not make sense as a demonstration of sheer transparent selfishness or self-interest unless we accept how complex the self is, how plural are its desires, how idiosyncratic and heterogeneous are its interests in itself, and how irreducible it is to an entity motivated by some abstract and uniform idea of pleasure.

Mandeville's invocation of the restlessness of self-defence is proto-Darwinian and helps focus some aspects of evolutionary psychology, and particularly the psychology of cooperation and competition. But it is to Smith's responses to Mandeville that we should turn. Hopes quotes Mandeville on the paradox or quasi-paradox of altruism or self-sacrifice:

> The Man of Manners picks not the best but rather takes the worst out of the Dish, and gets of every thing, unless it be forc'd upon him, always the most indifferent Share. By this Civility the Best remains for others, which being a Compliment to all that are present, every Body is pleas'd with it: the more they love themselves, the more they are forc'd to approve of his Behaviour, and Gratitude stepping in, they are obliged almost whether they will or not, to think favourably of him. After this manner, it is that the Well Bred man insinuates himself in the esteem of all the Companies he comes in, and if he gets nothing else by it, the Pleasure he receives in reflecting on the Applause which he knows is secretly given him, is to a Proud Man more than an Equivalent for his former Self-denial, and over-pays to Self-love with Interest, the loss it sustain'd in his Complaisance to others.[8]

The question is why does he prefer the secret applause to the sweetest apple he denies himself? And why do the others seem to prefer the compliment he makes to the apple he leaves them? As Hume pointed out, it is hard to see some narrow conception of self-interest in preferring the good will of others to the good things at hand.[9] What kind of pride is this that it behaves so self-effacingly in order to grant itself the pleasure of knowing that others are secretly applauding it for self-denial? How do we characterise the modesty of this pride? How can we evaluate the payback for this self-sacrifice? How is self-love here something different from the satisfaction one takes in having done the right thing? Is all such satisfaction simply to be disparaged as self-love? Perhaps the self *deserves* this love; perhaps it owes it to itself. It is 'overpayment' only if overpayment consists in too great a delight in one's own virtue, but it seems to me just as morally reasonable to see delight in one's own virtue as a virtue in itself and not the vice that Mandeville implies when he uses the language of overpayment with interest. Mandeville's argument is impressively circular. It follows the logic of the potlatch or of conspicuous consumption: the big spender, the person who overpays, does so out of pride. By overpaying others he always overpays his own pride as well which swells accordingly with self-love *because* it is so willing to overpay, because it has given itself a reputation as an overpayer. But the dynamics of competitive generosity Mandeville anticipates here cannot as easily be squared with the language of rational economic behaviour as Mandeville wishes.

Smith's characterisation is different: he says what is obvious, that the recompense in praise for the suffering one undergoes does not and cannot repay that suffering with interest, at least if your measure of worth or value is on the cod-Darwinian scale of what conduces to survival. If an unfairly injured or suffering man, by displaying aplomb under his misfortunes,

> follows that view which honour and dignity point out to him, Nature does not, indeed, leave him without a recompense. He enjoys his own complete self-approbation, and the applause of every candid and impartial spectator. By her unalterable laws, however, he still suffers; and the recompense which she bestows, though very considerable, is not sufficient completely to compensate the sufferings which those laws inflict. Neither is it fit that it should. If it did completely compensate them, he could, from self-interest, have no motive for avoiding an accident which must necessarily diminish his utility both to himself and to society; and Nature, from her parental care of both, meant that he should anxiously avoid all such accidents. He suffers, therefore, and though, in the agony of the paroxysm, he maintains, not only the manhood of his countenance, but the sedateness and sobriety of his judgment, it requires his utmost and most fatiguing exertions to do so.[10]

Where Mandeville saw actual profit in good or noble behavior, Smith's more subtle proto-Darwinian account of Nature's 'parental care' (which we can update to: evolution's bias towards reproductive success) makes such behaviour into a way of cutting losses, not of coming out ahead.

In the end their similarities are more important than their differences. In at least one very important respect their insights complement each other. Here is Mandeville again, on sympathy – a slightly longer version of the passage that Hopes quotes in his chapter:

> Love in the first Place signifies Affection, such as Parents and Nurses bear to Children, and Friends to one another; it consists in a Liking and Well-wishing to the Person beloved. We give an easy Construction to his Words and Actions, and feel a Proneness to excuse, and forgive his Faults, if we see any; his Interest we make on all Accounts our own, even to our Prejudice, and receive an inward Satisfaction for sympathizing with him in his Sorrows, as well as Joys. What I said

> last is not impossible, whatever it may seem to be; for when we are sincere in sharing with another in his Misfortunes, Self-Love makes us believe, that the Sufferings we feel must alleviate and lessen those of our Friend, and whilst this fond Reflection is soothing our Pain, a secret Pleasure arises from our grieving for the Person we love.[11]

This is slightly ambiguous, but I take Mandeville to be saying that the satisfaction we take in sympathy is irreducible to some other kind of selfishness – which means we are genuinely generous – but that there is also a hidden facet to that satisfaction which might be troubling, and which we therefore keep secret. I have no doubt that what he is saying is true, but Mandeville downplays the generosity to notice the 'secret Pleasure' of grieving. What is not quite clear is whether the pleasure comes from being able to feel more intensely the love we feel for the person we grieve for, or from our (more or less false) belief that our own suffering helps alleviates his through drawing it into ourselves. But he is certainly close to Smith in seeing that our love for the beloved person may cause us to act to our own prejudice, which is not the cynical or reductively selfish view one generally ascribes to him.

It is analyses like Mandeville's here, where (to use Philip Fisher's verb) we volunteer our own feeling on behalf of another, that Hume liked and recast in his own account of human emotion. Just by way of orientation, one could take Hume's example (which I discuss elsewhere and which Philip Fisher has also discussed) of the sympathy and anxiety we feel for a sleeping man about to be trampled to death by horses,[12] or Smith's example of the sick child whom the mother worries about far more than the child *can* worry about itself,[13] as examples of apotropaic worry or sympathy, emotions whose intensity consists in the fact that they try to endow themselves with enough magic desperation to ward off the danger which elicits them. We seek to supply the worry that those unknowingly in danger should be feeling; and in worrying for them as though that made a difference we can start seeing the social function of the kind of vicarious experience drama and narrative trade on. For reasons having to do with the evolution of cooperation, reasons that seem to be routed through the general phenomenon of what is called costly signalling, we prefer being known or being able to think ourselves, even in secret, able and willing to pay certain costs – in wealth or worth or value or care or love – than to be thought unable or unwilling to pay them, and this is true even when paying those costs is more expensive than not doing so, even when the return in admiration or love (or sexual favours) that such costly signals may garner is priced in. We pay them *because* they are more expensive than they are worth. One way that Mandeville and Smith are surprisingly similar to each other, despite their slightly different emphases, is that they both explicitly anticipate the paradox central to the modern theory of the evolution of cooperation. The dynamic that makes genuine cooperation possible is that we compete with each other to cooperate, to defer to each other. We are interested in putting our own interests last.[14]

Another example from Smith seems consonant with Mandeville in predicting the theory of the evolution of cooperation through the way it shows us ranking a kind of vicarious experience of ourselves (how we look to others) above our own direct experience of ourselves (the experience of unmediated pleasure or use or value or worth). In Part IV of the *Theory of Moral Sentiments* (one of the places where he invokes 'the invisible hand'),[15] Smith notes with approval the fact that our love even of utility frequently exceeds any reasonable valuation of what utility can do for us. He marvels at his discovery 'that this fitness, this happy contrivance of any production of art, should often be more valued, than the very end for which it was intended; and that the exact adjustment of the means for attaining any conveniency or pleasure, should frequently be more regarded, than that very conveniency or pleasure, in the attainment of which their whole merit would seem to consist'.[16] At least their whole merit might seem to Mandeville to consist, perhaps, in the conveniency or pleasure produced. The utility of the appearance of utility is itself, for Smith, a very *socially useful* contrivance of nature; it is essentially another example of how we take the view of the abstract (the impartial) spectator into account (here through our propensity to pay for abstract, impartial usefulness rather than simply consulting what would be most useful for *us*).

We will now consider the (intertemporal) debate between Mandeville's friend Joseph Addison and Dr Johnson about *King Lear*, before returning to an interesting solution to the evolutionary issue that *preferring not to follow our own preferences* (as we may now put it) brings up. Johnson, we know, objected to Addison's Aristotelian deprecation of 'poetic justice' in his remarks on the superiority of Shakespeare's *King Lear* to Tate's revision:

> Terrour and Commiseration leave a pleasing Anguish in the Mind; and fix the Audience in such a serious Composure of Thought, as is much more lasting and delightful than any little transient Starts of Joy and Satisfaction. Accordingly we find, that more of our *English* Tragedies have succeeded, in which the Favourites of the Audience sink under their Calamities, than those in which they recover themselves out of them. ... *King Lear* is an admirable Tragedy of the same Kind, as *Shakespear* wrote it; but as it is reformed according to the chymerical Notion of poetical Justice, in my humble Opinion it has lost half its Beauty.[17]

Addison's description notices and appeals to another and important consideration: the temporal dimension of satisfaction. Although he is not able to explain (or at least does not explain) the oxymoronic idea of 'pleasing Anguish', it seems to me that Mandeville's explanation (saving the cynicism) is sufficient, and indeed right: the primordial irreducibility of sympathy makes our anguish on behalf of others something pleasing. (It seems impossible that Addison really thinks pure terror would leave a pleasing anguish in the mind: he is talking, in a way that Aristotle did not, about sympathetic terror; that is, he is making terror a species of pity.) Knowing that there is no guarantee of a happy ending, a knowledge enforced by the idea that endings may be permanently sad, as in tragedy, changes our temporal relation to those we sympathise with. Happy endings, especially repeatedly happy endings, give rise only to little transient starts of joy and satisfaction, but serious composure of thought is more lasting and therefore more delightful. The part of sympathy that gives us pleasure, as Mandeville says, is directed at a more lasting future (the durable esteem of others or of the love we feel for them), and it is this that gives us serious composure of thought. Again, Addison is not actually talking about Aristotelian catharsis, but (if Mandeville is right) about what feels like a kind of alleviation of the sorrows of others through sympathising with them, an alleviation that is only alleviation and not termination: we care about Cordelia and Lear *now*, but what we care about is that this is what has happened to them; we care because their suffering was not rewarded, and this means that we care *for* them, still and continually. In other words (combining Mandeville and Addison) we can say that the puzzle of the delight and pleasure that we feel is at least half-solved by the sense that we have a more permanent relationship with them than we do with Tate's characters, and that such a relationship is important to us.

If Addison is aware of the temporality of such delight, so is Johnson. His response to Addison, in his general observation on *King Lear* in his edition of Shakespeare, is notorious, but worth our further consideration:

> Shakespeare has suffered the virtue of Cordelia to perish in a just cause, contrary to the natural ideas of justice, to the hope of the reader, and, what is yet more strange, to the faith of chronicles. Yet this conduct is justified by the Spectator, who blames Tate for giving Cordelia success and happiness in his alteration, and declares, that, in his opinion, 'the tragedy has lost half its beauty.' Dennis has remarked, whether justly or not, that, to secure the favourable reception of [Addison's tragedy] *Cato*, 'the town was poisoned with much false and abominable criticism,' and that endeavours had been used to discredit and decry poetical justice. A play in which the wicked prosper, and the virtuous miscarry, may doubtless be good, because it is a just representation of the common events of human life: but since all reasonable beings naturally love justice, I cannot easily be persuaded, that the observation of justice makes a play worse; or, that if other excellencies are equal, the audience will not always rise better pleased from the final triumph of persecuted virtue.
>
> In the present case the public has decided. Cordelia, from the time of Tate, has always retired with victory and felicity. And, if my sensations could add any thing to the general suffrage, I might relate that I was many years ago so shocked by Cordelia's death that I know not whether I ever endured to read again the last scenes of the play till I undertook to revise them as an editor.[18]

As most of us have felt, Johnson's report of how shocked he was by the death of Cordelia is a powerful piece of literary critical praise, all the more powerful for being intended as derogation. Perhaps we can feel some of Johnson's own ambivalence in the multiple uses he makes of the word *justice* and its cognates: Cordelia perishes in a *just* cause, but then Addison *justifies* Shakespeare's grim revision of the chronicles; Dennis may or may not be speaking *justly* in saying that Addison was self-dealing in decrying 'poetical justice'. All well and good, but then Johnson goes on that Shakespeare's play may indeed be 'a just representation' of life, and yet

THE DEATH OF CORDELIA AND THE ECONOMICS OF PREFERENCE

(strangely) those who 'naturally love justice' will not love this play, but will prefer to see what Johnson calls 'the observation of justice', *observation* slipping in meaning from its empirical sense of capacious view, that is, 'the act of observing, noting, or remarking', to its more normative sense of 'obedience; ritual practice'. This slide of meanings seems to be mediated through the way the word is used in Johnson's rubric 'general observation', where it means something like the 'Notion gained by observing; note; remark; animadversion.' (These are, of course, Johnson's three definitions of the term in his Dictionary.) The quasi-ritualistic practice of justice observed by revising *King Lear* to give it a happy ending, leaves the audience better pleased at the end of the play.

But for how long? Addison's point is that Shakespeare's version *fixes* us in a *lasting* composure of thought. Who would not rise better pleased with Tate's ending than with Shakespeare's? But who would find the emotional effect of Tate's version so durable – so unendurable – as that of Shakespeare's?

The intensity of Johnson's response to *King Lear*, and the serious Addisonian pleasure we take in it, shows the surprising centrality irreducibly vicarious experience sometimes assumes – the irreducibly vicarious experience of sympathy that is Smith's subject. We sympathise with intense sympathy, so that we sympathise with the sympathising mother in the example Smith offers just before he turns to sympathy for the dead:

> What are the pangs of a mother, when she hears the moanings of her infant that, during the agony of disease, cannot express what it feels? In her idea of what it suffers, she joins, to its real helplessness, her own consciousness of that helplessness, and her own terrors for the unknown consequences of its disorder; and out of all these, forms, for her own sorrow, the most complete image of misery and distress.[19]

The difference is that we would wish the source of the mother's anguish for the real agony of her infant lifted, but we take pleasure in Johnson's real anguish for unreal sorrow, although in other places Johnson does not fancy his unhappiness so unbearable. I suppose it is possible that Johnson is remembering this moment from Smith when he compares the experience of fictional theatrical emotion – which is a special case of vicarious experience, especially as the latter manifests itself in sympathy with the dead – to that of the mother imagining the death of her own child: 'If there be any fallacy, it is not that we fancy the players, but that we fancy ourselves unhappy for a moment; but we rather lament the possibility than suppose the presence of misery, as a mother weeps over her babe, when she remembers that death may take it from her.'[20] And we feel for the mothers – in Smith and Johnson – because of a kind of sympathy with sympathy itself, which is central to Smith's moral thinking. Smith further analyses this sort of sympathy with sympathy in the *Theory of Moral Sentiments* in his account of approbation as sympathetic approval of the feelings of others, and in particular in his discussion of approval or disapproval of the approbation or disapprobation of others.

Here we return to the virtuous circle of motivation that Smith has been urging against the tradition of Hobbes and Mandeville. We seek the approbation of those we approve of ourselves (the impartial spectator most of all); approbation is not itself a tautological good, but the motivation to a social good to which it is both means and end – not because it is an end in itself but because it is a facet of a larger end, which is mutual sympathy and cooperation. We approve of the approbation of those who approve of us if, and only if, we approve of them, and therefore if, and only if, they approve of the moral demands we make on them. The dynamics of approbation help explain and establish the irreducibly vicarious component of the beauty of utility: 'This account, therefore, of the origin of approbation and disapprobation, so far as it derives them from a regard to the order of society, runs into that principle which gives beauty to utility.'[21]

We will also sometimes approve of their disapprobation, says Smith.[22] But in the case of *King Lear* we can add a new wrinkle: *that we sometimes approve of their disapprobation of things that we ourselves approve of*, as I do of Johnson's disapprobation of Shakespeare's *King Lear*. I do not think Johnson is right: but I am glad that he feels the power of the play so strongly. (He is right to do that.)

If there is a paradox here, it is a paradox similar to the one that seems to be present in Mandeville, try as he might to deny it, a paradox now more obviously routed through intersubjectivity. But the idea was already intersubjective in Mandeville: we care about what others think of us, even in secret: we care in secret about what they think of us in secret.

Let us return to the question of the quantification of motivation that Mandeville and his predecessors mooted. If Hume and Smith and William James pretty decisively refute the purely arithmetic or quantitative account of motivation, we have to ask why they are not refuted in their turn by the Hobbesian demands of Darwinian evolution. Why does evolution not differentially reward those who are so constituted as to pursue their own interests most single-mindedly? Why do considerations of my own utility, or my own advantage, of my own prosperity not trump considerations of the utility, advantage and prosperity of others?

In one sense, as we have seen, such considerations are paramount, but only because others approve of those who do not pursue their own interests first and foremost. We get rewarded for not seeking reward. Though Mandeville would presumably agree with that idea, it simply displaces by one level the same question: why others take the pain and trouble to reward us for not seeking reward – pain and trouble which is greater than the profit they derive from our own self-denial. Very frequently, no one takes the last dainty in the dish, and all feel good about their mutual loss and mutual approbation.

The answer seems to be more or less what Smith says it is: that the mutual approbation which all feel for one another is better for the evolution of cooperation; but that it cannot arise out of a desire for advantage, because such desires would always trump the proclivity to cooperate. So how can cooperation evolve? Here we return to the theory of costly signalling, already incipient in Smith: if others approve of self-command, self-command will get a foothold on the evolutionary mountainside, and once it gets such a foothold it will manifest itself as (among other things) the unselfish and therefore costly approval of self-command.

How does it get this foothold? Costly signalling is an important aspect of sexual selection; but some costly signals lead to better general outcomes, outcomes for a whole population, than others, and it seems that the self-command which takes the form of actively disapproving of selfishness, and approving of self-command, is among the best.

But there is still a puzzle here about how to describe the psychology of self-denial – not why, but how the mind gives itself an incentive to discount its greatest incentives. Twenty-first-century readers of the work of Mandeville, Hutcheson, Hume and Smith might find a clue to the solution to this puzzle in the writing of George Ainslie, who has shown the universal prevalence in mammals and birds of *hyperbolic discounting* of future values in their evaluation of potential rewards and satisfaction.[23] The basic idea is this: we prefer immediate gratification to mathematically greater delayed gratification, even when compensated or even overcompensated for the delay. Almost everyone will prefer $100 today to $110 a week from today. And yet almost everyone will choose $110 fifty-three weeks from now to $100 in fifty-two weeks. These preferences are inconsistent with each other. But they suggest how immediacy overwhelms rational maximisation of one's own reward.

Vicarious experience tends to be immediate experience, to offer a Wildean formulation. Vicarious as to *whose* experience it is, it is nevertheless immediate in *time*. It is what we directly know or hear or see about someone's experience that concerns us, that engages our sympathy, and it does so at the moment that we sympathise. So the immediacy of that experience trumps the longer-term advantage we could exploit if we ignored others' immediate suffering or emotional needs. Immediacy gives others an importance they would not have for us if we were (all of us) being rational about payoffs.

The different temporal profiles of our motivations and satisfactions involve us in weighing them against each other, and in undertaking what Ainslie calls intertemporal bargaining. Such bargains turn out, paradoxically, to be the main cause of our ever preferring a greater but delayed satisfaction, since we are so consistently quick to choose a smaller but more immediate reward. Delayed satisfactions will often only trump immediate satisfactions if they can find some other immediate satisfaction to ally with. The glutton prefers the immediate pleasure of the delicacy in the dish to the longer term but vaguer self-approval that he will feel for himself in the future for his good behaviour; but the self-restrained guest understands that the company's approval, while it is long-term approval for good behaviour, is *also* something he knows he can reward himself with right now. If this sounds ultimately selfish, we can reverse the polarities of praise and blame. Self-command under adversity is a way to give oneself an immediate reward in the approval of the man in the breast or the impartial spectator, immediate reward which counteracts the far greater but also longer-term loss and concomitant temptation to despair. In a kind of virtuous inversion of panic, the rush of immediate approval looms up to block the effects of far greater but more distant loss. I believe that all emotional reaction is a short-term preference for immediate alleviation – to use Mandeville's word – of one's own sorrow or of the sorrow of others, or (usually) both.

Costly signalling is possible when we prefer the right kinds of immediate gratification (pride in self-command or in greatness of heart, for example, or emotional burden-sharing) to our obvious and serious cost: *Par délicatesse / J'ai perdu ma vie; It is a far, far better thing that I do*. In such cases our immediate preferences turn out – unexpectedly and wonderfully – to be preferences for generosity, self-abnegation, altruism, or self-denial; and may accurately be recognised as just that, by ourselves and others. This is a way of reconciling Smith and Mandeville.

The idea of temporal preferences also has to do with the gratifications we take in literature, and those gratifications show the dynamic of intertemporal bargaining and of its relation to vicarious experience. Johnson prefers the immediate gratification of Cordelia's survival. Addison prefers the longer-term gratification of being fixed in serious composure of thought. (If he wants this because it will ally with his immediate interest in seeing the success of *Cato*, we can feel, agreeing with him as we do, that this is a virtuous alliance.) As for us, we like Johnson's immediate dislike for Shakespeare's denouement. Johnson's extreme emotional response engages our sympathy – vicariously – and so bolsters our preference for Shakespeare, because he gave us the immediate pleasure of sympathising with Johnson's sorrow (and sympathy is a pleasure), while rebuking him for seeking to overcome that sorrow too quickly through recourse to Tate (because rebuke is also a pleasure). That pleasure supports our long-term preference for the greatness of Shakespeare's version, which we might otherwise reject. And it allows us to prefer the long term, which we almost never do by itself, because of the short-term, immediate and concentrated summation of the long duration Johnson refers to when he describes the many years he found *Lear* unendurable. That little immediate pleasure makes it possible for us to commit to the long-term reward of the unendurably great. Evolutionary psychology helps us see why, and so do Mandeville and Smith.

Notes

1. Darwin first discusses sexual selection in print in a preview of *Origin of Species*, in Charles Darwin, 'Extract from an Unpublished Work on Species', *Journal of the Proceedings of the Linnean Society of London. Zoology*, 3: 46–50 (1858), 50, http://darwin-online.org.uk/converted/pdf/1858_species_F350.pdf, accessed 1 November 2015.
2. See Albert O. Hirschman, *The Passions and the Interests: Political Arguments for Capitalism before Its Triumph* (Princeton, NJ: Princeton University Press, 1977).
3. Adam Smith, *An Inquiry into the Nature and Causes of the Wealth of Nations*, ed. Edwin Cannan, 5th edn (London: Methuen & Co., 1904), IV. vii. 3 (vol. 2, p. 95) and IV. ii (vol. 1, p. 422), www.econlib.org/library/Smith/smWN13.html, accessed 1 November 2015.
4. On sympathy for the dead, see Adam Smith, *The Theory of Moral Sentiments*, ed. R. P. Hanley (London: Penguin Books, 2009), part 1, sect. 1, ch. 1, pp. 17–18.
5. See William James, 'Pleasure and Pain as Springs of Action', *The Principles of Psychology* (New York: Henry Holt, 1908), vol. 2, pp. 549–59.
6. Smith, *Wealth of Nations*, vol. 1, bk IV, ch. 1 'Of the Principle of the Commercial, or Mercantile System', pp. 396–417.
7. Bernard Mandeville, *The Fable of the Bees*, ed. Phillip Harth (Harmondsworth: Penguin Books, 1970), pp. 158–9.
8. *Ibid.*, p. 111. See Jeffrey Hopes in this volume, Chapter 3, note 16.
9. David Hume, *An Enquiry Concerning the Principles of Morals: A Critical Edition*, Appendix 3, 'Some farther Considerations with regard to Justice', ed. Tom L. Beauchamp (Oxford; New York: Oxford University Press, 2006), pp. 96–101.
10. Smith, *Theory of Moral Sentiments*, part 3, ch. 3, pp. 170–1.
11. Mandeville, *Fable of the Bees*, p. 165. See Jeffrey Hopes in this volume, Chapter 3, note 17.
12. William Flesch, *Comeuppance: Costly Signaling, Altruistic Punishment, and Other Biological Components of Fiction* (Cambridge, MA: Harvard University Press, 2008), p. 117; David Hume, *A Treatise of Human Nature*, ed. L. A. Selby-Bigge, 2nd edn ed. P. H. Nidditch (Oxford: Clarendon Press, 1978), bk 2, part 2, sect. 9, pp. 385–6; Philip Fisher, *The Vehement Passions* (Princeton, NJ: Princeton University Press), 2002, pp. 142–6.
13. Smith, *Theory of Moral Sentiments*, part 1, sect. 1, ch. 1, §12, p. 17.
14. Mandeville, *Fable of the Bees*, p. 165. The best exposition of this idea is that of its inventors, Amotz and Avishag Zahavi, in their book *The Handicap Principle: A Missing Piece of Darwin's Puzzle* (New York: Oxford University Press, 1997).

15 Smith, *Theory of Moral Sentiments*, part 4, ch. 1, §10, p. 215.
16 *Ibid.*, part 4, ch. 1, §3, pp. 209–10.
17 *The Spectator*, ed. Donald F. Bond, vol. 1 (Oxford: Clarendon Press, 1965), no. 40 [Addison], Monday 16 April 1711, pp. 169–70.
18 *Johnson on Shakespeare*, ed. Arthur Sherbo, *The Yale Edition of the Works of Samuel Johnson*, vol. 8 (New Haven, CT and London: Yale University Press, 1968), p. 704.
19 Smith, *Theory of Moral Sentiments*, part 1, sect. 1, ch. 1, §12, p. 17.
20 'Preface to Shakespeare' [1765], *Johnson on Shakespeare*, ed. Sherbo, vol. 7, p. 78.
21 Smith, *Theory of Moral Sentiments*, part 7, sect. 3, ch. 1, §2, p. 372.
22 *Ibid.*, part 7, sect. 3, ch. 3, §14, p. 383.
23 See George Ainslie, *Breakdown of Will* (New York: Cambridge University Press, 2001) and William Flesch, 'Hyperbolic Discounting and Intertemporal Bargaining', in *Theory Aside*, eds Jason Potts and Daniel Stout (Durham, NC: Duke University Press, 2014), pp. 199–217.

PART II

Self-exploration in the Age of Reason: division and continuity

6

'Chaos dark and deep': grotesque selves and self-fashioning in Pope's *Dunciad*

Clark Lawlor

Pope and self-fashioning the body

Helen Deutsch has productively discussed Pope's construction of his own body in terms of deformity – one that Pope self-fashioned to his advantage as far as was possible:

> This poetic attention to sometimes ugly particulars is embodied by the author himself. His physical deformity becomes a vehicle for self-reflection, self-representation, and self-legitimation. The poet's body is both a trademark of his poetry's invisible property, and a sign of his own vulnerable visibility, rendering him at once an imitable original and a faulty imitation. Deformity frames the power of Pope's vision with its reminder of the observer's gaze.[1]

Deutsch's analysis mediates between the critical schools who make Pope reject (or abject) the feminine realm of the grotesque body, marketplace and mob, and those who praise him as a heroic champion of moral integrity.[2] The former have broadly taken their cue from Peter Stallybrass and Allon White's reworking of Mikhail Bakhtin and Julia Kristeva in their now-classic study, *The Politics and Poetics of Transgression*, while the latter follow in the monumental footsteps of Reuben Brower and Maynard Mack.[3] In both cases 'deformity as a self-consciously created figure for Pope's poetics patterned after the poet's own person is lost from sight'.[4] This chapter will argue that Alexander Pope's self – as depicted in his various *Dunciad*s – is a conflicted entity riven by the discourses of gender, physical norms based on classical precedent, the ever-rising middling orders, and consumer mercantile capitalism. Pope displaces his anxieties (consciously or not) about his own masculinity, poetic productivity and physical legitimacy, themselves structured partly by those broader discourses which generally constructed the Augustan self, onto a series of alternative selves, either grotesquely monstrous women, or chaotically effeminate men, most notably his poetic alter ego, the poet laureate Colley Cibber. Through the vehicle of literary representation, Pope was able to image and frame these threats to the self, and via that very narration of the unstable, othered and grotesque self, transformed it into an abject deformity that did not fall within the purview of Deutsch's notion of deformed self-fashioning. Some types of grotesquerie would aid Pope's control over his own image by exploiting that physical difference, while some types would be placed firmly beyond the reach of self-control. Whether readers accepted Pope's abject grotesque alternative selves as such is of course another question: the point here is that Pope developed his heroically deformed self against such inferior but threatening copies.

Ideas of the grotesque body and state

When Pope came to write the *Dunciad* the political, economic and medical contexts of his work had changed considerably from the glorious days of the Treaty of Utrecht and *Windsor Forest*. Times and selves had become grotesque, hybrid, abject. The first version of the *Dunciad*, which I will refer to as *Dunciad A*, came in three books and was published in 1728 just after the coronation of King George Augustus II in 1727.[5] This version of the poem rather gloomily leads to predictions of the dire consequences of the philistine Hanoverian succession on the elite preserve of classical values. As he states at the beginning of *Dunciad A*, 'Still Dunce the second reigns like Dunce the first' (I. 6): that is, George continued the Hanoverian succession, a succession that continued to be unfavourable for the Tories in opposition. With the arrival of a new king the Tories had hoped for a switch in favour away from Walpole (the Prime Minister) and the Whigs. Unfortunately for them this did not happen for at least two reasons. The attempt to install a new prime minister in the person of Lord Wilmington failed miserably, as he soon conclusively proved his incompetence; consequently the Whig ministry was safe when the Queen informed George that Walpole was the only man who could lever large increases in the civil list through parliament. In the year 1727 it must have seemed to the Tories that Walpole was unshakeable in his position. Another reason for their gloom was the fact that George, like his father before him, distrusted the Tories because the Hanoverians usually equated the Tory party with Jacobitism, due to Bolingbroke's attempt to secure the throne for James on the death of Queen Anne. All their efforts to ingratiate themselves in the separate court of the then Prince and Princess of Wales had come to nothing: even Pope had paid court to the Prince. The opposition quickly lapsed back into cynicism.

This politically grotesque time (to Pope at least) was paralleled by developments in the economics of the book trade and the response of the monarchy as supposed patrons of the arts to these developments. Pope felt that George II's court was prone to the same low tastes as the common audience of the 'literature' and dramatic entertainments being churned out by the Grub Street hacks. Hence both Pope's 'heroes', Theobald or 'Tibbald' of *Dunciad A* and Colley Cibber of the four-book 1743 *Dunciad B*, are mediators between the 'low' world of the drolls and the fair, and the elite world of the aristocracy of St James's Palace: 'Books and the Man I sing, the first who brings / The Smithfield Muses to the Ear of Kings (A. I. 1).' As Stallybrass and White point out, this is an area of cultural transgression: the boundaries between the discrete areas of classical learning of the elite and the grotesque farce of Bartholomew Fair which was based at Smithfield are breached in the very first lines of the poem.[6] Cibber, the hero of the revised version, is in many ways the more suitable of the two heroes because he had been appointed Poet Laureate under George II and yet produced sensational and lavish plays which would be attended by both court and commoner, including the King and Queen themselves. Theobald had also written a number of pantomimes despite being a rather more distinguished Shakespearean scholar than Pope himself. Defenders of classical values such as Pope and Swift could only find such a situation grotesque, an attack upon polite civilisation. Indeed Swift seems to have had a hand in encouraging Pope to bring the *Dunciad A* to fruition, as the

Twickenham editor observes.⁷ The newly burgeoning capitalistic market of Grub Street wrote not from a sense of classical standards, but from the sole perspective of making a profit by pandering to the lowest and, paradoxically in the case of George II, the highest common denominator, with the emphasis on 'common'. In his later works, argues Scott Hess, Pope cultivated a 'stance of authorial isolation' in order to negotiate a path between his need to present himself as a creative force independent of this market and yet his actual dependence on these very forces, 'an increasingly unknown and (for Pope) degraded commercial public'.⁸ This political and economic/cultural context for the poem is mirrored by its material context.

Pat Rogers has shown in his *Grub Street* and *Literature and Popular Culture* that the world of eighteenth-century London was grotesque in itself. Quite apart from the bizarre goings-on at the fairs such as the freak shows and the bear-baiting, there were the carnivalesque activities in the streets surrounding such events as executions, the Lord Mayor's day, and the ever-present threat of riots.⁹ Ned Ward gives a sense of Pope's experience of London life in his *London Spy* in which he describes the flinging of dead cats and filth by the mob at the Lord Mayor's show.¹⁰ The ludic activities of the great unwashed articulate clearly what Pope was defining himself against: the pleasures of the 'rabble' quite literally pollute all they encounter, and it was the conjunction of the mob with the monarchy in terms of pleasure that Pope feared and despised.¹¹

Medical developments did not help matters: following the demise of humoral theory, the rise of New Science, and such discoveries as the circulation of the blood by William Harvey in the seventeenth century, the body had been found to be nothing more than a hydromechanical system – or at least that was the fear. In fact most natural philosophers worked happily with the 'argument by design', the notion that such a finely ordered universe must have a creator.¹² Nevertheless such apparently specific knowledge of the body and its functionings created new anxieties about the possibility that the body lay mired in the messy mechanics of the physical world, and that it might return to its chaotic unformed state: a problem clearly expressed in the excremental 'games' of the *Dunciad* and the various alternative selves invoked by Pope.

Grotesque Goddesses

The greatest Popean anti-self in the poem is the greatest creative force in the poem – not a poet laureate, but the Goddess Dulness: Dulness is female, and she comes to embody the fears of the poet concerning a whole host of issues, including the poet's sexuality, creativity, the modern body and the material conditions of the book trade at the time. Susan Gubar's ground-breaking article 'The Female Monster in Augustan Satire' identified Dulness as the greatest in a line of female monsters who both create and uncreate, while Marilyn Francus's 'The Monstrous Mother: Reproductive Anxiety in Swift and Pope' has expanded the specifically maternal aspects of Dulness's identity.[13] Dulness provides the driving force for this great grotesque poem because she is inherently grotesque: she is a woman who has power; and, what is worse, has ultimate power. Dulness has the power of Divine Fiat, but her power fully betrays the destructive potential of her sex towards the rational light of the masculine self's knowledge and control: 'Light dies before thy uncreating word' (*B*. IV. 654). Not only is Dulness Goddess in her own universe, but she also has the ability to destroy what she has created. She is Satanic in her inversion of the male creative impulse, filled with pride in her own capacity to generate a world without any reference beyond herself, as she 'With self-applause her wild creation views' (*B*. I. 82). Unlike the permanence and beauty of God's creation, Dulness either destroys or forms 'momentary monsters' that 'rise and fall' (*B*. I. 83). This grotesque instability and fluidity of the feminine controls the world of the poem because it *is* the world of the poem. Even its structure is constantly collapsing and restarting due to Dulness's unstable tendency to create and then destroy and then create again, until the final book – when the ultimate consequence of grotesque female power comes to pass and classical civilisation is overwhelmed utterly.

The dark Isis

Dulness is the latest and greatest in a long line of female grotesques, as Susan Gubar has noted in her classic study, and the mythographic sources from which Pope constructs her composite figure are complex indeed. As Faulkner and Blair point out, the Great Mother or

Magna Mater is mentioned five times in the *Dunciad*, to say nothing of the vast body of allusions to various interlinked goddesses.[14] One of the many goddesses to which the Magna Mater has been linked is Isis, the Egyptian Queen of the moon and night, who is a tripartite goddess related to Diana Luna and Hecate. Douglas Brooks-Davies draws attention to the fact that Pope saw England as enduring the blackness of Isis as the Queen of the Night or Hecate rather than as the moon queen, Diana Luna, illuminating night's blackness.[15] Hecate is Daughter of Night, Queen of Hell and therefore identified with Proserpina, Goddess of witches and a destroyer of men. Dulness herself is 'Daughter of Chaos and eternal Night' (*B*. I. 12). Faulkner and Blair show that 'Hecate's presence is especially felt throughout the *Dunciad*', partly through the dog imagery which introduces the theme of rabid madness and blurs the distinction between mad dogs and the followers of Dulness who howl at the moon: 'Ralph to Cynthia howls' (*B*. III. 165).[16] Hecate was often confused with Cynthia, although her main connection is with the infernal darkness which pervades the *Dunciad*. Hecate is also implied by the magic practised by her followers, the dunces, who use excrement as 'magic juices' (*B*. II. 104).

Associated with the Isis/Hecate strain of imagery in the poem is Nox, another female deity who shares the darkness of the other two, and the symbol of the owl, Dulness's bird which lights upon Cibber's head after he has been anointed. The owl is suitably grotesque, associated with both 'natural' transgression and the carnivalesque masquerades: 'a monster of a fowl, / Something betwixt a Heideggre and owl' (*B*. I. 289–90). Heidegger was not only a promoter of masquerades, but also a provider of court entertainments of the kind that Pope so heartily despised. Nox and Isis are connected with sleep, dreams and visions. Dulness constantly brings an opiate sleep to her followers, and the poppy wreath won by Shadwell (*B*. III. 22) is a symbol of Nox and Sleep himself. Isis was noted for sending prophetic dreams to her followers, just as Cibber is given a vision of the future in the third book of the *Dunciad*. Hecate also was said to preside over dreams and watch her sleeping followers, as does Dulness. The various vapours (*B*. IV. 615) and 'fogs' (*B*. I. 262) that surround Dulness and are generated by her also confirm her link with these various goddesses and her love of caves and grottos where such gloom is naturally found. The fogs also relate the older humoral model of melancholia, where the noxious smoke of the burning black bile would ascend to cloud the mind and bring delusions, as we see in the Cave of Spleen in *The Rape of the Lock*, where Spleen herself prefigures Dulness in a more controlled and medicalised manner. Spleen is a bodily organ and a disease, whereas Dulness is a general sickness of society. Nox's black robe similarly symbolises the darkness, both physical and moral, that we find in the Goddess of Dulness.[17]

Grotesque underworlds

As in the Cave of Spleen, the *Dunciad* often becomes a grotesque feminised underworld, a womb-like grotto or cave where darkness and moral inversion are the norm. The vapours and fogs in the poem evoke similar responses and themes to those in the Cave of Spleen, where an unnatural female sexuality prevails. These dark goddesses reinforce the specifically female source of disaster that overtakes the world of the *Dunciad*. Thus, early on in the poem we meet the grotesque locale of 'The Cave of Poverty and Poetry' (*B*. I. 34) where Dulness oxymoronically shines 'in clouded Majesty' (*B*. I. 45) and spawns poetic creatures out of 'the Chaos dark and deep' (*B*. I. 55). As John Sitter says, this is a 'monstrous womb' that miscreates and inverts the natural order.[18] Like Hecate, Dulness performs the witchery of seasonal disruption, where 'heavy harvests nod beneath the snow' (*B*. I. 78). This Cave was shifted from Rag Fair in *A* to the environs of Bedlam in *B* to emphasise the mental instability of such a world, based on the inability of women to control their minds due to the paradoxically unruly rule of their bodies. Dulness is always closer to Nature than Culture, always on the outside of the civilised order which she constantly threatens to destroy from her mediatory position between civilisation and chaos. Like the protean 'Bards' (*B*. I. 37) – other Popean 'selves' – Dulness herself, and the Cave of Spleen before it, the Cave of Poverty and Poetry is a protean space, transformed by turns into a womb, primeval chaos, a play, a courtroom, a masquerade and so on. This metamorphic grotesque tendency further emphasises the lack of cultural boundaries that the physical topography mirrors. Sitter notes the connection between this locale and the Dome of Dulness which appears later on in the first book, the spiritual womb of the worldly Cave of Poverty and Poetry.[19] This too is an enclosed feminine space of 'the Great Mother' (*B*. I. 269) where distinctions between orders of things are collapsed, where a Cibber and a Shakespeare are indistinguishable (*B.* I. 285–6).

In the second book the grotesque topography of sinking into hellish darkness continues with the games. Amongst the general sliding around in excrement and mud, as the dunces sport in a kind of primal soup, Dulness hears the requests of her servants from 'her black grottos near the Temple-wall' (*B.* II. 98), a reference which invokes the caves and grottos of Cybele, who was often confused with Isis. Cybele was worshipped in these locations as well as in round temples. Curll takes advantage of Dulness's grotesquely rejuvenating sexuality by fishing 'her nether realms for Wit' (*B.* II. 101), although this Wit turns out to be suitably excremental as Dulness's fertility is not a productive one in terms of good literature. Here Cloacina acts as a kind of minor goddess who rules the sewers, an intermediate part of Dulness's complex character constituted by a series of echoing classical but debased selves. Pat Rogers observes that Cloacina is taken from Cloaca Venus, the purifier, but satirists treat her as a befouled Venus, building on the old misogynist adage that a woman is a temple built over a sewer, a suitable contrast between the classical surface and the grotesque underworld or nether realm.[20] As the sexual reference implies, woman becomes a kind of grotesque orifice which receives any kind of personal excretion and discharges yet another: women in the *Dunciad* are conduits for grotesque flows because they partake of these flows in their very nature, being always liable to collapse back into chaotic formlessness and therefore to contaminate men with their venereal pollutions. They are, as Mary Douglas would put it, 'matter out of place' – the dangers of materialism in the medical theory of the eighteenth century are never more apparent than here.[21] These underground locations are echoed in the underwater caverns of the mud-nymphs later on in the games, where the predatory excremental sexuality of the feminine continues as they suck in an admittedly willing male victim (*B.* II. 332). These caverns share the drugged and dream-like influence of Hecate and Nox, 'wafting Vapours from the Land of dreams' (*B.* II. 340) to lull all to sleep.

John Sitter notes the imagistic connection between the Dome and the Cave of the opening section and the underworld dominating the third book, where Cibber is actually transported to the banks of the Lethe in the Elysian shade, a realm that the 'plunging Prelate' has previously been shown by the mud-nymphs (*B.* II. 323, 339).[22] Based on the underworld of Virgil's *Aeneid,* as are most of Pope's subterranean set-pieces in some way, this realm is dominated by the grotesque excessive economy of Dulness's reproductive capacities as Cibber sees 'Millions and millions' (*B.* III. 31) of the souls of the dull. Yet again one is led to this female realm by a disorderly female guide, 'a slip-shod Sibyl' who meditates song 'in lofty madness' (*B.* III. 15–16). Like the mud-nymphs before her, she is a polluted figure, her disorderly clothing symbolising the mental disorder that the poetic woman must be experiencing in her grotesque state of creativity, rather than merely being the object of inspiration for the male author.

The fourth book continues the grotesque topography of the underworld by an ironic iconographic reversal of the binding of Discord and her female followers at the triumphant end of *Windsor Forest*. Instead of the disruptive feminine forces of Dulness being bound in fetters at the footstool of Reason or some other suitable deity, one finds that Dulness confines all such positive icons to an underworld of her own making:

> Beneath her foot-stool, *Science* groans in Chains,
> And *Wit* dreads Exile, Penalties and Pains.
> There foam'd rebellious *Logic*, gagg'd and bound,
> There, stript, fair *Rhet'ric* languish'd on the ground. (*B.* IV. 21)

Especially significant is the replacement of the good by the bad in terms of the female body: the classical body of 'fair' Rhetoric is violated by her grotesque counterpart, 'shameless *Billingsgate*', who steals her robes (*B.* IV. 26). As Sitter observes, the Renaissance pictorial tradition is inverted here. Normally, slack but sturdy chains would lead down from beneath Reason's footstool to personifications of various passions who constitute a harmonious miniature kingdom.[23] The underworld of Discord now becomes more of an overworld as the power of Dulness spreads beyond the confines of her subterranean haunts.

Grotesque mothers and grotesque sons

The poem, although driven by Dulness as the great female monster, also constructs the male grotesque body, and it does this in terms of gender. Dulness's offspring, the dunces, parallel the servants of

Cybele, the Great Mother, in their intellectual sterility. Faulkner and Blair explain that the Galli, mendicant priests of Cybele, were eunuchs, castration being part of the initiation into the cult.[24] Named after the River Gallus, whose waters were said to induce lunacy, they would travel in processions through the towns dancing ecstatically and making a great commotion. Amongst other practices, their secret sacrifices were considered obscene and orgiastic in nature. Faulkner and Blair note that 'classical writers looked upon the cult as generally offensive and lewd, and described the sexless priests as tricksters, vagabonds, and swindlers'.[25] Such a classical disapproval is one shared by Pope: he too gives his dunces the ability to make a hideous din as they learn 'the wond'rous pow'r of Noise' (*B.* II. 222).

Their obscenity is clear at every point, but particularly in the games. The nature of this obscenity becomes clearer when one also learns that the Galli are 'dressed as women, in long mantles'. Lucian considered them to be 'mountebanks and effeminate fellows'.[26] The dunces themselves are characterised as effeminate in their sexuality: castrated in mind, they are grotesque because they have accepted the role of a woman, and they are ruled by a woman who has usurped the power of a man. The male grotesque is therefore defined in terms of the feminine: the castrated dunces too are characterised by 'lack'. Pope subjects them to the process of feminisation when he depicts them locked in homosexual acts: 'Behold yon Pair, in strict embraces join'd' (*B.* III. 179). Similarly, the tickling contest to win a patron implies that the 'youth unknown to Phoebus' wins a secretaryship by touching his Grace's 'only tender part' (*B.* II. 213-20). The dunces, however, are not the only feminised males in the poem.

Cibber and Cybele

Self and genre are intimately related and self-constituting in the *Dunciad*: Pope's note to the first line of *Dunciad B* states that 'the Reader ought here to be cautioned, that the *Mother*, and not the *Son*, is the principal agent of this poem', answering Dennis's criticism that the hero of this mock-epic was not involved in the action. John Sitter develops this point by showing that Pope parodies the traditional epic notion that women in epic, such as Helen, Circe and Dido, 'embody a parochial, domestic selfishness which threatens the execution of a larger and more "significant" achievement'.[27] In the *Dunciad*, Dulness is the 'hero', while Cibber is feminised, adopting the passive role of the woman. Pope exploits, with poetic justice, the epic theory of one of his own dunces, Blackmore, who claimed that 'no Reason ... can be assign'd, why a Heroine may not be the Principal Person of an Epick'. Sitter suggests that Blackmore provides the rules for the inverted world of Dulness and Pope's anti-epic, complete with Popean anti-selves. It may be no coincidence that Blackmore was the author of a treatise on the spleen, that multifarious and protean disease that was so symptomatic of the world of dissolving, vaporous, yet material selves which it was Pope's mission to create in poetic form.

Cibber's relationship to Dulness is problematic in that he is both son and lover: as he nestles in her lap at the beginning of book three (B. III. 2), the scene recalls the connubial bliss of the newly 'Anointed' George and Caroline, and the child being cradled by his mother. Carolyn Williams notes that two of the 'mighty mothers' related to Dulness are Thetis, who proposes the prizes at Achilles' funeral games, and Venus, who shelters Aeneas in cloud to save him in battle. In both cases there is a sense that the heroes are in fact mothers' boys, manipulated and protected by their goddess matriarchs. Williams argues that Pope exploits the dubious aspects of the epic originals in order to stress the passivity of Cibber.[28]

Such an argument is reinforced by a further aspect of the Magna Mater myth. Cybele, in one version of her origins, was left to die on the top of Mount Cybele, nursed by wild animals and rescued by local shepherds. When she grows up she falls in love with Attys, a shepherd, who is killed by her father – the king of Phrygia – after their reunion. She then runs shrieking through the countryside, beating a tympanum. In her absence the Phrygians are struck by a plague which can only be lifted by the disinterment of Attys and the worship of Cybele with annual games and festivals in her honour. One can see the link with the reign of Dulness here, although Pope's goddess actually *brings* plagues and fogs rather than removes them.

Two other stories are more significant, however, in that they revolve around a castration myth, a myth which is clearly central to Pope's public image as a 'deformed' poet and to his personal self-fashioning – in which he attempts to overcome this threat to his masculinity. In the first, the aged goddess Cybele has a priest called Attys who breaks his vow of chastity to her and castrates himself behind a pine tree, subsequently dying from the wounds.

The goddess transforms him into a pine tree, which becomes sacred to her. The second story again describes an aged goddess, Cybele, falling in love with a young shepherd, Attys. He rejects her and agrees to marry the daughter of Midas, king of Pessinus. When Cybele discovers this she breaks down the city gates with her army and causes havoc inside, eventually castrating Attys when she finds him hiding behind a pine tree.[29]

In the *Dunciad* there is a chain of references that link Cibber to Attys. In at least one account of the myth, Attys is taken for Cybele's son as well as her lover. As Cibber lies in Dulness's lap his head is newly 'anointed', like a newly initiated priest. He is also an unchaste priest whose chastity is lost to Dulness herself (*B*. IV. 20). When Settle calls Cibber 'our own true Phoebus' (*B*. III. 323) the Attys myth is again brought into play because Attys was thought by some to mean the sun, thus comparing him with Apollo. Clearly Attys, like Cibber, can only be a false Apollo. Cibber is a poetic god *manqué*, lacking all the values of the true Apollo, the bringer of harmony and light.[30] Overall, Cibber is a grotesque, feminised hero, a suitable king for the similarly feminised dunces. All are passive in contrast to the guiding action of the Goddess, a castrating mother who strips them all of their potential masculinity. Cibber comes to be a mis-creating mother himself when the line of Dulness perpetuates itself: 'Embryo' and 'Abortion' of 'Ode' and 'Play' surround him in his study (*B*. I. 121–2). The *Dunciad* becomes a poem concerning the grotesquerie of motherhood and replication of selves when it is applied as a metaphor of literary production, and Cibber inhabits such a grotesque feminised body so that Pope does not.

Mothers and daughters: proliferating selves

The grotesquerie of Dulness's motherhood is not confined to Cibber/Attys, however. Her reproductive ability is a transgression of social codes in itself because Dulness is free of traditional male domestic controls. She reproduces without any male intervention or, worse still, she forces men to submit to her predatory sexuality, as the episode with Cibber demonstrates. Indeed, part of her affront to the concept of motherhood in patriarchy is her intensified or 'exaggerated femininity' as Catherine Ingrassia calls it.[31] The Magna Mater/Isis myth is again brought into play here in the form of

Diana of Ephesus, a nurturing maternal deity who wears a turreted crown, a veil and has lions depicted on the lower half of her column-like body. These symbols link her with Cybele, while the lotus blossoms at the bottom of the surrounding two columns connect her with Isis. The crescent moon brings Diana Luna into play, but her most significant feature is the grotesque multitude of breasts she invites the viewer towards.[32] She calls all of mankind to accept her fecundity, just as Dulness seeks to draw all men into her regressive maternity, which offers the solace of her deathly womb – the tomb of classical learning. Dulness seeks to replace nature itself with her own anti-nature of undifferentiated matter. Spinoza asserted that 'the purpose of Nature is to make men uniform, as children of a common mother', and this is what Dulness becomes through her mythical identity.[33]

The violation of 'classical' motherhood occurs in another way, which is related to the central theme of the laissez-faire economics which had overtaken the book trade in Pope's time. Ingrassia explains that, from the conservative view – which advocated a moral economy – the new economics of paper credit that had enabled the South Sea Bubble had feminised eighteenth-century economic man in a market environment where 'man symbolically gives free reign to his passions and allows his fate to be shaped by such allegorical female figures of disorder as Fortune and Luxury'.[34] Pope's celebration of capitalism in *Windsor Forest* has now become a condemnation of this system under the present corrupt monarchy and government. The dunces, as we have seen, are effeminate and rely upon just such an economics. Dulness herself becomes not just a mother, but a mother Strumpet, the Madam of the dunces, because she advocates the prostitution of literature to the market and its vulgar whims, its desires for grotesque entertainments. Bona Dea, another goddess identified with the Magna Mater, was worshipped at night and, when linked with the old Roman goddess Maia, was worshipped also on May Day. Dulness too is a goddess of the night and darkness and she holds the games at the place of former May Day festivities:

> Amid that area wide they took their stand,
> Where the tall may-pole once o'er-looked the Strand;
> But now (so ANNE and Piety ordain)
> A Church collects the saints of Drury-lane. (*B*. II. 27)

Anne's good work in replacing the site of pagan worship with a church is completely undone by Dulness, who reclaims it for the Drury Lane harlots to ply their trade once more, just as the dunces are encouraged to sell their polluted textual 'bodies'. We have already seen the opposition between the classical body of 'fair *Rhet'ric*' and whorish 'Billingsgate' (*B.* IV. 26).

Dulness is the mother of a number of devolved selves who appear at various stages of the poem. A network of grotesque women reinforces the idea that bad literature is effeminate and therefore threatening to culture generally. Eliza Haywood is another mother figure considered by Ingrassia to be 'Pope's living symbol of Dulness'.[35] Haywood conflates many qualities to which Pope objected: a successful novelist and hack, she had also pursued a less successful career in the theatre as an actress and playwright, consorting with many of Pope's enemies. Adding insult to injury, she had attacked Martha Blount, one of Pope's classical ideal women who embodied the traditional feminine values of passivity and silence. Haywood was the very antithesis of Martha, conforming to none of Pope's requirements for the ideal woman. Worse still, like Dulness, Haywood had no husband, or rather she had separated from him. Without a restraining male figure Haywood's offensive creative autonomy became a major target for Pope. Ingrassia suggests that Haywood should also be viewed in the light of the rise of the female novel, a doubly disturbing development for Pope because it brought together issues of female authorship and the capitalistic book market which would pander to any audience and any genre. Haywood is not introduced as an active figure in the *Dunciad*, however, but as the first prize in the pissing contest:

> See in the circle next, Eliza plac'd,
> Two babes of love close clinging to her waist;
> Fair as before her works she stands confess'd,
> In flow'rs and pearls by bounteous Kirkall dress'd.
> The Goddess then: 'Who best can send on high
> The salient spout, far-streaming to the sky;
> His be yon Juno of majestic size,
> With cow-like udders, and with ox-like eyes.
> This China Jordan let the chief o'ercome
> Replenish, not ingloriously, at home' (*B.* II. 157–66)

Rather than nourishing breasts or the pearls of virginity, Eliza shows 'two babes of love', which primarily suggests illegitimate creation, despite the Virgilian allusion. She possesses a grotesque fecundity – as the 'cow-like udders' imply. In a more sinister fashion, she is iconographically reminiscent of Nox, Sleep and Death, because Nox was often depicted holding two boys asleep, a white one on the right (Sleep) and a black one on the left (Death), with both of them having distorted legs.[36] This forcefully reminds one of Eliza's true mistress, the dark Isis. The economic connection is not lost either, as Haywood becomes a strumpet-mother, a literary prostitute who is the receptacle for the excretions of any man, waiting to be 'replenished' at home just like the chamber pot. Such flows also link her with Cloacina, the sewer goddess, another minor manifestation of Dulness. Should there be any doubt that Haywood is a willing participant in this literary/sexual economy, Pope informs us that 'the pleas'd dame' is led away 'soft-smiling' (*B*. II. 188), a happy authoress who has found a publisher (Curll) to accept her advances.[37]

Where does this leave Pope's own 'deformity', so well analysed by Deutsch? On one hand the 'disgrace' of his crippled body is entirely eclipsed by the multiplied shame of the various bodies of Dulness and her empire. Her subjects, both male and female, have become more transgressive and yet weirdly productive than Pope could ever be. By contrast, Pope comes out of the *Dunciad* smelling of roses rather than excrement – not for him the sewers, literal and metaphorical, that run throughout the poem. Waste matter is not deformity as such, but along with it go the grotesque forms – generated partly by mythical associations – of Dulness, Eliza Haywood and the rest. Despite the fact that Dulness is the 'hero' of the poem (following Blackmore's rules for epic), her feminised, castrated 'son' – Colley Cibber – provides the direct anti-self through which Pope can reveal his own, apparently deformed, physical self to be merely a side-show for the Dunces.

The true grotesque is the Cibberian self, the anti-Apollo who produces, and in some ways is, 'abortion' (*B*. I. 121–2). He is both castrated and maternal: Pope might have been seen as less than a man due to his tiny stature and curved spine (and the host of accompanying ailments), and indeed mocked his own status in that regard, but compared to Cibber Pope becomes a poetic hero, the defender of the nation (and world) against the rise of a new and dangerous empire, an empire that threatens to bury the self.

We end our analysis of the *Dunciad* with a stress on grotesquely feminised male selves: selves created by – and alternative to – the

Popean self. Pope prided himself on his independence from patrons, but also his ability to rise above the vulgarities of the literary marketplace, in a particularly delicate ideological manoeuvre. How could one escape the patronage system and not be captured by the capitalism of the book trade? How could Pope avoid prostituting himself in the manner of Dulness's alternative female selves, her 'slip-shod Sibyl[s]'? Pope certainly exploited his image as a deformed but authentic poet in the manner described by Helen Deutsch, but he also manipulated complex and deep-rooted classical, medical, popular, economic, gendered and sexualised discourses in order to construct a series of overdetermined alternative selves via the overarching trope of the grotesque. It was this grotesque matrix of selves that liberated Pope into the gloriously unstable creativity of his poetic masterpiece, the *Dunciad*. It is no small irony that the alternative selves of the Goddess Dulness and her poetic sons and daughters were required to build Pope's version of the epic self.

Notes

1 Helen Deutsch, *Resemblance and Disgrace: Alexander Pope and the Deformation of Culture* (Cambridge, MA: Harvard University Press, 1996), pp. 2–3.
2 Well-known general studies on the grotesque include: Mikhail Bakhtin, *Rabelais and his World*, trans. H. Iswolsky (Bloomington: Indiana University Press, 1984); Terry Castle, *Masquerade and Civilization: The Carnivalesque in Eighteenth-Century Culture and Fiction* (Stanford, CA: Stanford University Press, 1986); Arthur Clayborough, *The Grotesque in English Literature* (Oxford: Clarendon Press, 1965); Geoffrey Harpham, *On the Grotesque: Strategies of Contradiction in Art and Literature* (Princeton, NJ: Princeton University Press, 1982); Wolfgang Kayser, *The Grotesque in Art and Literature* (Bloomington, IN: Indiana University Press, 1963); Neil Rhodes, *Elizabethan Grotesque* (London: Routledge & Kegan Paul, 1980); Mary Russo, 'Female Grotesques: Carnival and Theory', in Teresa De Lauretis (ed.), *Feminist Studies/Critical Studies* (Bloomington, IN: Indiana University Press, 1986), pp. 213–29; Peter Stallybrass and Allon White, *The Politics and Poetics of Transgression* (London: Methuen, 1986); Tony Tanner, 'Reason and the Grotesque: Pope's *Dunciad*', *Critical Quarterly*, 7 (1965), 145–60.
3 Bakhtin, *Rabelais and his World*; Julia Kristeva, *Powers of Horror, an Essay in Abjection*, trans. Leon S. Roudiez (New York: Columbia University Press, 1982).

4 Deutsch, *Resemblance and Disgrace*, p. 4.
5 Alexander Pope, *The Twickenham Edition of the Poems of Alexander Pope*, vol. 5, ed. and intro. James Sutherland (London: Methuen, 1943): *Dunciad A*, pp. 1–245; *Dunciad B*, pp. 246–426. I will use the Twickenham edition as the default in this chapter, although in many ways Valerie Rumbold's excellent edition has superseded others: *The Dunciad in Four Books*, rev. edn (Harlow: Longman, 2009). References are given in the text, citing the version (*A* or *B*), book and line number.
6 Stallybrass and White, *The Politics and Poetics of Transgression*, p. 110.
7 Pope, *Twickenham Edition*, vol. 5, Introduction, p. xiv.
8 Scott Hess, *Authoring the Self: Self-Representation, Authorship, and the Print Market in British Poetry from Pope through Wordsworth* (New York and London: Routledge, 2005). Hess's wider and more contentious argument is that our present idea of a 'lyric', 'deep' or 'a specifically authorial self, [was] generated out of the conditions, tensions, and contingencies of print culture', p. 4.
9 See Pat Rogers, *Literature and Popular Culture in Eighteenth-Century England* (Brighton: Harvester Wheatsheaf, 1985), p. 14, and *Grub Street: Studies in a Subculture* (London: Methuen, 1972), pp. 99, 248 and 253.
10 Ned Ward, *The London Spy*, ed. Arthur Hayward (London: Cassell, 1927), p. 220.
11 For the problem of crowds in the *Dunciad* see Julian D. Ferraro, 'Crowds and Power and Pope', *The Review of English Studies*, 63:262 (2012), 779–96.
12 See Clark Lawlor, 'Poetry and Science', in Christine Gerrard (ed.), *Blackwell Companion to Eighteenth-Century Poetry* (Oxford: Blackwell, 2006), pp. 38–52.
13 See Susan Gubar, 'The Female Monster in Augustan Satire', *Signs*, 3 (1977), 391; Marilyn Francus, 'The Monstrous Mother: Reproductive Anxiety in Swift and Pope', *English Literary History*, 61:4 (Winter 1994), 829–51.
14 Thomas C. Faulkner and Rhonda S. Blair, 'The Classical and Mythographic Sources of Pope's Dulness', *Huntington Library Quarterly*, 43 (1979–80), 213.
15 Douglas Brooks-Davies, *Pope's* Dunciad *and the Queen of Night: a Study in Emotional Jacobitism* (Manchester: Manchester University Press, 1985), p. 6.
16 Faulkner and Blair, 'The Classical and Mythographic Sources of Pope's Dulness', 232.
17 *Ibid.*, 229–30 for more on this question.

18 Sitter, *The Poetry of Pope's* Dunciad (Minneapolis: University of Minnesota Press, 1971), p. 13.
19 *Ibid.*, p. 17.
20 Rogers, *Grub Street*, pp. 143-4.
21 Mary Douglas, *Purity and Danger: An Analysis of Concepts of Pollution and Taboo* (London: Routledge & Kegan Paul, 1966), and see Sophie Gee, *Making Waste: Leftovers and the Eighteenth-Century Imagination* (Princeton, NJ: Princeton University Press, 2010) for a more recent development of this concept in relation to both the *Dunciad* and wider eighteenth-century culture.
22 Sitter, *The Poetry of Pope's* Dunciad, pp. 20-1.
23 *Ibid.*, p. 44.
24 Faulkner and Blair, 'The Classical and Mythographic Sources of Pope's Dulness', 233-6.
25 *Ibid.*, 235.
26 *Ibid.*, 238.
27 Sitter, *The Poetry of Pope's* Dunciad, p. 59.
28 Carolyn D. Williams, 'Breaking Decorums: Belinda, Bays and Epic Effeminacy', in David Fairer (ed.), *Pope: New Contexts* (London & New York: Harvester Wheatsheaf, 1990), p. 75.
29 Faulkner and Blair, 'The Classical and Mythographic Sources of Pope's Dulness', 220-1.
30 *Ibid.*, 240.
31 Catherine Ingrassia, 'Women Writing/Writing Women: Pope, Dulness and 'Feminization' in *The Dunciad*'. *Eighteenth Century Life*, 14:3 (1990), 45.
32 Faulkner and Blair, 'The Classical and Mythographic Sources of Pope's Dulness', 234.
33 See Thomas Edwards Jr, *This Dark Estate: A Reading of Pope* (Berkeley, CA: University of California Press, 1963), p. 127.
34 Ingrassia, 'Women Writing/Writing Women', 41-2.
35 *Ibid.*, 51.
36 Faulkner and Blair, 'The Classical and Mythographic Sources of Pope's Dulness', 233.
37 Valerie Rumbold has perceptively argued that 'females among the human characters, minor divinities and personifications are imaged predominantly in terms of sexual and excremental (rather than literary) transgression, and the threat of female creativity is refocused away from women writers and onto Dulness herself, effectively marginalizing the importance of women's writing in comparison with traditional topics of anti-feminist satire'. 'Cut the Caterwauling: Women Writers (Not) in Pope's *Dunciads*', *The Review of English Studies*, New Series, 52:208 (Nov. 2001), 524, abstract.

7

In two minds: Johnson, Boswell and representations of the self

Allan Ingram

'My state of mind today', wrote Boswell in his journal in 1775, 'was still affected by Hartley and Priestley's metaphysics, and [I] was continually trying to perceive my faculties operating as machinery.'[1] The thought is a charming one, as if Boswell could suddenly spin round and catch himself out as a machine! One thing the notion makes clear, though, is how closely Boswell's thinking about himself was engaged with current ideas. Joseph Priestley's *Letters to a Philosophical Unbeliever*, dealing with issues of materialism and necessity, had only been published in 1774, while David Hartley's *Observations on Man*, in which he developed association of ideas, had been in print since 1749. We see a mind, one that was, it has to be said, always interested in itself, responding to recent ideas in terms of trying to take further its self-awareness of the intricacies of its own working. And this is the topic of this chapter: how far, and in what ways, both Samuel Johnson and James Boswell demonstrate consciousness of their own thought processes and the attitudes we can perceive towards those processes. It is a matter of how and where the individual mind is known, how far an identifiable sense of self can be fully recognised and endorsed, accepted, warts and all.

To turn to Johnson first, it is Boswell who provides a key image for one aspect of the nature of Johnson's mind and thought processes.

'His mind', writes Boswell (and I quote from the *Life of Johnson*, though the image had first appeared in his journal for October 1769):

> resembled the vast amphitheatre, the Colisæum at Rome. In the centre stood his judgement, which, like a mighty gladiator, combated those apprehensions that, like the wild beasts of the *Arena*, were all around in cells, ready to be let out upon him. After a conflict, he drove them back into their dens; but not killing them, they were still assailing him.[2]

The wild beasts, of course, are the apprehensions, indeed at times the terrors, Johnson certainly had concerning death, judgement, guilt, indolence and personal worth. As a mental warrior, he was energetic in forcing back such fears, and the gladiator image is a particularly appropriate one for a man whose cultural foundations were firmly in Ancient Rome. Yet, while there is energy in Johnson the writer and conversationalist as much as in Johnson the single combatant, it is not a comfortable energy. Recurrence is a key word here: the beasts keep re-appearing, the fight must be fought again and again, the repression must go on and on. The pattern, of assailment, triumph, retreat and re-assailment, is one, ultimately, of mental entrapment. The doubts will never be settled. Fear will always corrupt self-judgement, and energy will always be wasted in going over the same old ground with the same old ferocity, a ferocity necessary to keep down despair.

Boswell's perception reaches to a whole realm of issues in Johnson's writing. It touches the variety of literary forms in which he practised, from poetry in Latin to parliamentary reports, sermons, prefaces for other people's works, essays, biography, the editing of Shakespeare, the compiling of the *Dictionary*. Each calls for a different kind of creative energy, each, apparently, satisfies a different market, and, temporarily at least, a different psychological need. It reaches, equally, his extraordinary command over the English language, again evidenced through his prose styles, the *Dictionary*, his critical penetration and, of course, his conversation. If his linguistic and stylistic energies had been as effective in governing his demons as in taming English, there would have been no gladiator and no fights. The crucial question, though, is: how completely did Johnson recognise this? How far did Johnson truly inhabit the landscape of his own mind, understanding the nature of the terrain, and how this wall of words protected against this sheer cliff-face of despair?

Certainly, the preponderance of statements in his writing expressing the need for stoical endurance and for the expectation of disappointment makes it clear what Johnson's philosophical stance was, but this is not the same as a genuine awareness of how his mind worked, of how his self was constituted. There are, however, clues, and one such text is *Rambler* 32, published on Saturday 7 July 1750 – on 'the art of bearing calamities'. 'The cure', he writes,

> for the greatest part of human miseries is not radical, but palliative. Infelicity is involved in corporeal nature, and interwoven with our being; all attempts therefore to decline it wholly are useless and vain: the armies of pain send their arrows against us on every side, the choice is only between those which are more or less sharp, or tinged with poison of greater or less malignity; and the strongest armour which reason can supply, will only blunt their points, but cannot repel them.[3]

The prose is characteristically regulated, with the anticipated Johnsonian rhythms and the developed metaphor of assault and defence. The performance is a finished one and the moral message is quite clear. But, as elsewhere in Johnson, the gravity of the phrasing carries with it a more than general guarantee. This, it implies, is authentic, is based on hard experience and, moreover, is saying a great deal less than it could. The self-discipline needed to endure, to 'blunt' the 'points' of the pain and misery that are our lot, is also the self-restraint that holds back the keen sense of suffering that has led to this general truth and has imposed a necessary reticence on the expression of it. The writer, we come away believing, knows the true cost of endurance but, even while the beasts are in retreat, he will not be saying. The next paragraph of the essay, in fact, is particularly telling here: 'The great remedy which heaven has put in our hands is patience, by which, though we cannot lessen the torments of the body, we can in a great measure preserve the peace of the mind, and shall suffer only the natural and genuine force of an evil, without heightening its acrimony, or prolonging its effects.'[4] The true burden of human existence is in the mind, and the art of surviving is to preserve at all costs the integrity of personal mental hold. Physical suffering is one thing, but that is magnified by the mind, if one allows it. The art of suffering, in fact, is to seal it off, as it were, in the realm of the body.

Here, in a fresh light, is the sad case of the astronomer in *Rasselas*, convinced that he controls the weather and ignorant that he has been descending into madness. He becomes the subject of Imlac's observations, observations that bear a touching resemblance to Johnson's own case:

> Disorders of intellect ... happen much more often than superficial observers will easily believe. Perhaps, if we speak with rigorous exactness, no human mind is in its right state. There is no man whose imagination does not sometimes predominate over his reason, who can regulate his attention wholly by his will, and whose ideas will come and go at his command. No man will be found in whose mind airy notions do not sometimes tyrannise, and force him to hope or fear beyond the limits of sober probability.[5]

Here, in the elegant control of phrasing, the triple instancing of what no man is able to do, followed by the neat double of what all men experience, is the characteristic Johnson sleight of hand, the style attracting the ear so successfully that we are in danger of missing the full force of what he is saying: that the airy notions 'force him to hope or', especially, to 'fear beyond the limits of sober probability'. And it is in the last of these that the true Johnson, perhaps, is showing through, Boswell's 'gladiator' daring to hope that his fear has been overstated, over-endured, but all the while aware that his hope might equally have been absurdly optimistic. The dilemma is clear, and the passage concludes: 'All power of fancy over reason is a degree of insanity; but while this power is such as we can control and repress, it is not visible to others, nor considered as any depravation of the mental faculties: it is not pronounced madness but when it comes ungovernable, and apparently influences speech or action.'[6] Johnson, apparently oblivious of the eccentric figure he cuts, with his tics and obsessions, fears above all things in this world the stigma of insanity. Control is all, no matter what the provocation, whether outer or, more dangerously, inner.

Bertrand H. Bronson in a famous essay written many years ago now, 'Johnson Agonistes', quotes, with some distaste, the French historian and critic Hippolyte Taine, whose *Histoire de la littérature anglaise* had included severe remarks about Johnson's prose style:

> 'Whatever the work', he declared, Johnson 'always writes in the same style ... Classical prose attains its perfection in him ... Art

cannot be more finished, or nature more forced. No one has confined ideas in more strait compartments; none has given stronger relief to dissertation and proof ... none has more generally mutilated the flowing liberty of conversation and life by antitheses and technical words.'[7]

Bronson is dismissive of Taine's assessment, but admits 'a glimmer of truth': 'Johnson does almost always forcibly impose his pressure on what he says or writes. The swing of his phrases, even in trivialities, starts from the hips.'[8] This is the whole point: Johnson's stylistic control is masterful because it has to be. That does not stop it being elegant, but self-protection demands that ideas, and the language that expresses them, are obliged to remain firmly in their place, serving one purpose and one only. They can on no account be allowed free rein. That way the suggestiveness of Shakespearean verse lies, and that was what Johnson was capable of finding so disturbing. As he noted of the difference between lines on night in Dryden, as opposed to Shakespeare's *Macbeth*: 'He that reads Dryden finds himself lulled with serenity and disposed to solitude and contemplation. He that peruses Shakespeare looks round alarmed and starts to find himself alone.'[9]

Control, or in Boswell's image judgement, keeps down the mental anguish, the self-reproaches for wasted time, for lack of achievement, for idleness and the squandering of his talent. But above all control firmly keeps in the most appalling fear of all, Johnson's deepest and most abiding terror. As he puts it in conversation with Dr Adams in 1784, in a rare moment of genuine revelation into his mind (and the conversation is made into dialogue by Boswell in the *Life*):

> JOHNSON: As I cannot be *sure* that I have fulfilled the conditions on which salvation is granted, I am afraid I may be one of those who shall be damned.
>
> DR. ADAMS: What do you mean by damned?
>
> JOHNSON: (passionately and loudly) Sent to Hell, Sir, and punished everlastingly.[10]

The shock of the direction, 'passionately and loudly', is almost as great as the dreadful acknowledgement, made not only to Adams but also to his wife and, of course, to Boswell. Few moments in the biography have such directness, or reveal such depths of self-knowledge, depths that remain mere hints and gestures in so much of Johnson's published work and in his reported conversation.[11]

Johnson, as is well known, destroyed many of his private papers shortly before his death, and more were destroyed by Sir John Hawkins, one of his executors and his first biographer. But among those private expressions that did survive, diaries and prayers, the occasional revealing letter, are some that do show how completely Johnson was alert to the mind that is not, generally, on view in the published works. Here, for example, written in 1776, is a judgement of his own characteristics and his culpability, as he saw it, in too often acquiescing in what those characteristics dictated:

> My reigning sin, to which perhaps many others are appendent, is waste of time, and general sluggishness, to which I was always inclined and in part of my life have been almost compelled by morbid melancholy and disturbance of mind. Melancholy has had me in its paroxisms and remissions, but I have not improved the intervals, nor sufficiently resisted my natural inclinations, or sickly habits.[12]

Earlier in his life, in 1768, he actually considered writing 'the history of my melancholy', but added, 'On this I purpose to deliberate. I know not whether it may not too much disturb me.'[13] This bleak intention, of course, was never carried out, or if it was we have no trace of it. We make do with those self-assessments and summaries from the scraps that remain, like this from Easter Day 1777:

> When I survey my past life, I discover nothing but a barren waste of time with some disorders of body, and disturbances of the mind very near to madness; which I hope he that made me, will suffer to extenuate many faults, and excuse many deficiencies ... But I have very little reformed my practical life.[14]

All he can fall back on, as the judgement moves to a conclusion, is the hope of God's mercy: 'Have mercy upon me, O God, have mercy upon me; years and infirmities oppress me; terror and anxiety beset me. Have mercy upon me, my Creatour and my judge.'[15]

The restlessness of form, the concentration on intellectual outwardness, the burning of the papers, all this means that with Johnson we can find no real location for his expression of the known mind. His, I suggest, was a mind out of step with its time. He took all the energies of his age and reflected them in his work, and all the energies of past culture, but they were controlled, held down by the forces of religious orthodoxy in his thinking. No doubt in this respect he was well within the norms of many ordinary people of his period, who either sought the security of traditional beliefs and their expression when brought up against the challenges of new ways of thinking or of understanding the universe, or else ignored such challenges altogether and continued with the regular patterns of their lives.[16] It does mean, though, that energy in Johnson is not expended in going with the creative stream of his age, but rather in suppressing its possibly threatening implications, in marshalling instead the comforts of tradition in attempting to calm, over and over again, the awfulness of his personal doubts. Self, in other words, is that nagging uncertainty that refuses to be silenced, no matter how much of the English language Johnson deployed in the vain act of burying it.

With Boswell, it was quite otherwise. 'How easily and cleverly do I write just now!', he congratulates himself in his journal for 9 February 1763: 'I am really pleased with myself; words come skipping to me like lambs upon Moffat Hill; and I turn my periods smoothly and imperceptibly like a skilful wheelwright turning tops in a turning-loom. There's fancy! There's simile! In short, I am at present a genius.'[17] Boswell, far from being in dread of the inner self, found his own personality completely fascinating, determined to take views of it from every possible angle and in every situation, and to preserve it for his own later delectation – and for the opportunities of self-assessment:

> I have therefore determined to keep a daily journal in which I shall set down my various sentiments and my various conduct, which will be not only useful but very agreeable. It will give me a habit of application and improve me in expression; and knowing that I am forced to record my transactions will make me careful to do well. Or if I should go wrong, it will assist me in resolutions of doing better.[18]

The very idea that Johnson would ever have been capable of believing that a daily self-examination would be 'very agreeable' is enough to point to the gulf between these two senses of self, but Boswell's capacity for self-admiration, at least at this age (he was twenty-two) is boundless. He goes on, 'I shall here put down my thoughts on different subjects at different times, the whims that may seize me and the sallies of my luxuriant imagination.'[19] This, of course, is from his own preface to his first sustained journal, the *London*

Journal of 1762–63, and what Boswell would record in some of his later years is distinctly darker and tempered by experience, but the naive self-regard remains indicative of a mind that continued to see itself as an object of interest, even of enquiry, and one that he considered well worth expressing in regularly undertaken prose.

As a young man, confident and self-absorbed, Boswell found it inconceivable, too, that his own interest in himself would not be matched by the interest of others. On the Grand Tour in 1764, for example, he determines while going through Switzerland to meet both Rousseau and Voltaire. He writes in preparation to the former: 'I present myself, Sir, as a man of singular merit, as a man with a feeling heart, a lively but melancholy spirit. Ah, if all that I have suffered does not give me singular merit in the eyes of Monsieur Rousseau, why was I made as I am? Why did he write as he has written?'[20]

Rousseau, he declares, has 'a perfect knowledge of all the principles of body and mind, of their movements, their sentiments; in short, of everything they can do, of everything they can acquire which truly affects man as man. And yet, Sir, I dare present myself before you. I dare to put myself to the test.'[21] And he draws towards his conclusion with a heightened peroration intended, clearly, to demonstrate his own worthiness in Rousseauian terms, but also, with the Scots sentiments, and the astonishingly high self-valuation, in firmly Boswellian terms, for the requested interview:

> Your writings, Sir, have melted my heart, have elevated my soul, have fired my imagination. Believe me, you will be glad to have seen me. You know what Scots pride is. Sir, I am coming to see you in order to make myself worthy of a nation that has produced a Fletcher of Saltoun and a Lord Marischal. Forgive me, Sir, I feel myself moved. I cannot restrain myself. O dear Saint-Preux! Enlightened Mentor! Eloquent and amiable Rousseau! I have a presentiment that a truly noble friendship will be born today ... Open your door, then, Sir, to a man who dares to tell you that he deserves to enter it. Place your confidence in a stranger who is different. You will not regret it.[22]

He subsequently meets Rousseau, sending him a long sketch of his life, written in French, and enjoying a series of interviews with him. He also, incidentally, conducts a passionate affair with Rousseau's housekeeper/mistress when sharing transport with her in his return to England – 'Yesterday morning had gone to bed very early, and had done it once: thirteen in all. Was really affectionate to her.'[23]

The point here is not that Boswell displays any high degree of self-knowledge – quite the contrary: he demonstrates again his considerable capacity for self-delusion. He does, though, show a remarkable ability to access sentiments and rhetorical devices that he knows will project to himself the self that he thinks – and above all hopes – is James Boswell, Esq. At one point in the *London Journal*, having spent time writing letters to a series of correspondents, he declares: 'I have touched every man on the proper key, and yet have used no deceit.'[24] The distinction is a fine one, but the wider significance of the remark is that the man for whom he possessed the finest ear for 'the proper key' was James Boswell. The long process of being proved wrong had scarcely begun while he was on the Grand Tour between 1764 and 1766, even after the severe melancholy of his time in Utrecht, where he was supposedly studying for the Scots bar. At this point, his melancholy cast is seen more as the shade in the eye-catching portrait he fondly assumed to be himself.

So – and again the contrast with Johnson is strong – Boswell fills his journal not only with expressions of astonishment at his own variousness but also the raw experiences that gave that variousness scope to develop. There is travel, work, aspiration, disappointment, family, friends, drink and sex, and especially drink and sex. It is all grist to the Boswellian mill. He is aware, for example, of his own taste for witnessing other people in extreme situations and in noting their reactions. So he conducts the famous deathbed interview with David Hume in 1776, hoping, rather fatuously, to hear him miraculously repent of his atheistic views.[25] So, too, while in London, he records indulging his fascination with criminal classes, especially with daring young men. He visits Newgate: 'In the cells were Paul Lewis for robbery and Hannah Diego for theft ... Paul, who had been in the sea-service and was called Captain, was a genteel, spirited young fellow. He was just a Macheath.'[26] Especially, one might add, with daring young men who resembled literary models, and particularly when they were models Boswell himself, in the wilds of his 'luxuriant imagination', aspired to match. And he is fascinated by executions, the most extreme of extreme situations. So taken is he by Lewis that he cannot resist, the next day, going along to Tyburn to be a spectator at his execution, even though, in his own variousness, he is aware how it will affect him.

> My curiosity to see the melancholy spectacle of the executions was so strong that I could not resist it, although I was sensible that I would suffer much from it. In my younger years I had read in the *Lives of the Convicts* so much about Tyburn that I had a sort of horrid eagerness to be there. I also wished to see the last behaviour of Paul Lewis, the handsome fellow who I had seen the day before. Accordingly I took Captain Temple with me, and he and I got upon a scaffold very near the fatal tree, so that we could clearly see all the dismal scene. There was a most prodigious crowd of spectators.[27]

He is amply, and predictably, repaid: 'I was most terribly shocked', he records, 'and thrown into a very deep melancholy.'[28] He is so affected, in fact, that he cannot face the night alone: 'I went home and changed my clothes. But gloomy terrors came upon me so much as night approached that I durst not stay by myself; so I went and had a bed (or rather half a one) from honest Erskine, which he most kindly gave me.'[29] Indeed, the next night he is 'still in horror, and so slept this night with' his friend George Dempster. The following morning he 'awaked as usual heavy, confused, and splenetic', whereupon Dempster 'prescribed to me to cut two or three brisk capers round the room, which I did, and found attended with most agreeable effects. It expelled the phlegm from my heart, gave my blood a free circulation, and my spirits a brisk flow; so that I was all at once made happy.' So much for Paul Lewis. 'I must remember this', observes Boswell, 'and practice it.'[30]

It is, indeed, in regard to his own melancholy that Boswell is most attentive in his journals, and in this respect he again differs markedly from Johnson, as far as we can tell: Boswell takes every opportunity to observe himself and to try to understand why and in what ways he is a melancholy man. He details his symptoms repeatedly, as in July 1781, when he finds himself brought down in the company of the Earl of Eglinton:

> Had some pleasure in observing the Earl's sense and spirit, but was saddened by speculative clouds composed of the uncertainty of life, the forgetfulness of things years after their happening, and such dreary truths. Wondered how I had ever been active and keen in anything ... I was grievously hypochondriac in the evening.[31]

The journal, indeed, becomes at times the vehicle for self-scrutiny in terms of his melancholy – and always while actually undergoing the suffering. Johnson might have done the same, but it seems unlikely, and any evidence is lost. Where Boswell goes far beyond what Johnson might have attempted, though, is in also publishing his experience and analyses of melancholy – publishing them anonymously, under the name of the Hypochondriack, but publishing nevertheless. For six years, between 1777 and 1783, Boswell wrote a monthly essay for the *London Magazine* as 'The Hypochondriack', and, while they cover many topics, a number of them are devoted to the experience of melancholy. Not only does he write one essay while labouring under the agonies of it, but he recognises, from the outset, that he is addressing almost a community of fellow sufferers – 'my atrabilious brethren', he calls them at one point, referring to '*we Hypochondriacks*',[32] and beginning the particular essay written 'in a state of very dismal depression' by speculating that 'there may perhaps be some of my unhappy brethren just as ill as myself, to whom it may be soothing to know that I now write at all'.[33]

The details Boswell then goes on to give are every bit as revealing as those remaining private pieces from Johnson's diaries and prayers. He selects 'some of those thoughts, the multitude of which confounds and overwhelms the mind of the Hypochondriack'.[34] The thoughts, needless to say, are directly at odds with the jaunty young man of the earlier journals, and the otherwise self-satisfied hedonist of his non-melancholy periods. 'His opinion of himself', he begins, 'is low and desponding … He imagines that every body thinks meanly of him.'[35] This is the man who declared to Rousseau that he would not regret meeting with him. He points, too, to the stark contrast between his state of mind now and when he is well: 'He envies the condition of numbers, whom, when in a sound state of mind, he sees to be far inferior to him. He regrets his having ever attempted distinction and excellence in any way, because the effect of his former exertions now serves only to make his insignificance more vexing to him.'[36] He is, moreover, trapped in a perpetual present within his own imagination: the past was a waste of time, filled with vain attempts at distinction, while the future offers no 'prospect of more agreeable days': 'There is a cloud as far as he can perceive, and he supposes it will be charged with thicker vapour, the longer it continues.'[37] This, clearly, is some reminder of the 'barren waste of time' that Johnson perceives when he surveys his 'past life'. The power of Johnson's utterance, though, is that there is apparently no way out. In Boswell's case, in spite of his declaring that 'hope hides itself in the dark cloud',[38] there does after all appear, only a page later, the release to a positive state of mind:

> In the multitude of such thoughts as these, when the Hypochondriack is sunk in helpless and hopeless wretchedness ... how blessed is the relief which he may have from the divine comforts of religion! From the comforts of GOD, the Father of Spirits, the Creator and Governour of the Universe, whose mercy is over all his other works, and who graciously hears the prayers of the afflicted.[39]

If the repetition here of the characteristics of the Almighty, echoing as it does the *Book of Common Prayer*, can be suspected as rhetorical devices designed to build up Boswell's own sense of the validity of what he is saying, it still fails to match, in terms of conveying mental authenticity, the pitiful helplessness of Johnson's wretched 'Have mercy upon me, my Creatour and my judge', with the dreadful unspoken assumption that he might not do so.

One significant point, though, that Boswell does make in this remarkable essay is that the hypochondriac retains a high degree of self-awareness: 'Though his reason be entire enough, and he knows that his mind is sick, his gloomy imagination is so powerful that he cannot disentangle himself from its influence, and he is in effect persuaded that its hideous representations of life are true.'[40] Boswell, as so often, keeps one eye on himself even while totally self-absorbed: it may be, as here, that the observing eye is as anguished as the observed, but observing it is, capable of recall and reflection even when the observed has faded from the memory, only remaining, in this instance, as a record on the published page. Susan Manning has written of what Boswell owed to David Hume in terms of his conception of identity. For Hume, she argues, 'The self exists because through memory and imagination it constructs itself. Consciousness of identity is itself all the identity which may safely be posited.'[41] His 'philosophy of personal identity', she continues, 'gave Boswell a way of describing himself in the double roles of spectator and actor, participant and observer, at once able to receive sensations and to reflect upon them'.[42] While Manning is principally discussing Boswell as we read him in the journals, her observation exactly applies, too, to at least this essay in his

Hypochondriack series: the essayist displays himself, deeply within himself, for the benefit of his readers, yes, but also very much for himself.

Boswell, then, is not only very ready to attempt the scrutiny of his own mind but, in some measure, to do so in public. Even the *London Journal* was originally written for a friend, John Johnstone, and sent back to Edinburgh from London in batches. He has far fewer internal mental barriers than Johnson, and a much greater readiness to try things out in writing – which is also to say he has less judgement, less self-respect and less sheer terror at what might lie within. Above all, unlike Johnson, he is ready to go beyond the orthodox in terms of religion. Here, for example, he recounts his ongoing reactions to hearing the Presbyterian preacher Robert Walker at New Church, Edinburgh, in 1775:

> In the afternoon Mr. Walker endeavoured to prove that the eternity of punishment was nowise inconsistent with GOD's goodness ... 'But alas!' thought I, 'What shall be said as to men of wavering faith and strong passions?' ... But I found that my mind had internal force enough to dissipate the mist. I steadily thought that eternity of punishment *could not be*, according to my notions of the divinity.[43]

Johnson would not only have been incapable of writing such a sentiment, he would have been constitutionally unable to think it. To do so would be to give in to the wild beasts – or even, as everything fell apart, to have joined them.

Boswell's editors, in fact, point out of that final sentence that 'With a return of orthodoxy, Boswell inked out this and the preceding sentence.'[44] But in this, more than in anything, is the difference between the two selves: Johnson would never go there; Boswell tries it out and thinks better of it, and in the gap between the writing and the inking out we see the mind working, just as we do, more subtly, in the measured cadences and developed metaphors of Johnsonian prose, the elaborate means whereby he disguised what he might really have been feeling, had he been free to acknowledge it to himself.

'Self' is one of the longest entries in Johnson's *Dictionary*: it runs to over four columns, almost three of them given over to quotations – from Shakespeare, Milton, Denham, Addison, Pope and others. The most interesting of the eight definitions, though, is the seventh: 'It signifies the individual, as subject to his own contemplation or action.'[45] Among the five illustrative quotations are two from one of Johnson's favourite sources, Locke's *An Essay Concerning Human Understanding*; 'Since consciousness always accompanies thinking, and it is that that makes every one to be what he calls *self*, and thereby distinguishes himself from all other thinking things; in this alone consists personal identity, i.e. the sameness of a rational being.' And 'It is by the consciousness it has of its present thoughts and actions, that it is *self* to it *self* now, and so will be the same *self*, as far as the same consciousness can extend to actions past or to come.' Johnson, it would seem, endorses the concept of the coherent self, of an identity that has duration and memory, even if one suspects he would prefer it were otherwise. He could then forget, perhaps, the endlessly repetitive struggles with the beasts, the catalogue of wasted time and the failures to do justice to his talents, or to keep his word to himself, and the doubts over the fate of his soul. In that context, consciousness of self is the greatest burden of living.

Two minds, then, two mentalities, two uses of literary space, two exemplars of literary language of a revealing kind, one for what it tells us quite frankly and, usually, unashamedly, and the other for what it is, not at all frankly, trying to hide. Two minds, in fact, with a lot in common, including conservative principles in politics and in religion, with Boswell, in some things, actually less radical than Johnson – his position on slavery, for example, on which he wrote his ridiculous poem *No Abolition of Slavery: or, The Universal Empire of Love* in 1791. But Boswell was far more completely a creature of his own time than Johnson, precisely because he lacked Johnson's inbuilt safety mechanisms. At a period when scientific discovery and philosophical speculation were making huge changes in public awareness, and, towards the end of the century, when movements towards Romanticism were beginning to blow apart a traditional sense of the self, Boswell, for all his limitations, was set in the mould of the new, as demonstrated by his great biography, where Johnson, Boswell's subject, was, for all his intelligence, learning and energy, a man, and a self, of a past age.

Notes

1 James Boswell, *Boswell: The Ominous Years, 1774–1776*, eds Charles Ryskamp and F. A. Pottle (New York: Heinemann, 1963), p. 212.

2. James Boswell, *Life of Johnson*, eds R. W. Chapman and Pat Rogers (Oxford: Oxford University Press, 1980), p. 427.
3. Samuel Johnson, *The Rambler*, 32 (London: C. & J. Rivington *et al.*, 1823, 3 vols), 1, p. 209.
4. *Ibid.*, 1, p. 209.
5. Samuel Johnson, *Rasselas, Prince of Abissinia*, ed. J. P. Hardy (Oxford: Oxford University Press, 1968), p. 104.
6. *Ibid.*, pp. 104–5.
7. Bertrand H. Bronson, 'Johnson Agonistes', in *Johnson Agonistes and Other Essays* (Cambridge: Cambridge University Press, 1946, reprinted 2012), p. 3, quoting Hippolyte Taine, *Histoire de la littérature anglaise*, bk 3, ch. 6, trans. H. Van Laun (New York, 1925 edn).
8. *Ibid.*, p. 4.
9. Samuel Johnson, *Dr Johnson on Shakespeare*, ed. W. K. Wimsatt (Harmondsworth: Penguin Books, 1969), p. 132.
10. Boswell, *Life of Johnson*, p. 1296.
11. On this, see especially Robert DeMaria Jr, *The Life of Samuel Johnson: A Critical Biography* (Oxford: Blackwell, 1993), pp. 257–8.
12. Samuel Johnson, 'Diaries and Prayers', in Allan Ingram (ed.), *Patterns of Madness in the Eighteenth Century: A Reader* (Liverpool: Liverpool University Press, 1998), p. 110.
13. *Ibid.*, p. 110.
14. *Ibid.*, p. 110.
15. *Ibid.*, p. 111.
16. On the ways in which recent research has re-established religion and the role of the church as central to many people's lives in this period, see Jeremy Gregory, 'Religion: Faith in the Age of Reason', *Journal for Eighteenth-Century Studies*, 34:4 (Dec. 2011), 435–43, especially 439–40.
17. James Boswell, *Boswell's London Journal 1762–1763*, ed. F. A. Pottle (Harmondsworth: Penguin Books, 1966), p. 211.
18. *Ibid.*, p. 65.
19. *Ibid.*, p. 65.
20. James Boswell, *Boswell on the Grand Tour, Germany and Switzerland, 1764*, ed. F. A. Pottle (London: Heinemann, 1953), p. 214.
21. *Ibid.*, p. 214.
22. *Ibid.*, pp. 214–15.
23. James Boswell, *Boswell on the Grand Tour, Italy, Corsica and France, 1765–1766*, eds Frank Brady and F. A. Pottle (London: Heinemann, 1955), pp. 294–5.
24. James Boswell, *Boswell's London Journal 1762–1763*, ed. F. A. Pottle, p. 353.
25. See Richard B. Schwarz, 'Boswell and Hume: the Deathbed Interview', in Greg Clingham (ed.), *New Light on Boswell: Critical and Historical*

Essays on the Occasion of the Bicentenary of The Life of Johnson (Cambridge: Cambridge University Press, 1991), pp. 116–25, for a useful discussion of this.
26 Boswell, *Boswell's London Journal 1762–1763*, ed. Pottle, pp. 274–5.
27 *Ibid.*, p. 275.
28 *Ibid.*, p. 275.
29 *Ibid.*, p. 276.
30 *Ibid.*, p. 276.
31 James Boswell, *Boswell Laird of Auchinleck 1778–1782*, eds Joseph W. Reed and Frederick Pottle (Edinburgh: Edinburgh University Press, 1993), p. 386.
32 James Boswell, *Boswell's Column 1777–1783*, ed. Margery Bailey (London: William Kimber, 1951), p. 43.
33 *Ibid.*, p. 207.
34 *Ibid.*, p. 208.
35 *Ibid.*, p. 208.
36 *Ibid.*, p. 208.
37 *Ibid.*, p. 208.
38 *Ibid.*, p. 209.
39 *Ibid.*, p. 210.
40 *Ibid.*, p. 209.
41 Susan Manning, '" This Philosophical Melancholy": Style and Self in Boswell and Hume', in Clingham (ed.), *New Light on Boswell*, p. 129.
42 *Ibid.*, p. 131.
43 Boswell, *Boswell: The Ominous Years, 1774–1776*, pp. 199–200. Original emphasis.
44 *Ibid.*, p. 200, note.
45 Samuel Johnson, *A Dictionary of the English Language*, vol. 2 (London: Johnson, Dilly et al., 1755, 1799 edn), entry under 'Self', pp. 548–50.

8

'The place where my present hopes began to dawn': space, limitation and the perception of female selfhood in Samuel Richardson's *Pamela*

Barbara Puschmann-Nalenz

Introduction

The genre of the epistolary novel already emphasises authenticity and the importance of the self that is externalised by communicating it in writing. This chapter seeks to investigate the relation between place and formation of the female self represented in Pamela's letters and journal, with the focus on topographical distinctions between the house and outdoor places. It has been observed that 'authors have long exploited the multiple meanings of the garden, and, in particular, the metaphor of the attempted seduction of the heroine, in the garden'.[1] Margaret Doody in her seminal study of Richardson's novels even defined the pastoral theme as one of the strongest unifying forces at work in *Pamela*.[2] She claimed that the central character and the fable of the novel match the pastoral comedy which is in part defined by its love theme and a happy ending, although the humble country girl as heroine does not immediately align with the pastoral genre;[3] comments by other characters about Pamela as 'funny' and 'comical' also place her outside it. Even 'Pamela's rural surroundings are very ordinary',[4] considering the announced 'Subjects, in Genteel Life' of the 1801 edition's title page. Pastoral harmony, it is true, obtains a victory in the end, assessed through the main characters' second visit to the Bedford summerhouse, with Pamela as Mr B.'s wife.[5]

When Doody remarks about the marriage of Pamela and Mr B. that '[t]he *mock*-pastoral comedy, unusual, amusing, sometimes grotesque, now shades into the traditional pastoral comedy',[6] Richardson's or 'the editor's' intentions as proclaimed in *Pamela* are supplanted.[7] As recent scholarship maintains,[8] he did not mean to parody or ridicule the pastoral in his work. Addressing the portrayal of idyllic nature in the later part of *Pamela* with its 'glimpse of glorified rural life, with its implications of natural beauty, peace, and love',[9] the pastoral tradition admittedly eclipses didactic intentions.[10]

Without evading this discussion about the pastoral or the research on the different versions of *Pamela*, it is the intrinsic objective of this chapter to work out a mapping of the female self by an exploration of the 'inside'/'outside' relation prior to the protagonists' wedding. The investigation proceeds with special regard to the connection between spatial position, the emotional condition and self-awareness of its titular heroine.

The main thesis of this chapter, corroborated by an analysis of four incidents, is that in *Pamela* introversion and extroversion show a correspondence to the protagonist's spatial situatedness, and the starting point to substantiate it lies in the often-stated emotional contradictoriness of Pamela's utterances. Moreover, their indeterminate fierceness shifts considerably from the first to the later editions of the novel. 'To read between the lines' has been a response pursued by the earliest critics of *Pamela*,[11] and to interpret what remains implicit. For instance, hardly any reader of Pamela's letters – the first one is Mr B. – can overlook that she unintentionally betrays an attraction Mr B. has for her from the start. The focus of my analysis therefore lies on conflicts *inside* the letter-writer. This does not disavow Patricia McKee's argument that the described emotions and the way of mediating them through letters define Pamela's self as 'dependent from and inseparable from others'.[12] One of the most imperative determinants is for Pamela the moral commandment of obedience, and therefore the question whom to obey – the paternal law of the distant father who can only be reached by symbolic representation but who is also the proxy of the religious education governing her decisions, or the resident master to whom she is obliged by socio-economic, cultural and legal rules? Moral principles, including that of patriarchy and regard for social status – personalised in the mostly absent paternal figure of the letter writer's addressee whose unceasing inner presence dictates much of what she writes – contrast with ambivalent feelings towards Mr B. Thereby severe tensions are created not only *between* Pamela and the other characters, first of all her male antagonist, but *inside* her. Additionally, as has been observed by Richardson's prominent contemporaries, Henry Fielding and Eliza Heywood, pretty but helpless Pamela's insistence on her virtue and innocence must be considered her means to exert some power.

First crisis: the Bedford house

An important instrument for the representation of emotionality in *Pamela* is the crossing of boundaries both in the literal and the metaphorical sense. Transgression as a *leitmotif* pervades the whole novel, with the apparently harmonising ending repeatedly exposed by minor characters, nameless readers and famous critics alike as a socially transgressive misalliance and insult to polite society and good name. The triumph of bourgeois morality and religious principles over the hegemonic claim of the master class may at times obscure Pamela's inward struggle which is finally also resolved, above all by Mr B.'s defiance of conventions and social hierarchies.[13] As I will show in textual details, the exceeding of limits becomes most intense in scenes where the confinement motif is curbed and the house – whether prison or palace – temporarily departed from.[14] The setting for an unbridled emotionality is in *Pamela* preferably a 'natural', unrestrained environment. Above all, movement, either as escape into or walking in the garden, whether as a journey from Bedford to Lincolnshire or a ramble with Mr B. in his chariot, prompts an outpouring of passion in Pamela. While the closet, the place of introspection where Richardson's heroines sit down to write their representations of events, dialogues and feelings, has variously become the object of literary criticism or the history of art and design,[15] this article focuses on areas out of doors that give Pamela the opportunity to come out of the 'shell'[16] which encloses her interior.[17] This chapter will argue that border-crossing in *Pamela* and by its heroine becomes plainly manifest where outdoor space allows expansiveness to the female character, and unrestricted emotion gathers momentum.

Mr B.'s summerhouse at his Bedford estate as well as Clarissa's ivy summerhouse are to be seen as rooms where privacy or pensive solitude can be attained and every third party's control diminished.[18] What is more important for *Pamela*: the protagonist's self-control is also diminished. Not only does the seducer Mr B. during his first visit at the summerhouse violate limits – from Pamela's perspective – when he kisses and caresses her, but Pamela herself reproaches him twice for having tempted her 'to forget myself' during his advances – certainly an ambiguous phrase continued by a suggestive 'and what belongs to me'.[19] On the surface this expresses that she is led to ignore her social position as a lower-class servant and contradict her master. Disobedience was the Original Sin committed in the Garden of Eden. Indeed her persistent impertinence and her reproaches towards Mr B., which she reports in her letters and often refers to as her 'boldness', represent a social transgression which he angrily observes and condemns as a lack of respect. Only in later moments when he is in an especially humorous mood soon to be dispersed can he call her 'my pretty teacher',[20] thereby ironically indicating her impudence in her reversal of roles. Richardson's authorial mind adopts the hypothetical perspective of the male aristocrat as imagined by Pamela and alternatively that of the female servant herself. Fictional cross-dressing regarding class and gender is strikingly present on the story level as on the level of narrative production.

When, instead of accompanying Pamela back to her parents, Mr B.'s coachman at his master's order takes her to his Lincolnshire estate, the gap between the two characters – in the geographical as well as the social sense – seems to have broadened:[21] Mr B.'s proudly announced intention soon to go to Court to be made a lord[22] contrasts with Pamela's disdain for him as an immoral and dishonourable master. The rustic heroine certainly lays claim to authority and the narrative voice.[23]

At this point the novel's 'editor' thinks it necessary to interfere by explaining intentions and conditions the heroine is still ignorant of, thus creating a discrepancy of awareness: 'Here it is necessary the reader should know, that when Mr B. found Pamela's virtue was not to be subdued, and he had in vain tried to conquer his passion for her, he had ordered his Lincolnshire coachman to bring his travelling chariot from thence'.[24] Henceforth Mr B. deceitfully chooses abduction in order to bend her to his will. This journey actually leads her deeper into the range of Mr B.'s power, which reaches far beyond his Bedford house and the borders of the county.

It also removes her from the home of her lately deceased lady, her seducer's mother, whose kindliness had left a trace in Mrs Jervis's motherly temper, and takes her decisively into her young master's hegemonic sphere. The exertion of social, economic and political power by the squire, to whom those whom she meets on her way are also obliged,[25] disavows geographical distance. In Pamela's universe Mr B.'s sovereignty, at the Lincolnshire estate exacerbated by the wicked Mrs Jewkes, ranks second only to the spiritual authority exercised by religion and filial duty – and is thus contested for the top position.

The Lincolnshire estate

The garden and the pond: Scene 1

In the 'journal', which represents the female protagonist's consciousness, Pamela depicts her situation in this house as the place of 'my Bondage', 'my heavy Restraint', and 'my imprisonment'.[26] The plans for her flight from it, where even the window of Pamela's closet is barred, are in detail communicated to her diary before being acted out; they mingle with thoughts about suicide as the ultimate escape. Since the heroine appears as a consumer of novels and adventurous tales[27] she can seize upon their inspirations and cunningly devise ways to deceive the inhabitants of the house about her breakout. The 'sad relation' which follows her abortive attempt to get away, written as an entry in her diary 'in my now doubly-secured closet' a few days later,[28] because letters are not allowed to reach the world outside, expands on the rhetoric of self-pity and necrophilia, mixed with religiously motivated contrition and self-reproach. The act of writing down her experience undeniably contains an element of self-fashioning – the fashioning of a self that is exposed as inconsistent and not at all sure of itself.

As soon as she leaves the domestic interior behind, if only for a short time, (melo)drama is bound to be staged in *Pamela*, so that here outdoor spaces do not guarantee a relaxed atmosphere and state of mind, but rather an excess of contradictory feelings. The garden into which she jumps from her prison at night offers a hiding place for her writings, emblematically 'under a rose-bush'.[29] After having been severely injured by a brick when she tries to overcome the borderline of Mr B.'s spatial hegemony, the garden wall,[30] Pamela reaches the pond into which she flings some of her clothes to deceive her persecutors and where she subsequently wants to throw herself at midnight. Though she refers to a tale about a seaman who leapt overboard,[31] it is the discrepant image of Ophelia which emerges in readers' minds: the desperate maiden who drowned herself. This garden is not symbolic of paradise.

The heroine's repeated wavering between sentiment (freshly presented in her writing) and sensibility (evinced on further reflection) has prepared the narratee for her sudden change between hesitating reflection and sentimentally fantasising the sight of 'the dead corpse of the miserable Pamela',[32] of her seducer shedding tears and everybody recognising her true value and innocence after her suicide. Possibly to become 'the subject of their ballads and their elegies'[33] testifies to her lively imagination and, moreover, to the waiting-maid's literary education; yet, paying tribute to humbleness, she prefers the idea 'that my memory, for the sake of my dear father and mother, may quickly slide into oblivion!'[34] Humbling herself or 'making no claims for self whatsoever', Pamela reverses once again her previous act of self-possession or self-assessment.[35] By religious teaching and her physical bruises she is finally deterred from her sinful suicidal inclinations and seeks 'shelter' – from her own urges as from the threat which the 'outside' poses to her. It is her spatial situatedness which plays a key role in this verbalised outburst of passion:

> What then, presumptuous Pamela, dost thou *here*? thought I: quit with speed these perilous banks, and fly from these dashing waters, that seem in their meaning murmurs, this still night, to reproach thy rashness! Tempt not God's goodness on the mossy banks, which have been witnesses of thy guilty purpose; and while thou hast power left thee, avoid the temptation, lest thy grand enemy, now, by Divine Grace, repulsed, return to the assault with a force that thy weakness may not be able to resist! ...
> And so saying, I arose; but was so stiff with my hurts ... that with great pain I got from this pond, which now I think of with terror; and bending my limping steps towards the house, took refuge in the corner of an out-house ....[36]

Richardson does not present his readers with an explicit Christian allegory such as John Bunyan's *The Pilgrim's Progress*, yet like The Slough of Despond the site of Pamela's despair in Mr B.'s Lincolnshire garden – she later calls it the place of her 'sinful despondence'[37] – invokes the idea of offence against Christian doctrine. In sight of a fish-pond that is little more than a puddle the same distorting perspective of Pamela to which Doody points[38] is at work in the above passages ('perilous banks', 'dashing waters'). The heroine flees from the outdoor spot, where she has been tempted by the 'grand enemy' and takes refuge in a habitation, seeking protection from the 'outside' perils in a shack near the house. It is in this hut that Pamela follows the accustomed Protestant duty of an introspective examination of conscience. It culminates in her statement that, although a successful liberation from the captivity by her master would have been a sign of God's grace towards her, 'I have more abundant reason to praise him, that I have been delivered from a worse enemy – *Myself!*'[39] For later readers the ambivalences and multiple inner struggles portray the girl as participating in the topical concept of the individual and a responsible self, by which the predominance of a belonging to unshakeable religious and social structures is problematised; in this scene Pamela gains self-knowledge and experiences humility because of her attempt to violate fundamental (religious) boundaries by the sin of pride, her being 'presumptuous'. To consider her own self as her enemy, because the good self was almost subdued by her evil self that had been leading to sinful self-destruction, parallels the struggle of other binary oppositions represented in the novel.

Richardson repeatedly surprises his readers with the indeterminacy of the meaning of spatial surroundings, in this context through the versatility of nature, which in its gloominess at midnight evokes the Gothic. While the above-quoted experience of a vehement fit of emotion is described as taking place in the garden which appears here as a *locus terribilis* instead of a *locus amoenus*, Pamela's producing its written account is situated in the prison of the double-locked closet – the closet that also symbolises the female focaliser's consciousness and individuality.[40] Though her withdrawal from the world is in general 'extremely conversational'[41] and communicative, she converses there above all with her own self. She continually constructs it from different and conflicting imperatives: the patriarchal rooted in religion that opposes the social prerogative, to which is added the personal attraction she has felt at the beginning for Mr B.,[42] whom she describes as a fallen angel, but whom she cannot hate even now.[43] The philosophical concept of the individual self that had been in England publicly under debate since it plainly surfaced around the beginning of the eighteenth century makes itself felt in these disputes as controversial yet appealing. The collective cultural awareness thus parallels in a sense this representation of a young person's private struggle for her individuality, which bestows on the narrative the colour of what in twentieth-century literary criticism is called a 'coming-of-age novel' – a genre in which movement and spatial displacement including inevitable dangers are crucial.[44]

The garden and the pond: Scene 2
The indoor scene following Pamela's rejection of Mr B.'s proposal of a mock-marriage[45] shows him using intrigues and force in entering the bed(room) she shares with Mrs Jewkes under the disguise of the maid Nan (Ann) after he has overheard Pamela's 'prattle',[46] by which she reaffirms her wish to remain chaste and withstand Mr B.'s offer.[47] Restriction and compulsion subsequently draw near death. When she has barely recovered from her faints and is almost thought dead once more, which frightens the gentleman and prevents him from raping her, Pamela overhears Mr B. explaining his change of strategy to the housekeeper, to whom he proclaims his intention to see the girl 'thawed by kindness'. He now wants 'to melt her by love',[48] after her icy resistance to his use of force. When Mr B. starts to put his words into deed by leading her outside the following morning Pamela's aversion is made much more obvious for the readers of the 1801 version – 'the text that sought to remove their grounds of objection'.[49] There the wording would satisfy the most critical of contemporaneous implied or flesh-and-blood readers in regard to the heroine's steadfastness, innocence and circumspection. She is once more torn between the obligation to comply with her master's wish and her suspicion of his immoral intentions. The passage which carefully prepares the realisation of her seducer's true plans to procure a moment of the closest intimacy with Pamela during this stroll in the garden is considerably longer with the additions in the 1801 text than in the edition of 1740 which provoked Fielding's *Shamela, The Anti-Pamela* and similar satirical responses. In the earlier versions it becomes clear that Pamela again cannot trust *herself* in this situation outside the house, whereas the revised text displays a defensive attitude in her description of the scene: '"We will take a walk in the garden," said he, taking my hand, and led me into it. What signified denying to go? Should he have base designs, thought I, I am as much in danger in the house, with

such a vile woman, as in the garden.'⁵⁰ The house and domestic space, also in its symbolic sense, will not protect her any longer.

A juxtaposition of the core sentences of 1740 and 1801 shows telling differences in Pamela's demeanour and feelings, which reflect on the addressing of emotion in the female consciousness:

> After walking about, he led me into a little alcove, on the farther part of the garden; *and really made me afraid of myself*; for he began to be very teasing, and made me sit on his knee; and was so often kissing me that I said, 'Sir, I don't like to be here at all, I assure you. Indeed you make me afraid!'⁵¹

The posthumous edition is altered in a wordier, extenuating way:

> After walking about, he led me into a little alcove in the further part of the garden, which having a passage through it, *I the less resisted; and still the less, as he had led me through once without stopping;* but then stopping in it, he began to be very teazing. He made me sit on his knee; *and still on my struggling against such a freedom*, he bid me rely on his honour, solemnly assuring me that I might. But then kissing me very often, *though I resisted every time*, I told him, at last, and would have got from him, that I would not stay with him in this place, I would not be so freely used.⁵²

In the 1740 version Pamela's verbal rejection and her body language offer less defiance, and she fearfully seems almost to succumb to her master's seduction. In the 1801 edition of the same scene Pamela's reference to her previous experience can show that she believes a walk in the garden and to the alcove is harmless, as she and Mr B. had undertaken it before without him molesting her. To emphasise even more his present unforeseen desire ('but then stopping') – in contrast to his former politeness – and stress her immovable virtue, the narrative repetitively underlines the girl's physical and verbal resistance to Mr B.'s flattering words and approaches. It uses refined language stimulating the reader's fantasy by mere hints at the squire's procedure: in the end, 'He held me fast notwithstanding, professing honour all the time with his mouth, though his actions did not correspond.'⁵³

In the ensuing quarrel Mr B. angrily reverses Pamela's remonstrance that *he* is taking too great liberties that are not in accord with the code of honour his position demands. The concepts of class, gender and status reveal themselves as increasingly fluctuating, a characteristic linguistically indicated by the frequent contradictions and mutations signalled in adverbs such as 'but', 'yet' or 'notwithstanding'. It becomes, above all, a demonstration of the changeability and contradictoriness of feelings as well as their volatile epistolary representation by Pamela – analogous to that of the 'eye-watering' novelistic revisions by her creator[54] – that she writes on the same night about a surprising change of consciousness and behaviour which has occurred. This momentary peripety of the plot is caused in Pamela's own self while walking and – according to Pamela – equally in Mr B. The location of this miraculous alteration is again the garden, with Pamela as the observer, agent and reporter of every detail:

> My master took two or three turns about the room, musing and more thoughtful than ever before I had seen him; and at last he went out, saying, 'I am going into the garden: you know, Pamela, what I said to you before dinner.' ...
> Notwithstanding I had no reason to be pleased with his treatment of me before dinner, yet I made haste to attend him.
> I found him walking by the side of that very pond, which, through a sinful despondence, had like to have been so fatal to me. And it was by the side of this pond, and not far from the place where I had that dreadful conflict, that my present hopes, if I am not to be betrayed by them, began to dawn.[55]

As the quotation shows, the reversal of Pamela's view is also peripatetic in the literal sense, with the imagery taken from pensive movement ('walking' etc.), or diurnal change ('dawn') approaching a pastoral scene. Mr B.'s confession of love for Pamela and especially the expression of his growing conviction that she is truly virtuous and honest bring forth her suppressed sympathies for the man; yet, once more wavering 'back', upon 'return' into her 'closet' with the internal presence of the dominant father figure, back to her scruples, she realises and has to admit that she has fallen in love with her master.[56] Attending to the exploration of the passions – by a male authorial intrusion into the female mind and an occasionally intrusive 'editor' of the narrative – this representation of a mixture of frightening and pleasant sensations by the letter writer is ambitious and exceeds the proclaimed moral and didactic goals.

More turns in mood and expectations are yet in store after Mr B.'s confession, which is mingled with his jealousy, that he loves and cannot live without Pamela. When he professes sincerity it is only 'at present',[57] changeable and unreliable in a moment of outgoing protestations from both parties. The crucial aim to get hold of Pamela's secret records leads to Mr B.'s almost stripping her of her clothes, and though her doubts consequently increase and her wish to go back to her parents is renewed, she finally hands her papers over to Mr B. in another garden scene, once more at the side of the pond, where Mr B. reads the account of her despair as well as her 'thanks for escaping from *myself*'.[58] That she is unable to resolve the struggles in her own consciousness and still fears that Mr B. will dishonour her causes his outbreak of anger that terminates the pastoral scene – harmony is still at a distance, although the peak of despair lies behind her. Since Pamela cannot be his wife for reasons of class and will not be his mistress she must suffer the pains of unrequited love and spatial separation from Mr B. While she tries to unify her inner self which resembles a battlefield of conflicting rules, ethical demands and inclinations, she once more moves spatially away by leaving the estate. This meandering movement – mirroring the change of feelings and proclivities – does by no means prescribe an ending in tune with pastoral romance. The crisis that leads to Mr B.'s resolution in the double sense grows out of spatial distance and illness – nature's revolt –, so that on her way to her parents Pamela returns to him on his urgent request. Again she means to teach him, but cures him instead. As soon as he is well enough to 'take a turn after breakfast, in the chariot'[59] Pamela must come outside with him once more to engage in another blaze of emotion.

The ride in Mr B.'s chariot

'I have to relate to you of what passed in this charming airing.'[60] When Pamela writes this sentence and the extremely long letter to her parents she is eventually freed from her fears of a mock-marriage or some other 'contract' which she cannot accept because it includes sex before marriage.[61] Social obstacles, however, remain as the barrier which hinders Pamela from accepting the marriage proposal. Her final protestation of self-humiliation – affected modesty to some of her critics – shows the ascension of the 'true Pamela',[62] who is not merely self-confident but promotes all her gifts and talents that she will gaily and gratefully display as Mr B.'s wife. During the excursion, Mr B.'s confession to Pamela that her 'kind compliance' with his wish to have her by him in his illness has 'rivetted my affections to you, and induced me to open to you, in this free and unreserved manner, my whole heart' prompts her to give up all restraint in her avowal of love for her master.[63] In this moment of B.'s self-liberation from social conventions and Pamela's 'coming-out-of-the-closet', her self-reflexive recognition is expressed with imagery taken from nature and seizing Mr B.'s own use of metaphorical expression: 'I knew not myself the state of my own heart, till your kindness to me melted away, as I may say, the chilling frost that prudence and love of virtue had cast about the buds of – What shall I say?'[64] Instead of death and torpor symbolised by frost, spring – both in the sense of the growing vegetation and streaming water – emblematically asserts life. Because Pamela's emotions are now harmonised with her moral principles no divergence shows in her articulated feeling between what she tells Mr B. or what she writes her parents: 'My heart was like a too full river, which overflows its banks. My gratitude, at the moment, got the better of my fear, and carried my shamefacedness away before it, as the river does every thing that opposes it.'[65] The former image of the frightening 'dashing waters' is replaced by a stream of unrestricted positive feelings.

'The chariot brought us home at near the hour of two' reads the conclusion to this final *volta* which takes place during another peripatetic ramble that dissolves the static positions of the two characters.[66] It puts an end to the inner conflicts of the heroine and exhibits Mr B. as a decisive man who gives his personal happiness priority over considerations of family and class, though not without corroborative thoughts that his union with Pamela will be naturally fruitful and continue the lineage.

After this crucial 'turn' the quality of spatial movements, once inscribed with intense fear and defiance, patently changes: flight, escape or eviction are ousted by delightful pleasure trips in Mr B.'s coach and chariot. Journeys to the chapel, whose renovation is Pamela's immediate project before the wedding ceremony – once called 'foolish' by the bridegroom[67] – further underline the reconciliation which includes the end of the aristocrat's deriding haughtiness towards religion and Christian doctrine;[68] to generously restore the order of the building 'shell' hints at Pamela's personal impact. Their 'little airings' into the surrounding countryside emphasise the smallness of her world, while during these outings she learns about the Grand Tour her master completed as a bachelor and the education he had received as things of the past. These narrative representations do not attain the elevated sophistication of the pastoral genre, nor do they continue the psychological drama of the earlier scenes, but further indulge in the 'native Simplicity' praised by early readers.[69] Crowning these excursions, the return to Bedford epitomises the novelty of Pamela's life: 'What a delightful change was this journey to that which, so contrary to all my wishes, and so much to my apprehensions, carried me hence to the Lincolnshire house!'[70] Pleasant walks around the Bedford estate now contrast with her desperate moments in the Lincolnshire garden. Generous and pacified, Pamela in one of these 'little airings' transcends boundaries of middle-class propriety in forgiving Mr B.'s moral trespassing and befriending his little daughter.[71] Satisfying though it may be for virtuous bourgeois reader expectations, this happy ending lacks the narrative tension of the inner struggle with temptations and outbursts of passion in the open air.

Conclusion

Probing the concept of narrated selfhood, this chapter suggests that the publication date of *Pamela* occupies an especially remarkable position in the history of ideas. In 1739 to 1740, about the same time as the first edition of Richardson's epistolary novel, David Hume had published *A Treatise of Human Nature*, in which the Scottish philosopher develops the idea that the self cannot be considered anything separate from sense perceptions.[72] Section VI, Part IV of Book 1 of the *Treatise*, which is entitled 'Of personal identity', expresses Hume's doubt about the opinion of 'some philosophers' who consider the 'self' a certainty. He argues: 'But self or person is not any one impression, but that to which our several impressions and ideas are suppos'd to have a reference.' There exists no 'simple and continu'd' self, because all impressions are ephemeral. He continues: 'But setting aside some metaphysicians of this kind, I may venture to affirm of the rest of mankind, that they are nothing but a bundle or collection of different perceptions, which succeed each other with an inconceivable rapidity, and are in a perceptual flux and movement.' 'Bundle' (of clothes) is a key word also in *Pamela*, which signifies her optional selves.[73] Alain Bony draws attention to the disclosure Patricia M. Spacks had made in her study *Imagining a Self*, namely that the early modern English novel imaginatively confirms the psychological and moral coherence of the individual at precisely the moment when Hume was to question a metaphysical concept of the individual. Bony adds that this circumstance may be interpreted either as an oppositional or a complementary pattern of the relation between philosophy and fiction.[74] On the one hand this observation, I contend, would reaffirm the statement that literature is conservative in the sense that it preserves ideas and concepts that are being superseded by more recent developments in different scientific or empirical fields. On the other hand, the heroine's mind having become what I called a contested space of good and evil, of Christian religion and English middle-class striving for cultural – including moral – hegemony, Pamela's inner self strongly resembles a 'bundle of sensations'. Both her rationality and her exercise of 'the passions' colliding with her master's exercise of power add further tension. Hume's statement – 'When I turn my reflection on *myself*, I never can perceive this *self* without some one or more perceptions; nor can I ever perceive any thing but the perceptions. 'Tis the composition of these, therefore, which forms the self'[75] – is reflected in the representations of Pamela's multiple and inconsistent internal conditions. Paradoxically, yet consequently, we see her 'affirming her self's significance in endless words'.[76] In her letters the heroine fights for the continuity of her precarious 'self' that must not become the object of Mr B.'s decisions, '*nor act like one who is doubtful of her own mind*', but indisputably the notion of the self-reflexive individual that Pamela recognises 'in the glass' contains mutability.[77] That the protagonist insists on performing what she considers her own self elucidates how the idea of selfhood is in the novel not conceived of as an illusion, even though the unified self appeared illusionary to the philosopher. Eighteenth-century fiction actually relied on an awareness of 'selfhood' as shown in *Pamela*. The narrative demonstrates the emerging freedom of the individual, male or female, with constant negotiations between individuality and Pamela's relationality through filial, religious, marital, parental and social duties. The trope of personal identity as a mere 'situation' at the intersection of diverse perspectives and discourses,[78] however, was reserved for late modernist and postmodern literature with its partiality for subversion, fragmentation and incoherence.

Notes

1 Karen Lipsedge, *Domestic Space in Eighteenth-Century British Novels* (Basingstoke: Palgrave Macmillan, 2012), p. 131; see also J. Butler, 'The Garden: Early Symbol of Clarissa's Complicity', *Studies in English Literature*, 24 (1984), 527–44.
2 Margaret Anne Doody, *A Natural Passion: A Study of the Novels of Samuel Richardson* (Oxford: Clarendon Press, 1974), p. 36.
3 For a discussion of the connection between Philip Sidney's *Arcadia* and *Pamela* see G. Beer, '*Pamela*: Re-thinking *Arcadia*', in Margaret Anne Doody and Peter Sabor (eds), *Samuel Richardson: Tercentenary Essays* (Cambridge: Cambridge University Press, 1989), pp. 23–39.
4 Doody, *Natural Passion*, p. 56.
5 Lipsedge, *Domestic Space*, pp. 142–4.
6 Doody, *Natural Passion*, p. 63 (added emphasis).
7 Regarding these aims see 'Preface by the Editor', in the T. Keymer and A. Wakely edition of the 1740 text (Oxford: Oxford University Press, 2001), pp. 3–4. That the representations of femininity in the pastoral genre often contained satire or parody is discussed in B. Latimer, *Making Gender, Culture, and the Self in the Fiction of Samuel Richardson: The Novel Individual* (Farnham: Ashgate, 2013), esp. pp. 29–31. Her argument that Richardson and his heroine intended parodistic effects is debatable; I tend to consider it a conclusion of 'the unreliable reader'.
8 See Thomas Keymer and Peter Sabor, Pamela *in the Marketplace: Literary Controversy and Print Culture in Eighteenth-Century Britain and Ireland* (Cambridge: Cambridge University Press, 2005) and Beer, 'Re-thinking *Arcadia*'.
9 Doody, *Natural Passion*, p. 63.
10 Lipsedge, *Domestic Space*, p. 143.
11 Thomas Keymer, *Richardson's* Clarissa *and the Eighteenth-Century Reader* (Cambridge: Cambridge University Press, 1992, repr. 1993), p. 20.
12 Patricia McKee, 'Corresponding Freedoms: Language and the Self in Pamela', *English Literary History*, 52:3 (1985), 622.
13 Heidi Giles draws attention to the striking frequency of the lemma 'resolve' in the novel in 'Resolving the Institution of Marriage in Eighteenth-Century Courtship Novels', *Rocky Mountain Review*, 66:1 (2012), 76–82.
14 Michael McKeon remarks how much '*Pamela*'s metaphoric language … repeatedly translates the theme of private conflict into the emotive register of the public and the political'. See McKeon, 'Richardson's *Pamela* and Political Allegory', in Lisa Zunshine and Jocelyn Harris

(eds), *Approaches to Teaching the Novels of Samuel Richardson* (New York: Modern Language Association, 2006), p. 103. Morris Golden discusses in 'Public Context and Imagining Self in *Pamela* and *Shamela*', *English Literary Studies*, 53:2 (1986), 311–29, whether Richardson with his representation of controversial topics of the Hanoverian rule approaches a political allegory. Keymer also sees volatile political issues addressed on a small scale, e.g. control and censorship, treason and rebellion ('Introduction', *Pamela; or, Virtue Rewarded*, Keymer and Wakely (eds), pp. ix–xx).

15 See for example K. Lipsedge, '"Enter into thy closet": Women, Closet Culture, and the Eighteenth-Century English Novel', in John Styles and Amanda Vickery (eds), *Gender, Taste, and Material Culture in Britain and North America: 1700–1830* (New Haven, CT: Yale University Press, 2006), pp. 107–22; also Lipsedge, *Domestic Space*, pp. 95–6 and 98–114.

16 Gaston Bachelard, *The Poetics of Space* [1957], trans. Maria Jolas (Boston, MA: Beacon Press, 1994), Chapter 5, 'Shells', pp. 105–35.

17 Circumscribed or contained spaces like the Bedford summerhouse or Clarissa's dairy-house with its symbolic meaning for her emerging self and the ivy summerhouse at Harlowe Place provide examples where the meaning of places on the fringe of the domestic interior, which can be seen as variations on the 'house-as-shelter' *topos* in Richardson, has been addressed. See Lipsedge, *Domestic Space*, pp. 133 and 136–44; Lipsedge, '"I was also absent at my dairy-house": The Representation and Symbolic Function of the Dairy House in Samuel Richardson's *Clarissa*', *Eighteenth-Century Fiction*, 22:1 (2009), 29–48; Lipsedge, 'A Place of Refuge, Seduction or Danger? The Representation of the Ivy Summer-House in Samuel Richardson's *Clarissa*', *Journal of Design History*, 19:3 (2006), 185–96.

18 See Lipsedge, *Domestic Space*, pp. 131–3.

19 *Pamela; or, Virtue Rewarded*, ed. Sabor (London: Penguin Books, 1980, repr. 1985), p. 55. The Penguin edition quoted throughout refers to the 1801 text; it contains the first two volumes (of Richardson's projected four) of *Pamela*, published in 1740.

20 *Ibid.*, p. 101.

21 Margaret Doody points to the distortion of the image of higher ranks brought about by the perspective of Pamela who wishes to see in Mr B. her protector and superior: 'He is the ruler of her small world, but the reader realizes that this fox-hunting young country squire would be considered something of a bumpkin himself at St James's.' Yet this is apparently more due to his youth than his upbringing or family, which, according to arrogant Mrs Davers, is 'no upstart family. It is as ancient as the best in the kingdom.' (1801: p. 293): Mr B.'s representation can

be regarded as uneven or inconsistent through Pamela's view. See M. Doody, 'Introduction', Richardson, *Pamela; or, Virtue Rewarded*, ed. Peter Sabor (London: Penguin, 1980, repr. 1985), p. 15.
22 *Pamela; or, Virtue Rewarded*, ed. Sabor, p. 100.
23 *Ibid.*, pp. 121–3.
24 *Ibid.*, p. 123.
25 *Ibid.*, p. 143.
26 *Ibid.*, pp. 183, 200 and 207.
27 *Ibid.*, p. 124.
28 *Ibid.*, p. 209.
29 *Ibid.*, p. 209.
30 The garden and especially its wall – like the chapel – are in a state of neglect and not only 'old' (*ibid.*, p. 210) but old-fashioned. A walled garden instead of a sunk fence or 'ha-ha' as in the more fashionable English landscape garden connotes a careless and neglectful proprietor.
31 *Ibid.*, p. 208.
32 *Ibid.*, p. 212.
33 *Ibid.*, p. 212.
34 *Ibid.*, p. 212.
35 See McKee, 'Corresponding Freedoms', 632. I wish to disagree with McKee's statement that Pamela displays an 'absence of selfhood' altogether in her present condition. The protagonist constantly oscillates between 'too much' and 'nothing at all' in regard to selfhood and thereby shows the instability of her self-awareness, the uncertainty where to place her self in the cultural and social framework, and the pressure on her mind.
36 *Pamela; or, Virtue Rewarded*, ed. Sabor, pp. 213–14 (emphasis in original).
37 *Ibid.*, p. 250.
38 See note 21.
39 *Pamela; or, Virtue Rewarded*, ed. Sabor, p. 214 (original emphasis).
40 Simon Varey, *Space and the Eighteenth-Century Novel* (Cambridge: Cambridge University Press, 1990), p. 189.
41 Roy Roussel, 'Reflections on the Letter: The Reconciliation of Distance and Presence in *Pamela*', *English Literary History*, 41:3 (1974), 376.
42 *Pamela; or, Virtue Rewarded*, ed. Sabor, p. 52.
43 *Ibid.*, p. 218.
44 Patricia McKee in an existentialist reading variously points to the fact that both Pamela and Mr B. are 'young people' in the process of negotiating determination and freedom ('Corresponding Freedoms', *passim*), which is supported by a language of exchange. The negotiations become most visible on the pages following the flight scene, where Mr

B.'s proposals of a mock-marriage and Pamela's answers are opposed (*Pamela; or, Virtue Rewarded*, ed. Sabor, pp. 227–31). A psychological line of argumentation such as McKee's becomes anachronistic, however, where it ignores the backdrop of eighteenth-century English society and literature.
45 *Ibid.*, pp. 227–31.
46 *Ibid.*, p. 238.
47 Terry Castle presents a psycho-sexual interpretation of the novel's gender-confusion in 'P/B: *Pamela* as Sexual Fiction', *Studies in English Literature*, 22 (1982), 471; see also McKee, 'Corresponding Freedoms', 630–1. Castle also attaches obvious Freudian meaning to the lock-and-key symbolism ubiquitous in the Lincolnshire part ('P/B: *Pamela* as Sexual Fiction', 483). Generally, spatial violation is ascribed great importance in the novel, for example when Mrs Davers enters her brother's bedroom and insults his newly wed wife. See Varey, *Space and the Eighteenth-Century Novel*, p. 190.
48 *Pamela; or, Virtue Rewarded*, ed. Sabor, p. 246.
49 Thomas Keymer, 'Assorted Versions of Assaulted Virgins; or: Textual Instability and Teaching', in Zunshine and Harris (eds), *Approaches to Teaching the Novels of Samuel Richardson* (New York: Modern Language Association, 2006), p. 30.
50 *Pamela; or, Virtue Rewarded*, ed. Sabor, p. 247.
51 Richardson, *Pamela; or, Virtue Rewarded* (London: Dent, 1914, repr. 1962, 1966), vol. I, p. 183 (added emphasis); see also Samuel Richardson, *Pamela*, ed. T. Keymer (Oxford: Oxford University Press, 2001), vol. I, p. 208. Both editions reproduce the 1740 text.
52 *Pamela; or, Virtue Rewarded*, ed. Sabor, p. 247 (added emphasis).
53 *Ibid.*, p. 247.
54 Keymer, 'Assorted Versions', p. 26.
55 *Pamela; or, Virtue Rewarded*, ed. Sabor, p. 250.
56 *Ibid.*, p. 252.
57 *Ibid.*, p. 253.
58 *Ibid.*, p. 276 (original emphasis).
59 *Ibid.*, p. 295.
60 *Ibid.*, p. 296.
61 *Ibid.*, p. 230.
62 *Ibid.*, pp. 299–301.
63 *Ibid.*, pp. 306–7.
64 *Ibid.*, p. 307.
65 *Ibid.*, p. 311.
66 *Ibid.*, p. 309.
67 *Ibid.*, p. 230.
68 Richardson was an Anglican, but was influenced by Puritanism. Keymer comments on his pamphlets against playhouses as worthy of Jeremy

Collier and calls his *The Apprentice's Vade Mecum of 1733 and '35* with passages against play-going 'a conduct manual conspicuously short on elegance, though long on advice' ('Introduction', *Pamela; or, Virtue Rewarded*, Keymer and Wakely (eds), p. xii).
69 'To the Editor of Pamela', in Richardson, *Pamela*, eds T. Keymer and A. Wakely (Oxford: Oxford University Press, 2001), p. 8.
70 *Pamela; or, Virtue Rewarded*, ed. Sabor, p. 477.
71 *Ibid.*, pp. 495–500.
72 David Hume, *A Treatise of Human Nature*, eds David Fate Norton and Mary J. Norton (Oxford: Oxford University Press, 2009), 'Of personal identity', pp. 164–71. The quotes in the following lines are from pages 164–5.
73 See *Encyclopædia Britannica*, 'Bundle theory', www.britannica.com/topic/bundle-theory, accessed 28 May 2015.
74 Patricia Meyer Spacks, *Imagining a Self: Autobiography and Novel in Eighteenth-Century England* (Cambridge, MA: Harvard University Press, 1976), p. 2; A. Bony, 'Philosophie et discours littéraire: identité personnelle et conscience de soi chez Hume et dans l'essai périodique', in Robert Ellrodt (ed.), *Genèse de la conscience moderne. Études sur le développement de la conscience de soi dans les littératures du monde occidental* (Paris: Presses Universitaires de France, 1983), p. 185.
75 Hume, *Treatise of Human Nature*, p. 399 (original emphasis).
76 Spacks, *Imagining a Self*, p. 227; cf. note 45.
77 *Pamela; or, Virtue Rewarded*, ed. Sabor, pp. 227 and 229 (original emphasis).
78 Latimer, *Making Gender*, p. 31.

9

The discursive construction of the self in Shaftesbury and Sterne: *Tristram Shandy* and the quest for identity

Gioiella Bruni Roccia

Locke, Sterne, and the concept of personal identity

The problematic nature of selfhood has puzzled man since antiquity. The long eighteenth century, however, witnessed a renewed interest in the philosophical and psychological problem of the 'self'[1] and the related notions of subjectivity and self-consciousness – all issues and discussions so brilliantly parodied in *The Life and Opinions of Tristram Shandy, Gentleman*. This chapter proposes a re-reading of Laurence Sterne's masterpiece in the light of the contemporary debate about selfhood, starting from what can be regarded as a pivotal point: Locke's theory of personal identity.

In the second edition of *An Essay Concerning Human Understanding* (1694), John Locke provided the earliest systematic account of the problem of personal identity in the history of modern philosophy. In Book II, Chapter 27, 'Of Identity and Diversity', the author declares that the notion of the *self* rests entirely in consciousness.[2] The salient characteristic of this view is the use of memory or remembering in order to elaborate the concept of personal identity, that is, the concept of what makes us the same person over time. According to Locke, remaining the same person ('the same *self*') is a matter of psychological continuity: it is by the consciousness of one's present thoughts and actions that the self is conceived, and it is through the continuous link of memory that the self is extended back to past consciousness.³ In other words, identity is retained through uninterrupted history. This apparently simple idea is often made explicit in terms of overlapping chains of causal and cognitive connections between beliefs, desires, intentions, experiential memories, character traits, and so forth. Thus, passing from theory to representation(s) of the 'self' in the course of the century, this Lockean view seems to be well suited for experimental narratives conducted from a first-person perspective, such as *The Life and Opinions of Tristram Shandy, Gentleman*.

Indeed, Sterne's comic masterpiece offers a subtle parody of the Lockean concept of personal identity, exaggerating the role of memory and its extending back to past experience. The *incipit* of the novel suffices to convey the sense of this retrieval operated by Tristram, who is both the narrator of his *Life and Opinions* and the subject of the thoughts, feelings and regrets that motivate his writing. From the very beginning, the consciousness of the first-person narrator – the *self* – is proposed as the authentic object of the story being told:

> I wish either my father or my mother, or indeed both of them, as they were in duty both equally bound to it, had minded what they were about when they begot me; had they duly consider'd how much depended upon what they were then doing;—that not only the production of a rational Being was concern'd in it, but that possibly the happy formation and temperature of his body, perhaps his genius and the very cast of his mind; …—Had they duly weighed and considered all this, and proceeded accordingly,—I am verily persuaded I should have made a quite different figure in the world, from that, in which the reader is likely to see me.⁴

'I wish either my father or my mother …': no *incipit* could more eloquently introduce the topic of memory which extends to the retrieval of the entire existence of the self. The act of writing *The Life and Opinions of Tristram Shandy* begins with a verb of desire: and this desire coincides with a retrospective view, with an expression of regret for what might have been but did not happen. 'I wish': as shown in the quoted passage, the opening verb appears to enclose the whole 'Being' of the authorial persona, going back to the initial moment of (biological) conception and projecting its effects on the present action of writing. It is precisely this *reductio ad absurdum* that emphasises the limits of Locke's theory of personal identity, founded on a supposed continuity of consciousness. The parodistic operation carried out by Sterne reaches its climax in the second chapter of the novel, where the hero makes his appearance in the person of the *homunculus*: this Latin expression refers to the miniature human figure which early microscopists believed they saw in a spermatozoon. Thus, addressing the reader directly, Laurence Sterne ridicules the excesses of the contemporary debate about the self as an autonomous, rights-bearing individual:

> The HOMUNCULUS, Sir, in how-ever low and ludicrous a light he may appear, in this age of levity, to the eye of folly or prejudice;—to the eye of reason in scientifick research, he stands confess'd—a BEING guarded and circumscribed with rights: —The minutest philosophers, who, by the bye, have the most enlarged understandings ... shew us incontestably, That the HOMUNCULUS is created by the same hand—engender'd in the same course of nature, —endowed with the same loco-motive powers and faculties with us.[5]

Evidently, what is of primary interest to Sterne is not so much the concept of personal identity as such – in what it consists and how psychological continuity is to be understood – as rather the way of representing that complex, enigmatic and elusive reality called 'self'. If Locke questions himself about the idea of the sameness of consciousness, the creator of *Tristram Shandy* stages the plurality of the self and its manifold manifestations. 'We are a restless set of beings', Sterne writes in his sermon *The History of Jacob*, 'and as we are likely to continue so to the end of the world.'[6] In other words, the variety of characters that appear in *Tristram Shandy* is nothing but the breaking down into different identities of the *restless* and divided self. Each character embodies a partial self: the authorial persona takes on the task of interpreting and reconstructing the multiplicity of the voices and faces in the idiosyncratic puzzle of his writing. It is precisely through this process of analysis and recollection that the identity of Tristram Shandy is revealed. The personality of the main character does not emerge from what is recounted of him and of his family, but is gradually shaped through the very peculiar way in which the narrator relives his own past.

While Locke emphasises the role of memory over time in his attempt to define the concept of personal identity, Tristram-Sterne tends to spatialise the history of his life in order to oppose the passing of time and thus reassemble the 'pieces' of his self. An eloquent image of this spatialisation of life is offered in the seventh volume of the novel, which is entirely occupied with a humorous account of Tristram's tour on the Continent. An epigraph taken from Pliny the Younger, placed at the beginning of the volume, cleverly illustrates the meaning that this operation assumes in relation to the whole work: 'Non enim excursus hic eius, sed opus ipsum est.' ('For this is not a digression from it, but the work itself.')[7] In other words, the act of travelling implies a spatial dislocation which symbolically alludes to the wandering style of Tristram's narrative as such. In truth, from the opening sentence of the novel, the writing of *The Life and Opinions* takes the shape of a journey against time, a journey into the labyrinth of consciousness in search of one's own self. It is therefore no coincidence that right here, in a famous chapter of the seventh volume, the author dramatises with incomparable irony the crucial problem of personal identity:

—My good friend, quoth—as sure as I am I—and you are you—
—And who are you? said he.—Don't puzzle me; said I.[8]

The direct question about the self is destined to remain unanswered, at least in the pages of *Tristram Shandy*, leaving the way open to the image of a fragmentary, unstable, contradictory nature of self-hood. The expression used by Tristram to elude the most disturbing question – 'Don't *puzzle* me' – refers us back to the seemingly inexplicable sense of his writing: a true *puzzle* which, at this point, becomes a transparent metaphor for the unfathomable mystery of human consciousness and the impossibility of reducing it, in Lockean terms, to a 'clear and distinct idea'.[9]

Shaftesbury and the path of self-knowledge

Despite the veiled allusion to Locke's theory of personal identity within a novel which explicitly refers to *An Essay Concerning Human Understanding*, the most important influence on Sterne's narrative seems to be the practice of self-examination recommended by Shaftesbury. A moral imperative of self-knowledge and character formation, typically derived from the Socratic and Stoic tradition, is at the core of Shaftesburian philosophy. According to this view, each person must make an inward journey or descent into the self as an essential preliminary to any other moral questions:

Men must acquire a very peculiar and strong habit of turning their eye inwards in order to explore the interior regions and recesses of the mind, the hollow caverns of deep thought, the private seats of fancy, and the wastes and wildernesses as well as the more fruitful and cultivated tracts of the obscure climate.[10]

In his essay *Soliloquy, or Advice to an Author*, published in 1710, Shaftesbury argues that true self-knowledge must primarily deal with the examination of the passions, since – as the philosopher puts it – they 'affect my character and make me different with respect to myself and others'.[11] And he goes on to articulate his argument, trying to explore the essence of the *self*:

> ... it is the known province of philosophy to teach us ourselves, keep us the self-same persons and so *regulate our governing fancies, passions and humours* as to make us comprehensible to ourselves and knowable by other features than those of a bare countenance. For it is not certainly by virtue of our face merely that we are ourselves. It is not we who change when our complexion or shape changes. But there is that which, being wholly metamorphosed and converted, we are thereby in reality transformed and lost.[12]

Thus, in order to control and 'regulate our governing fancies, passions and humours' and thereby construct a coherent self, Shaftesbury revives the ancient Stoic concept of self-discourse as a means of moral improvement. This technique of inner conversation or 'soliloquy' – modelled on Marcus Aurelius's *Meditations* – must be practised as a form of mental examination and therapeutic exercise, or rather as a psychic surgery. Through 'self-dissection' the individual 'becomes two distinct persons'.[13] This division of the *self* into two parts, of which one teaches and raises questions, while the other answers and learns, goes back to the model of the Socratic dialogue. Indeed, maieutics is *par excellence* the art of questioning, the art of debating: at the end of the dialectical path, Socrates's interlocutor is divided, as if he were split into two, forced to distance himself from his assumptions and unquestioned beliefs. Similarly, the exercise of the soliloquy or inner dialogue aims at objectifying the individual consciousness, presenting the ordinary man with an opportunity to rearrange his preconceived judgements and to reassess his hierarchy of values. It is a work carried out on oneself, whose primary purpose is to fix a coherent identity against any form of alienation, against any pretext deriving from received opinions and false convictions. More precisely, following the Stoic tradition, the practice of inner dialogue is aimed at disciplining the imaginations that inhabit the human mind, which often reveal themselves to be so powerful as to direct our thoughts in one way or another. To put it differently, the art of soliloquy corresponds to that intelligent use of critical judgement by which we deflate our subjective 'fancies' and substitute adequate or objective representations for them.

Thus, for the author of *Soliloquy*, self-knowledge consists essentially in self-questioning. Far from being transparent to ourselves, we have to question our own desires and implicit judgements in order to make them declare and express what they really mean. Usually, our thoughts and imaginations 'conceal half their meaning'[14] and hide themselves behind the ambiguous way of whispering insinuations and confused murmurs. As Shaftesbury writes in his essay:

> One would think there was nothing easier for us than to know our own minds and understand what our main scope was, what we plainly drove at and what we proposed to ourselves, as our end, in every occurrence of our lives. But our thoughts have generally such an obscure implicit language that it is the hardest thing in the world to make them speak out distinctly. For this reason, the right method is to give them voice and accent.[15]

To put it briefly, the task of inward conversation is to make explicit what usually remains silent, obscure, unexpressed. On the scene of the inner theatre, through a typical process of personification and staging, this discursive practice assumes an intrinsically dramatic and rhetorical structure:

> And here it is that our sovereign remedy and *gymnastic method of soliloquy* takes its rise when, by a certain powerful figure of inward rhetoric, the mind apostrophizes its own fancies, raises them in their proper shapes and personages and addresses them familiarly, without the least ceremony or respect. By this means, it will soon happen that two formed parties will erect themselves within. For the imaginations or fancies being thus roundly treated are forced to declare themselves and take party.[16]

Thanks to the procedure of self-discourse, our implicit evaluations and fancies 'are forced to declare themselves' openly, so that they can be criticised. If the art of soliloquy may essentially be viewed as a self-persuasive practice, rhetoric becomes a precious technique within this process. The quoted passage clearly shows how the efficacy of the 'gymnastic method of soliloquy' stems from the dialogic and linguistic nature of this *mental* exercise, which invariably tends to configure itself in the neat and concrete form of verbal expression. Indeed, the process of putting our feelings and imaginations into words enables us to control our unconscious minds, which otherwise might exert a powerful influence on our attitudes and behaviour.

Needless to say, the admonition to practice this sort of self-examination or soliloquy can be traced back to the Delphic inscription, 'Know Thyself'. It is important to notice, however, that the classical motto is tellingly rephrased, in Shaftesbury's essay, as 'Recognize yourself!', which in its turn is made explicit by a compelling imperative: 'Divide yourself!' or 'Be two!'[17] In this way, the English philosopher emphasises the achievement of a dialectical, inter-subjective process in which the phase of *disagreement* plays an essential role. The point of dividing oneself into two parts, with the need to express and confront antagonistic positions and attitudes, aims to reach the kind of consensus that results from rational discussion. As Shaftesbury strikingly claims in *Soliloquy*, 'The disagreement makes me my own.'[18] In other words, the ultimate purpose of inward dialogue is to achieve integrity and self-unity within one's own mind.

The importance of such a conception in relation to Laurence Sterne's masterpiece can hardly be overestimated. Bringing together ancient and modern learning, the narrator of *Tristram Shandy* makes inner dialogue the basic underlying principle of his own writing, as well as of his search for identity. Right from the beginning of the story, the protagonist questions himself on the sense of his coming into the world, expressing a biased and distorted view of reality. A negative perception of himself and of the world transpires from the first chapters of the novel:

—*I wish* I had been born in the Moon, or in any of the planets, ... for it could not well have fared worse with me in any of them (tho' I will not answer for *Venus*) than it has in this vile, dirty planet of ours,—which o' my conscience, with reverence be it spoken, *I take to be* made up of the shreds and clippings of the rest;—not but the planet is well enough, provided a man could be born in it to a great title or to a great estate; or could any how contrive to be called up to publick charges, and employments of dignity or power;—but that is not my case; ...—for which cause *I affirm it over again* to be one

> of the vilest worlds that ever was made;—for *I can truly say*, that from the first hour I drew my breath in it, to this, that I can now scarce draw it at all ...;—I have been the continual sport of what the world calls Fortune.[19]

In any case, the very act of writing his life, and above all his opinions, can be interpreted as a self-reflexive exercise in the Shaftesburian sense. It is worth noting, in the quoted passage, the gradual intensification of the narrator's inner attitudes: from the expression of an impossible desire ('*I wish* I had been born in the Moon') to a paradoxical conviction ('*I take to be* made up of the shreds and clippings of the rest'), from a repeated assertion ('I affirm it over again') to a strong declaration ('I can truly say'). This climax is even more significant when considering that it marks the passage from self-discourse to the actual dialogue with a virtual interlocutor – an imaginary friend, a sort of *alter ego* who is represented by the 'implied reader'.[20] As a matter of fact, in the chapter that immediately follows, Tristram Shandy assumes his proper narrative identity postulating a progressive, collaborative relationship with an ideal reader. Thus, addressing his hypothetical interlocutor, the narrator claims the right to 'tell *his* story *his* own way':

> I have undertaken, you see, to write not only my life, but my opinions also; hoping and expecting that your knowledge of my character, and of what kind of a mortal I am, by the one, would give you a better relish for the other: As you proceed further with me, the slight acquaintance which is now beginning betwixt us, will grow into familiarity; and that, unless one of us is in fault, will terminate in friendship.—*O diem præclarum!*—then nothing which has touched me will be thought trifling in its nature, or tedious in its telling. Therefore, my dear friend and companion, if you should think me somewhat sparing of my narrative on my first setting out,—bear with me,—and let me go on, and *tell my story my own way*.[21]

Dialogue and conversation in Shaftesbury and Sterne

Indeed, what appears to be continuously thematised throughout *The Life and Opinions of Tristram Shandy* is the relationship between the narrator and the reader. Therefore, the model of conversation is proposed in order to affirm the role of the reader as a true participant in the construction of the story. Or at least, such an intention is programmatically declared in one of Sterne's most frequently quoted passages:

> Writing, when properly managed (as you may be sure I think mine is) is but a different name for conversation: As no one, who knows what he is about in good company, would venture to talk all;—so no author, who understands the just boundaries of decorum and good breeding, would presume to think all: The truest respect which you can pay to the reader's understanding, is *to halve this matter amicably*, and leave him something to imagine, in his turn, as well as yourself.[22]

Far from being a mere adjunctive element, the presence of the reader inside the text is essential to the constitution of a full dialogical dimension, from which Tristram himself derives his truthfulness, his intrinsic uniqueness and personal identity. The influence of Shaftesbury is perceivable in the passage quoted above, most evident on the literal level, but also revealed by the close connection between the key notion of conversation, implying equality and reciprocity, and the ethical category of sympathy. 'To halve this matter amicably' is the method proposed by Tristram-Sterne to the perceptive reader in order to encourage his or her sympathetic participation. The very wording of this meaningful expression recalls Shaftesbury's *Soliloquy, or Advice to an Author*, since the verb used explicitly denotes the 'division' implied by the Socratic dialogue, which the English philosopher revives as the most appropriate method of knowledge and self-knowledge for the modern era.[23]

In Shaftesbury's view, the construction of the self is essentially inter-subjective and dialectical, involving at least the practice of inward conversation, if not actual interpersonal discourse. Since our true passions and opinions are not immediately clear and self-evident to us, we must have recourse to a sort of discursive therapy in the form of soliloquy or dialogue. According to Shaftesbury, only through dialogue can preconceptions and false opinions be unmasked. Through dialogue and conversation the deceitful use of language, the reductive use of names and labels to classify people and human behaviour can be brought to light and corrected. But this form of critique, this ability of discerning the real value of persons and opinions, passing through a multiplicity of different perspectives, must be grounded upon the moral virtue of sympathy.[24]

In his own philosophical dialogue, *The Moralists*, Shaftesbury offers a telling example of this process, since both interlocutors become dynamic embodiments of the philosopher's viewpoints. The dialogic form enables the author to present the argument from various angles and to create a context within which the opposing tendencies can be reconciled. As the work begins, each character seems to be locked in a unique, rigid view of his own identity. The situation of dialogic exchange, however, requires that each participant undergo a mutual modification of his previous conception so as to internalise aspects of the other's identity. Moreover, the circular structure of the work is aimed at overcoming what may appear as an irreducible opposition. Finally, as a result of this educative process, the reader is asked to be more than a spectator; in fact, he is encouraged to abandon his conception of the self as a singular, monolithic identity and to share to some extent the role of the other.[25]

Shaftesbury's valuable lesson becomes even more significant when applied to Sterne's novel. 'I write to instruct',[26] the narrator declares at the beginning of the second volume of *Tristram Shandy*. At the core of this pedagogical instruction is the crucial question of *how to read* 'this rhapsodical work':[27] or, to put it in other words, how to participate in such a complicated discursive construction. The subject matter of the story being narrated, with all its interruptions, digressions, suspensions, constitutes the internal dimension of *The Life and Opinions of Tristram Shandy*. However, on this level too, inside the narrative itself, what is truly thematised is the relationship between the members of the Shandy family, recollected and relived by Tristram through an authentic and intimate conversation. But the reader must learn how to behave and interact properly in order to be admitted into the domesticity of Shandy Hall. This is also the essential condition that enables the reader to pass from an exterior dialogical level, the formal level of the relation with the author, to the inward dimension of a more familiar conversation. If we now return to the passage already quoted from chapter XI, in the second volume of *Tristram Shandy*, we can observe the way in which this educational progress of the reader is developed:

> For my own part, I am eternally paying him compliments of this kind, and do all that lies in my power to keep his imagination as busy as my own.

'Tis his turn now;—I have given an ample description of Dr. *Slop*'s sad overthrow, and of his sad appearance in the back parlour;—his imagination must now go on with it for a while.²⁸

When looking at the actions of other people, we can imagine how we would feel in their situation. This is precisely what Tristram-Sterne expects of his reader, inviting him to use his imagination in order to take part in the scene depicted. When the narrator proposes 'to halve this matter amicably', actually he is inviting the reader to a sympathetic participation in the events narrated, so as to share the emotions and sentiments of the characters and of the person who tells the story. In short, he wants the reader to identify himself with the characters and situations described:

> Let the reader imagine then, that Dr. *Slop* has told his tale;—and in what words, and with what aggravations his fancy chooses:—Let him suppose that *Obadiah* has told his tale also, and with such rueful looks of affected concern, as he thinks will best contrast the two figures as they stand by each other: Let him imagine that my father has stepp'd up stairs to see my mother:—And, *to conclude this work of imagination,*—let him imagine the Doctor wash'd,—rubb'd down,—condoled with,—felicitated,—got into a pair of *Obadiah*'s pumps, stepping forwards towards the door, upon the very point of entering upon action.²⁹

Evidently, the reader is not asked to cooperate in the material construction of the story. He is not expected to interfere in what the story is about, or to suggest the way in which the events and actions should follow one another. All that is perfectly established by the author, as this brilliant piece of self-irony shows. The reader, instead, is required to place himself in the situation of the characters, to enter into their bodies and their minds in such a way as to feel their sensations, to share their emotions, to participate in their feelings. Even more, in Sterne's words, in order 'to conclude this work of imagination', the reader should perform and enact that extraordinary tension towards visualisation and auralisation that is inscribed in the written page, with the aim of conveying the sense of a face-to-face relationship. This is the reader's responsibility towards a literary work intended and proposed as conversation. Ultimately, the basic assumption of Sterne's novel is that 'conversation', *cum-versari*, implies the willingness to-stay-in-the-situation-with-the-other, looking at him and feeling with him; and this is the proper meaning of *sympathy*, the moral virtue that Shaftesbury considers indispensable for the formation of a unified and harmonious self.

Tristram Shandy as a quest for identity

At the very heart of *Tristram Shandy* there is a passionate search for identity, which is indissolubly interconnected with the crucial issues of self-knowledge and the role of language in constructing the self. From the opening lines of the narrative, 'I wish either my father or my mother ...', right up to the ending, the writing of *The Life and Opinions* is carried forward by Tristram's quest for self-understanding: and the reader is the figure called upon to answer this fundamental desire. But the reader must learn how to participate in this discursive construction of identity. Indeed, by calling attention to the writing process itself, Sterne's self-conscious novel reminds us of Paul Ricoeur's illuminating assertion on the significance and implications of the narrated life:

> The narrative constructs the identity of the character, what can be called his or her narrative identity, in constructing that of the story told. *It is the identity of the story that makes the identity of the character.*[30]

Put another way: Tristram's quest for identity begins and ends with the attempt to define the uniqueness of his work, that is, to recognise himself as the narrator of his *Life and Opinions*. In its intrinsically meta-fictional nature, Sterne's masterpiece displays various attempts at self-defining, using phrases for naming and qualifying the work and illustrating the laws of its own composition with diagrams and models and verbal explanations. But 'to define—is to distrust',[31] according to Tristram. Nevertheless, all these attempts to describe the work, to explain what it is about and the way it is constructed, to characterise it from a particular point of view – 'this dramatic work', 'this rhapsodical work', 'this book of books'[32] – all this recurring effort of naming *The Life and Opinions of Tristram Shandy, Gentleman* in the very act of producing it, is essential to the intimate purpose of Sterne's writing. All these tentative definitions, though ironically elusive, contradictory, confounding, contribute to creating quite a subtle interplay of names which reciprocally recall one another throughout Sterne's narrative, intermixing and moving their object continuously under the reader's eye. Significantly, this self-reflexive attitude pervades the whole work up to the end of the last volume, where the final inconclusive expression 'a COCK and a BULL',[33] put in Yorick's mouth when answering a question of Tristram's mother, leads the reader back to the very beginning of the story: 'I wish either my father or my mother ...'

Names really affect human existence in the Shandean universe: not so much the Christian name given to a baby, as Walter Shandy thought, as the nouns by which men understand and perceive reality, since they express and convey opinions, and opinions are responsible for the condition of happiness or unhappiness of men, according to Epictetus.[34] The act of naming is of crucial importance in the general design of *Tristram Shandy*, in so far as it reveals the deceit inherent in any definition, the implicit pretension of any monological and denotative language to fix opinions in a definite form. Finally, any attempt at naming human life and experience proves to be unjust, unless it implies as a constitutive component the implicit reference to another voice, to a different perspective, to *a different name*. And it is precisely this acknowledgement of the intrinsic *otherness* of any human word – of its unavoidable subjectivity and ambiguity – that founds the all-embracing definition of Sterne's masterpiece: 'Writing, when properly managed (as you may be sure I think mine is) is but *a different name* for conversation'.[35]

This indeed can be considered a meaningful expression of the intrinsically dialogical nature of any human word, of any speech act, whatever form it may assume. The very way in which this definition is worded should be intended not as a synonymic substitution – one name in place of another, one concept in place of another – but as a continuity, as a sort of metonymic relation, as an ideal, hypothetical progression of writing towards conversation. It is this self-conscious dynamism, which brings writing towards reading and reading towards writing in the name of conversation, that reveals the ethical tension inherent in the very act of writing, 'when properly managed'. In other words, we might say that Tristram's writing is redeemed from its hobby-horsical tendency, namely from the risk of a narcissistic involution, because of its radical orientation towards an interlocutor. It is precisely this tension towards the *other*, this desire for the other's responsive understanding – in the words of Bakhtin and Ricoeur[36] – that turns writing into conversation.

Thus, as we have noticed, Sterne's conversational work is characterised by an unpredictable, unstable, ever-changing structure that defies any claim to a clear and fixed definition. Similarly Tristram Shandy, as the hero and narrator of his own *Life and Opinions*, displays an idiosyncratic, fluctuating, kaleidoscopic identity formation that reflects, to some extent, a fractured and wounded family context. In Paul Ricoeur's view, 'narrative identity' follows the dialectical movement of the story;[37] therefore, in conformity with the dialogical strategies governing the narrative process as a whole, Tristram's identity is shaped through discursive, inter-subjective relationships. Indeed, while the title of the novel suggests the idea of an autobiographical narrative, in *Tristram Shandy* we do not really read about the protagonist's life, but about hilarious episodes that are mainly concerned with the lives of his father and uncle. From the very beginning of *The Life and Opinions*, Tristram explores his own identity by representing the members of his family: 'I wish either my father or my mother ...'[38]

As already observed, the opening act of wishing is of the utmost importance to introduce the crucial topic of personal identity, inasmuch as it emphasises the distance between the imagined self and the actual self. From this perspective, Tristram's metanarrative underlines the general necessity of telling the story of one's life in order to achieve self-awareness through the knowledge and acceptance of the past. The process of arranging and reworking former events, shaping them into a compelling though fragmentary story, can lead to a plausible construction and understanding of the self. It is not without reason that the greatest part of Sterne's novel is devoted to describing in detail all the disasters of Tristram's first years: his interrupted conception, his adventurous birth, the choice of his name, his bungled christening, the accident with the sash-window that circumcises him. Furthermore, the narration of these events is literally interwoven with the voices of the Shandy family, and the narrator is called upon to interpret them, acknowledging the absolute singularity and *otherness* of each person. It is precisely this recognition of the other's identity, achieved through an underlying interior conversation, that constitutes the principle of Tristram's *dialogical self*. In truth, when interpreting the actions and verbal behaviours of his closer relatives, Tristram reconstructs his own 'self' through an authentic inter-subjective relationship.

If there is a progression in the story being told, this should be sought in the dynamic adaptation and evolution of the narrator's consciousness. It has often been pointed out that the third volume of *Tristram Shandy* plays a crucial role in the general economy of the novel, inasmuch as it introduces the long-awaited birth of the hero. It is no coincidence, therefore, that the *incipit* of the third volume appears to signal unequivocally a new beginning:

> —'I wish, Dr. *Slop*,' quoth my uncle *Toby* (repeating his wish for Dr. *Slop* a second time, and with a degree of more zeal and earnestness in his manner of wishing, than he had wished it at first) —'I wish, Dr. *Slop*,' quoth my uncle *Toby*, '*you had seen what prodigious armies we had in Flanders.*"
>
> My uncle *Toby*'s wish did Dr. *Slop* a disservice which his heart never intended any man, —Sir, it confounded him—and thereby putting his ideas first into confusion, and then to flight, he could not rally them again for the soul of him.[39]

The insistent iteration of 'I wish', declined in all possible forms and put in Toby's mouth at the very moment of Tristram's birth, is intended to cast ridicule on the absurdity of human wishes. But the expression of this unseasonable desire is not merely aimed at parodying uncle Toby's passionate interest in military matters.[40] The meaningful repetition of the optative 'I wish', which marks the very beginning of Sterne's work, eloquently reveals the narrator's intention of reconsidering and reshaping the whole story from a different standpoint. In approaching the heart of his history, Tristram re-reads the initial phases in the light of a new wisdom, having acquired a more comprehensive understanding through the dialogical relationship with the members of his family. The willing disposition to accept and appreciate the existence of the others in his own life, including the weight of their respective hobby-horses or whimsical obsessions, allows Tristram to recognise, in the voice of uncle Toby, his own inner voice and his personal wish. Indeed, the inter-subjective process of discovering others opens the way for a deeper awareness of oneself and the world, as shown in one of the most delightful descriptions of the Shandy family. Towards the end of the third volume, Tristram sets about depicting what he defines as one of the most amusing scenes of his family's usual ménage: a scene which dramatises the relationship between his father and uncle Toby. However, before introducing the characters, the narrator pauses for a moment in order to make a solemn declaration – and at this point he removes his cap:

> There was not any one scene more entertaining in our family,—and to do it justice in this point;—and I here put off my cap and lay it

upon the table close beside my ink-horn, on purpose to make my declaration to the world concerning this one article, the more solemn,—that I believe in my soul (unless my love and partiality to my understanding blinds me) the hand of the supreme Maker and first Designer of all things, never made or put a family together, ... where the characters of it were cast or contrasted with so dramatic a felicity as ours was, for this end; or in which the capacities of affording such exquisite scenes, and the powers of shifting them perpetually from morning to night, were lodged and intrusted with so unlimited a confidence, as in the SHANDY-FAMILY.[41]

It is the opening paragraph of Chapter 39, where Tristram's progress towards self-reconciliation appears to reach its goal, having passed through the stages of antagonistic contrast and disagreement. The narrator's preliminary gesture of taking off his fool's cap is significant: the very act of taking on the role of the fool, and then leaving it, presupposes the Shaftesburian 'Divide Yourself – Be two' in order to achieve integrity and self-unity. At this point, from his rediscovered identity, Tristram is able to rise above the subject matter and proclaim a renewed confidence in his own capacity to discover and construct the 'true self'.

Notes

1 See E. J. Hundert, 'The European Enlightenment and the History of the Self', in Roy Porter (ed.), *Rewriting the Self: Histories from the Renaissance to the Present* (London: Routledge, 1997), pp. 72–83.

2 'When we see, hear, smell, taste, feel, meditate, or will any thing, we know that we do so. Thus it is always as to our present Sensations and Perceptions: And by this everyone is to himself that which he calls *self* ... For since consciousness always accompanies thinking, and 'tis that, that makes every one to be, what he calls *self*; and thereby distinguishes himself from all other thinking things, in this alone consists *personal Identity*, *i.e.* the sameness of a rational Being: And as far as this consciousness can be extended backwards to any past Action or Thought, so far reaches the Identity of that *Person*; it is the same *self* now it was then; and 'tis by the same *self* with this present one that now reflects on it, that that Action was done.' John Locke, *An Essay Concerning Human Understanding*, ed. Peter H. Nidditch (Oxford: Clarendon Press, 1979), bk II, ch. 27, §9, p. 335.

3 For earlier discussions see Henry E. Allison, 'Locke's Theory of Personal Identity: A Re-Examination', *Journal of the History of Ideas*, 27:1 (Jan.–March 1966), 41–58; Margaret Atherton, 'Locke's Theory of

Personal Identity', *Midwest Studies in Philosophy*, 8:1 (Sept. 1983), 273–93. For more recent discussions, see also Marya Schechtman, 'Memory and Identity', *Philosophical Studies*, 153:1 (2010), 65–79; Johan E. Gustafsson, 'Did Locke Defend the Memory Continuity Criterion of Personal Identity?', *Locke Studies*, 10 (2010), 113–29; Shelley Weinberg, 'Locke on Personal Identity', *Philosophy Compass*, 6:6 (2011), 398–407.

4 Laurence Sterne, *The Life and Opinions of Tristram Shandy, Gentleman*, eds Melvyn New and Joan New (Gainesville: University Presses of Florida, 1978), I. 1, p. 1. All the references to the text of *Tristram Shandy* are to Sterne's original volume and chapter numbers, followed by the page number in the Florida edition.

5 *Ibid.*, I. 2, pp. 2–3.

6 Laurence Sterne, *The Sermons of Laurence Sterne*, ed. Melvyn New (Gainesville: University Presses of Florida, 1996), p. 213.

7 Sterne, *Tristram Shandy*, VII. p. 573.

8 *Ibid.*, VII. 33, p. 633.

9 A recurring expression in Locke's *Essay Concerning Human Understanding*. In particular, the author dwells upon the specific meaning of this phrase in 'The Epistle to the Reader', pp. 12–14 in the Nidditch edition.

10 Anthony Ashley Cooper (the Third Earl of Shaftesbury), *Characteristics of Men, Manners, Opinions, Times* [1711], ed. Lawrence E. Klein (Cambridge: Cambridge University Press, 1999), p. 427. This passage is taken from *Miscellaneous Reflections on the Preceding Treatises and Other Critical Subjects*, a sort of metatextual commentary that concludes the *Characteristics*.

11 *Ibid.*, p. 132.

12 *Ibid.*, p. 127. Added emphasis.

13 *Ibid.*, p. 72.

14 *Ibid.*, pp. 84–5.

15 *Ibid.*, pp. 77–8.

16 *Ibid.*, p. 84. Added emphasis.

17 *Ibid.*, p. 77.

18 *Ibid.*, p. 145.

19 Sterne, *Tristram Shandy*, I. 5, p. 8. Added emphasis.

20 This concept was introduced by Wolfgang Iser in one of his most influential books, *The Implied Reader: Patterns of Communication in Prose Fiction from Bunyan to Beckett* (Baltimore, MD: Johns Hopkins University Press, 1978).

21 Sterne, *Tristram Shandy*, I. 6, p. 9. Added emphasis.

22 *Ibid.*, II. 11, p. 125. Added emphasis.

23 See Flavio Gregori, *Il wit nel* Tristram Shandy: *totalità e dialogo* (Roma: Edizioni dell'Ateneo, 1987).

24 For more extended discussion, see Lawrence E. Klein, *Shaftesbury and the Culture of Politeness: Moral Discourse and Cultural Politics in Early Eighteenth-Century England* (Cambridge: Cambridge University Press, 1994); Isabel Rivers, 'Shaftesbury and the Defence of Natural Affection', *Reason, Grace and Sentiment: A Study of the Language of Religion and Ethics in England, 1660–1780*, vol. 2, *Shaftesbury to Hume* (Cambridge: Cambridge University Press, 2000), pp. 85–152.
25 For an insightful treatment see Michael Prince, *Philosophical Dialogue in the British Enlightenment. Theology, Aesthetics, and the Novel* (Cambridge: Cambridge University Press, 1996), especially the chapter entitled 'Shaftesbury's *The Moralists*: a dialogue upon dialogue', pp. 47–73.
26 Sterne, *Tristram Shandy*, II. 2, p. 98.
27 *Ibid.*, I. 13, p. 39.
28 *Ibid.*, II. 11, p. 126.
29 *Ibid.*, II. 11, p. 126. Added emphasis apart from the names.
30 Paul Ricoeur, *Oneself as Another* (Chicago: University of Chicago Press, 1995), pp. 147–8. Added emphasis.
31 Sterne, *Tristram Shandy*, III. 31, p. 258.
32 *Ibid.*, I. 10, p. 18; I. 13, p. 39; III. 31, p. 258.
33 *Ibid.*, IX. 33, p. 809.
34 It is well known that the first two volumes of *Tristram Shandy* appeared with a famous motto from the *Enchiridion* of Epictetus: 'Not things, but opinions about things, trouble men.'
35 Sterne, *Tristram Shandy*, II. 11, p. 125. Added emphasis.
36 See Mikhail M. Bakhtin, *The Dialogic Imagination: Four Essays* (Austin, TX: University of Texas Press, 1981); Ricoeur, *Oneself as Another*; and also Ricoeur's last book, *The Course of Recognition* (Cambridge, MA: Harvard University Press, 2007).
37 See Paul Ricoeur, 'Narrative Identity', *Philosophy Today*, 35:1 (Spring 1991), 73–81.
38 See Rocío Gutiérrez Sumillera, 'Tristram's Identity Revisited', *Babel-Afial*, 17 (2008), 77–98.
39 Sterne, *Tristram Shandy*, III. 1, p. 185.
40 On the concept of 'hobby-horse' see Luigi Cazzato, '*Tristram Shandy* and the Epistemology of the Hobby-Horse', *Textus*, 16:2 (2003), 213–32.
41 Sterne, *Tristram Shandy*, III. 39, pp. 278–9.

PART III

Romantic wanderings: the self in search of (its) place

10

The anxiety of the self and the exile of the soul in Blake and Wordsworth

Laura Quinney

> ... the inability of the self to arrive at or be in equilibrium and rest by itself ...
> Kierkegaard, *The Sickness Unto Death*[1]

> I was not born here I come and go
> W. S. Merwin, 'Cold Spring Morning'[2]

Wordsworth and Blake are both inheritors of Enlightenment anatomies of the self (Locke, Hume, Hartley), and each of them writes about divisions within the self, and yet each is also partial to older concepts of the soul, less Christian than Gnostic and Neoplatonic. Instead of opposing them, each poet in his own way draws on these rival legacies in his exploration of selfhood and of the self's relation to itself. The two legacies come together in the connection Blake and Wordsworth find between self-alienation (the self's anxious experience of itself as incoherent) and alienation in the world (the self's feeling of homelessness or what the Gnostic and Neoplatonic tradition calls 'the exile of the soul'). Though it can be shown that both poets knew the essential ideas of the Neoplatonists and the Gnostics, my point here is not to trace out an intellectual debt. Wordsworth and Blake were not so much influenced by those ancient ideas as attracted to them because the ideas corroborated their own basic intuitions, and provided terms with which to address a fundamental interest, which they shared, in the bewilderment of selfhood.[3] For Wordsworth and Blake, and arguably for Romantic thinking in general, estrangement from what appears to be the alien 'outside' turns out to complement the more tortuous forms of inner estrangement, wherein the self is made anxious not by its relation to anything other than it, but by its own being and its relation to itself.

In his book *The Gnostic Religion*, Hans Jonas uses the term 'existential alienation' to name the feeling that the world is not one's home. As a religious idea, existential alienation is explained by metaphysics: the true home of the 'soul' is in a divine realm beyond this one, the soul has fallen or 'descended' into this world, and it has as its goal a return from exile to the higher world where it belongs. (For the sake of argument, let us define 'soul' as the essential humanity and identity of any individual person, usually understood in a religious context as possessing uniqueness, immortality and a divine origin.) As far as we know, the first religions to talk of the alienated soul were the Orphic and Pythagorean. Both were dualistic, anticipating the soul/body dualism that lies deep in the ontology of Platonism and subsequently influenced Christianity. The body itself is seen as a mere vehicle of the soul, foreign in its nature and even inimical to the soul, in so far as it, the body, is matter, and participates with the rest of the material world in dragging the soul down to its level. As Pierre Courcelle has shown, the Orphics compared the body to a prison,[4] while the Pythagoreans liked to pun on the similarity of the Greek words for 'body' and 'tomb' (*soma* and *sema*). Socrates cites the Orphic comparison sympathetically in the *Cratylus*: 'I think it is most likely the followers of Orpheus who gave the body its name [prison], with the idea that the soul is being punished for something, and that the body is an enclosure or prison in which the soul is securely kept.'[5] The general idea of the division of interests between body and soul runs throughout Plato. In one image, Plato likens the body to a cadaver that threatens to infect the soul with gangrene. This image is sufficiently grotesque, but according to Courcelle,[6] Aristotle 'improved' on it in giving the ultimate statement of Greek disdain for the body: 'For indeed the conjunction of the soul with the body looks very much like this. For as the Etruscans are said often to torture captives by chaining dead bodies face to face with the living, fitting part to part, so the soul seems to be extended throughout and affixed to all the sensitive members of the body. Mankind possesses nothing divine or blessed that is of any account except what there is in us of mind and understanding: this alone of our possessions seems to be immortal, this alone divine.'[7]

It may be, nonetheless, that the Orphics and Pythagoreans did not elaborate much on the notion of the soul. Walter Burkert reports that there is surprisingly little evidence of concrete doctrine, suggesting that 'ancient mysteries were a personal, but not necessarily a spiritual form of religion'.[8] Their attraction turned on offering a cathartic emotional experience, 'a chance to break out of the enclosed and barren ways of predictable existence' and 'to create a context of sense in a banal, depressing and often absurd world'.[9] The rituals of mystery counteracted anxiety and despair by giving the individual, the self or soul (the 'person' in 'personal religion') a stake in a new and different reality. It is Plato who made the exile of the soul a definite idea taking its place amid a set of interrelated philosophical claims. In the *Phaedo* and the *Phaedrus*, particularly, Socrates attributes to the 'purified' soul a longing to rejoin the divine 'intelligible' world from which it came, where the gods repose and knowledge is truth. We know we came from this other world because we have, or rather 'recollect', traces of absolute knowledge we cannot have gained through experience. These are traces of the Ideas which by definition are purely ideal, or intelligible, and the recollection of them can induce in us a kind of nostalgia. In the *Republic*, Socrates's interlocutor, Glaucon, objects when he realises that the ideal city is just that – merely ideal – 'it can't be accommodated anywhere in the world'. Socrates responds that its value lies precisely in its ideality – not because it provides a model to aspire to – but because ideality itself allows the soul to rejoin its origin and true nature, temporarily: 'It may be, however, that it [the perfect city] is retained in heaven as a paradigm for those who desire to see it and, through seeing it, to return from exile.'[10] The Greek word translated as 'return from exile' is *katoikein*, to go home. We 'go home' in being lifted, mentally, beyond the material world into the realm of the wholly immaterial. The pathos of this notion is poetic. Indeed, Wordsworth makes use of it in 'Ode: Intimations of Immortality from Recollections of Early Childhood'. Gnosticism adds that the soul was unwillingly thrust into the abyss of materiality by either a lesser or an evil god. The material world tries to seduce the soul into forgetting its divine provenance, but existential alienation can prompt the soul into an 'awakening' by which it recalls its origins, questions its empirical selfhood, and learns to repudiate the spurious Creation.

Existential alienation turns on a sense of ontological difference – between the nature of the self and the nature of the world – and therefore it is at once of an impersonal order and of the most dramatic relevance to the self. (The 'Intimations Ode' conveys the power of this combination.) Feelings like ennui, nostalgia and disillusionment, even sadness over the transience of things, may involve some empirical self-disgust, or some reflection on the nature of the self; but they do not *entail* either. They might leave the status of the experiencing subject out of consideration altogether. In existential alienation, by contrast, it is thought about the status of the self which inspires feeling, and the feeling is inseparable from the philosophical intuition: the soul is pained, and through an ontological recognition it is able to explain to itself the source of its pain: it is incompatible in nature with the world in which it finds itself. One might assume that the knowledge of a soul would be reassuring, even without the transcendental consequences. But reassurance does not always follow. As a consequence of discovering its alien status, the Soul or self also finds, to its dismay, that it is inchoate, scattered across time and space, lacking identity, autonomy and force. Paradoxically something remains – what identifies itself as 'the self' – to suffer this philosophical disappointment and desire to express it.

We should thus distinguish 'existential alienation' from the social alienation often associated with Romanticism. Social alienation is the feeling that one does not belong in a particular place or a particular society. Existential alienation is the feeling that one does not belong in the world at all. At its highest level of self-consciousness, existential alienation recognises an ontological impasse: it is *as a soul* that one does not belong in the world. Alienation is necessary and permanent because it follows from the nature of one's being. Social alienation tends to shade into existential alienation in Wordsworth, but as it turns out he himself is careful to discriminate between them. In 'Lines written a few miles above Tintern Abbey', he says his memories have brought him 'sensations sweet' during his 'hours of weariness' in 'lonely rooms, and mid the din / Of towns and cities' (26–8).[11] The association of loneliness, weariness and noise, the invasion of stimuli, points to estrangement from his surroundings – that is, to alienation of a local and personal kind.

194

The opening passage of *The Prelude* describes urban alienation in the same, now familiar terms: Wordsworth rejoices that he has 'escaped / From the vast city, where I long had pined / A discontented sojourner' (1850: 1, 6–8); (note the word 'sojourner', meaning visitor, one who is only passing through).[12] He celebrates his liberation from a life that was particularly uncongenial to him:

> Trances of thought and mountings of the mind
> Come fast upon me: it is shaken off,
> That burthen of my own unnatural self,
> The heavy weight of many a weary day
> Not mine, and such as were not made for me. (1850: 1.19–23)

Placement in the line emphasises the last phrase: city life is unsuitable *for me* (contrast Stevens's generalisation in *Notes Toward a Supreme Fiction*: 'we live in a place / That is not our own and, much more, not ourselves'[13]). He can shed his alienation by changing his venue.

In 'Tintern Abbey', Wordsworth uses some of the same vocabulary as in this passage from *The Prelude* – burden, heaviness, weight – but it is by way of differentiating between his individual urban alienation and a form of oppression that seems not only larger and deeper but more impersonal. After describing his sweet sensations and their power, he moves up a level, asserting that his memories gave him 'another gift, / Of aspect more sublime' (37–8): they brought on 'that blessed mood' which lifts 'the burthen of the mystery' and 'the heavy and the weary weight / Of all this unintelligible world' (38–41). Wordsworth thus discriminates between his urban loneliness and a kind of philosophical panic (which might be felt anywhere) in which the 'world' has become incoherent and human existence, a perplexing enigma. The 'serene and blessed mood' heals this existential alienation by suppressing consciousness of body – the seat of estrangement in so far as it seems separate, frail and embattled in the world – in order to replace it with the easy being of an assimilated 'living soul':

> —that serene and blessed mood,
> In which the affections gently lead us on,
> Until, the breath of this corporeal frame,
> And even the motion of our human blood
> Almost suspended, we are laid asleep
> In body, and become a living soul:
> While with an eye made quiet by the power

Of harmony, and the deep power of joy,
We see into the life of things. (42–50)

I do not see mysticism in this passage so much as a theoretical solution to the dilemma of alienation. The soul is reconciled to existence when it can feel itself to be undivided from the material world, living in it as in its element because it has uncovered the immaterial dimension of materiality ('the life of things'). The nervous eye, once an open aperture through which the alien world besieged the soul, has been 'made quiet' by a new harmony with it. To be 'a living soul' is not to be a world-making Idealist soul, but to be a soul confident that it shares its own vitality with the 'life' in things.

As we would expect, we can also look at Book Seven of *The Prelude* ('Residence in London') to study the relationship between urban anxiety and existential alienation. Here again we find that the latter transcends the former. The Blind Beggar scene, Book Seven's 'moment of time' or passage of sublimity, dramatises the transition: overcome by the human surfeit of the crowd, and his own isolation within it – 'The face of every one / That passes by me is a mystery!' (1850: 7.628–9) – Wordsworth has a sudden apprehension that promotes his disquiet to a higher state of feeling, one with a philosophical purchase, where epistemological and existential questions come into play:

> lost
> Amid the moving pageant, I was smitten
> Abruptly, with the view (a sight not rare)
> Of a blind Beggar, who, with upright face,
> Stood, propped against a wall, upon his chest
> Wearing a written paper, to explain
> His story, whence he came, and who he was.
> Caught by the spectacle my mind turned round
> As with the might of waters; an apt type
> This label seemed of the utmost we can know,
> Both of ourselves and of the universe;
> And, on the shape of that unmoving man,
> His steadfast face and sightless eyes, I gazed,
> As if admonished from another world. (1850: 7.636–49)

If, with his identification and simple personal narrative, the beggar exemplifies 'the utmost we can know', then we can know very little.

Each of us has a hold of only a few facts about his or her individual empirical self – where you were born, what they call you, what befell. Wordsworth raises the stakes considerably by adding that this is the utmost we can know 'Both of ourselves and of the universe', which implies that there lies an abyss of darkness on either side of consciousness, within and without.

With this thought, we plunge back into the experience of the Gnostic subject, adrift and homeless, bewildered both by selfhood and by material existence. The Blind Beggar now becomes for Wordsworth a symbol of this existential vagrancy, and at the same time he becomes an alter ego, a likeness and an image in reverse of Wordsworth himself. Like the old man in *Resolution and Independence*, he suffers a fate Wordsworth shares in some measure and greatly fears, but musters an equilibrium in the face of it (he is 'unmoving' and 'steadfast') that Wordsworth longs to emulate. The mirror-image of the Blind Beggar, in his equanimity, bears witness to the anxiety Wordsworth feels: in characteristic terms, he 'gazes' on the sight, riveted, with an intensity proportionate to his need. But also he cannot let the sight go because it is addressed to him in the imperative mode, directed towards him and requiring something of him; he feels 'as if admonished from another world'. With nice equivocation, 'admonish' means to warn, to reprimand, and to urge, as if to say: you have done wrong, and here is how you must do better, or else. (In 'Resolution and Independence', Wordsworth is recalled from self-pity and despair by the 'apt admonishment' (112) of the Leech-Gatherer's appearance.) In true Gnostic fashion, the consciousness of existential alienation – call it the vertiginous loneliness of the soul – has called up 'another world', a higher reality to which the soul can refer itself, at the cost of acknowledging its current disability and its neglect of its own vocation.

Wordsworth sometimes celebrates this rifting of existence, in which total alienation opens a view unto a higher reality. In the episodes of childhood 'idealism' he described to Isabella Fenwick in his gloss on the 'Intimations Ode', the sequence is reversed:[14] absorption in another reality estranges Wordsworth from the surrounding world, but the logic of anxious isolation precipitating transcendence dominates the climaxes of the 'sublime' passages in *The Prelude,* from the boat-stealing scene to the ascent of Mount

Snowdon. Just to remind you, here is the characteristic conclusion of the ode to Imagination in Book Six:

> In such strength
> Of usurpation, in such visitings
> Of awful promise, when the light of sense
> Goes out in flashes that have shewn to us
> The invisible world, doth greatness make abode,
> There harbours whether we be young or old.
> Our destiny, our nature, and our home,
> Is with infinitude—and only there. (1805: 6.532–9)

The plot is familiar: a violent disruption of appearances leads to metaphysical transport. The figure of the 'flash' or 'glimpse' is also characteristic: the higher world that the lost soul may take to be its real 'home' cannot inhabit this world, and thus, short of madness, it can be only briefly intuited, or, as in the Snowdon episode, visited by way of metaphor:

> and from the shore
> At distance not the third part of a mile
> Was a blue chasm, a fracture in the vapour,
> A deep and gloomy breathing-place, through which
> Mounted the roar of waters, torrents, streams
> Innumerable, roaring with one voice.
> The universal spectacle throughout
> Was shaped for admiration and delight,
> Grand in itself alone, but in that breach
> Through which the homeless voice of waters rose,
> That dark deep thoroughfare, had Nature lodged
> The soul, the imagination of the whole. (1805: 13.54–65)

In this passage, Wordsworth literalises the idea of the 'fracture' or the 'breach' through which appears the intimation of a world not part of this one where the soul has its proper being (conflated here with 'imagination', as also in the passage from Book Six). This time he figures the intimation as a sound, not a sight – a life-giving 'breath', a dramatic 'voice of waters'. The voice appears as 'homeless' because its source, hidden in the 'dark deep thoroughfare', remains invisible, but also because, to Wordsworth, powerful sounds always seem like noble spectres, adrift and phantasmal. ('With what strange utterance did the loud dry wind / Blow through my ear!' (1850: 1.337–8).

Thus Wordsworth complements his language of tantalising appearance – of 'flash' and 'glimpse' – with the language of ghosts: phantoms and shadows, 'visitings' and insubstantial manifestations. He rather rigorously uses figures of temporary accommodation – 'abode', 'lodge', 'visit', 'sojourn', 'lurk' – to describe the relationship of the other realities to this world, to which they do not belong, where they are, in fact, 'homeless'. Figuratively, their homelessness stands in for the soul's own: this is made plain in the Snowdon passage, where Wordsworth offers 'the homeless voice of waters' as a metaphor for the imagination, the 'soul' of the whole human being. But it is also suggested by the many passages in which Wordsworth describes the contents of the inner life in his 'ghostly' idiom – as for example, this passage on writerly ambition, from the first book of the 1805 *Prelude*:

> I had hopes
> Still higher, that with a frame of outward life
> I might endue, might fix in a visible home,
> Some portion of those phantoms of conceit,
> That had been floating loose about so long,
> And to such beings temperately deal forth
> The many feelings that oppressed my heart. (1805: 1.127–33)

Here we have an economical version of a major theme in *The Prelude:* how the psyche is haunted by itself. Thus by its own nature it is displaced from the world. This thought brings us back around to the deeper connection underlying the shared figures of phantom visitation: the soul that feels itself to be alien or away-from-home, nearly unreal, mirrors itself in another order of being which necessarily appears here as utterly strange, flickering and insubstantial.

The association with ghosts means that every glimpse of the other world admonishes. On this hinge turns the fact that each celebration conceals a reservation – a recognition of irremediable loss and vocational paradox, as the logic of the 'Intimations Ode' makes clear, but is also already suggested by the metaphor of the 'glimpse'. Existential alienation has been authorised by an epiphany: but now, how to go back to living? The soul's vocation has been revealed, but is it consistent with mundane experience? In fact, Wordsworth has to be 'admonished' (reprimanded) because, falling into temporality, he has lapsed and forgotten. The 'Intimations Ode' argues explicitly that earthly life effaces primordial memory, leading to loss of self-consciousness and neglect of transcendental vocation: 'The homely Nurse doth all she can / To make her Foster-child, her Inmate Man, / Forget the glories he hath known, / And that imperial palace whence he came' (81–4). But it cannot be all the fault of Nature, for otherwise the soul would not deserve reprimand. It is guilty, somehow, of participating in its accommodation.

The 'Intimations Ode' does not use the word 'admonish' but the kind of childhood epiphany it honours has the structure of admonishment. Spontaneous disorientation – a sudden, brief foray into an immaterial world – serves to forcibly remind the soul of the 'High instincts' which properly belong to it:

> Not for these I raise
> The song of thanks and praise;
> But for those obstinate questionings
> Of sense and outward things,
> Fallings from us, vanishings;
> Blank misgivings of a Creature
> Moving about in worlds not realiz'd,
> High instincts, before which our mortal Nature
> Did tremble like a guilty Thing surpriz'd. (142–50)

'Our mortal nature' evidently feels reprimanded, since it 'tremble[s] like a guilty thing surpriz'd'. The literary allusions in this phrase – to Satan and to the ghost of Hamlet's father – serve to underscore the force of the word 'surpriz'd': to be caught out, to be taken in the act. But they also point to a deep sense of guilt, deeper than this situation seems to warrant. For what has our mortal nature done but to live the mortal life that was thrust upon it? What dreadful thing was it caught in the midst of doing? Following the Gnostic paradigm, our 'mortal nature' is guilty of appropriating our whole identity, collaborating with a lesser reality, confusing life with the life of the body and the material world. In this way it induces us to forget our 'High instincts'. It is guilty, in short, of being itself – a guilt so radical that it is, dialectically, innocence.

I will return later in the chapter to the notion of the primal guilt of consciousness. In the 'Intimations Ode', the immediate fault is spiritual amnesia: a subsiding into this life on the part of our 'mortal nature'. A glimpse of the other world calls it to account. However much Wordsworth may delight in the 'strength / Of usurpation' (1805: 6.532–3) by which imagination seizes upon invisible reality, the experience remains equivocal, for it liberates the anxieties of consciousness from their assuaging suppression. Lifted up into another world only after a short time to fall back down, it must now recognise its proper alienation – its restlessness, guilt and dread – and it must cleave to them, lest it betray itself again. Although it is the ghost of Hamlet's father which, at the cock-crow, 'started like a guilty thing upon a fearful summons', it is Hamlet himself who has been fearfully summoned by the ghost, admonished to undertake a task he comes to doubt, and in the end fails to perform (he avenges his mother's death, not his father's, upon his uncle). Like Hamlet, our mortal nature has been 'summoned' to a task that will be hard to pursue, once it returns to life in motion, because the charge is anachronistic. Our mortal nature is no more one to renounce the world than Hamlet is to enact the stilted plot of a revenge tragedy. In fact, it has no choice, since there is no living in the other world now. (That is what it means for it to be the *other* world.) Thus, paradoxically, if it perseveres in its task and does not betray itself, it is condemned not only to alienation, but to uneasy conscience and self-mistrust. Whatever compensations Wordsworth may discover in the 'Intimations Ode', and whatever forms of reconciliation he may embrace, he is committed by the logic of his Platonic scheme to self-doubting vigilance. 'Thoughts that do often lie too deep for tears' (206) are not subject to catharsis; they cannot be bewept and laid to rest. The task is endless: compare Kierkegaard's 'becoming subjective', where the *vocation* of subjectivity is to be made anxious by itself.[15]

Alienation and self-mistrust: here again is the abyss of darkness on either side of consciousness, within and without. For, to take up the theme adumbrated above, existential alienation and self-division accompany one another. But this is a complicated business, and there is more than one way to explain it. In the 'Intimations Ode', admonishment awakens guilt, and guilt is inherently self-divisive. To put it more expansively: the phrase 'our *mortal* nature' hints at the presence in us of a different 'nature', an immortal nature harbouring 'High instincts', *before which* our mortal nature trembles like the traitor before the throne. This distinction is related to the Gnostic separation of true and false selves, or of the real and the accreted soul, though it seems hardly so clean in Wordsworth, because only the 'true' soul knows its guilt in the Gnostic paradigm, where in Wordsworth it is 'mortal nature' which feels admonished. Nonetheless, in so far as our mortal nature is taught to guard against its inclinations – to beware complacency – it must divide the sentinel in itself from the sluggard. Tellingly, the new moral focus has what an older vocabulary might term a 'stiffening' quality, an emphasis on final things which concentrates the mind in place of the penetrating 'High instincts':

> We will grieve not, rather find
> Strength in what remains behind,
> In the primal sympathy
> Which having been must ever be,
> In the soothing thoughts that spring
> Out of human suffering,
> In the faith that looks through death,
> In years that bring the philosophic mind. (182–9)

The immediate meaning here is that the 'philosophic mind', armed with 'the faith that looks through death', can place human suffering in the proper perspective and thus 'soothe' the anguish of it, by recalling the immortality of the soul. But the whole passage suggests that the real recompense is philosophical depth itself, the elevation of the mind that beholds truth unswervingly. This Stoical gravitas substitutes for flights of transcendence, exchanging depth for height, and morality for sublimity. Though lesser, it has the merit of training the intelligence on subjects that estrange it from immediacy, and thus sustain the requisite distance and autonomy. The sentinel survives in the philosophic mind. Its thoughts of human suffering are 'soothing' to it in so far as they assure it has not lost the battle with stultification. It has evaded the 'earthly freight' (129) that custom or habituation imposes, lying upon the soul 'with a weight, / Heavy as frost, and deep almost as life!' (130–1) because it thinks beyond life; it goes deeper than life, 'too deep for tears' (206).

Success is to maintain a double consciousness, a being in the present ('Then, sing ye Birds, sing, sing a joyous song!' (171), and an abstracted Philosophy, 'an eye / That hath kept watch o'er man's mortality' (200–1). Wordsworth often wants to say that the two blend harmoniously, but there remains an implicit tension between them, because that very tension is required to create and sustain the autonomy of the philosophic mind, since the philosophic mind defines itself *against* our accommodating nature. Its continued existence depends on its continued estrangement from the world, using 'estrangement' in the etymological sense – it is of a different nature, it is a stranger to the world – but also remembering that this difference is supposed to be hierarchical: it is better than the world, and endangered by it.

Existential alienation divides the self against itself. In the Gnostic paradigm, the moment of initial bewilderment gives way to a doctrinal distinction between true and false selves. But reassurance does not always follow. The interplay between the true and false selves can be complicated, as we have seen, and can be a source of anxiety in itself. With existential alienation comes an awareness of the mutability of the self over time. A gulf opens up between the past, 'naive' self and the present 'awakened' one. The observing self registers a distance from the self having a revelation in the present, while the epiphanic self looks back and registers a distance from the 'naive' self in the past – several different 'naive' selves, in fact, at several different moments. Self-separation occurs along horizontal as well as vertical axes: across levels of self-consciousness in the present (horizontal) and down a time-line into the past (vertical).

Romantic 'poems of revisitation' are particularly intent on studying this kind of self-confrontation. As developed earlier in the eighteenth century, the 'poem of revisitation' portrays the return of the adult to a place familiar in childhood, and usually explores the melancholy awareness of time passing, and of the dramatic difference between the child and the adult self. Wordsworth and Coleridge adapted this model in poems where the catalyst of self-recognition, the forms of self-division, and the stakes involved, are both more dramatic and more subtle. But they begin with the same basic lament: against my will, time has parted me from myself. (Anyone who has read Proust will recognise this as one of his central themes.)

The 'Intimations Ode' is one of Wordsworth's late poems of revisitation, beginning with a lament about the way in which time has forced involuntary changes upon him. The earlier 'Tintern Abbey' explores the proliferation of selves more vertiginously. The premise of the poem is that Wordsworth has returned to a place of blessed memory with happy anticipation, but has somehow been disappointed. With emphatic deictics ('this' and 'these'), he points to the identity of what he sees now with what he has seen. The more he insists on identity, the more we recognise that he is trying to convince himself of it, because though the scene may look the same to him, it does not feel the same. He is not having the experience he expected to have. He anticipated a homecoming of sorts, but everything, though physically the same, wears a strange face. He is floating free, but scrabbling to re-establish connection. Within the lonely landscape is a formation that seems to image a greater loneliness: the cliffs stand out against 'a wild secluded scene' and on this scene they 'impress / Thoughts of more deep seclusion' (6–7). When he sees the cliffs this way, he is thinking of himself, though he may not know it. He is the one on whom the 'seclusion' of the scene has induced 'thoughts of more deep seclusion', namely his own, as the anomalous or foreign element, driven back into his inner world, as only a consciousness can be.

That withdrawal is exactly what we see in the next verse paragraph, as his thoughts fall deeply inward, to memories of what the memory of this landscape had meant to him in the intervening times. The passage sounds like celebration: but we must remember that this whole set of memories appears under the rubric: 'this [may be] but a vain belief' (51–2). The 'belief', evidently, is that he was remembering something real when the memories of this place sustained him. If he was not remembering something real, as his present sense of alienation suggests, then he was nourishing himself on fantasy, and much in his understanding of self and world is now subject to question, as in any loss of faith. He looks back at himself in a series of memories; and wonders if that self was naive, even deluded. Or, to be more accurate, the self of the past five years dissolves into a group of different selves, each confined to its own temporal location: the past selves who remembered the scene, at different times – 'in hours of weariness' (28), the lost selves who knew 'unremembered pleasure' (32), or who perhaps performed 'unremembered acts / Of kindness and of love' (35–6), the self which suffered under 'the burthen of the mystery' (39), the one who ascended into a 'serene and blessed mood' (42), 'laid asleep / In body' and becomes 'a living soul' (46–7). These different selves or consciousnesses seem discrete, not really integrated into a whole, even though it is a present self who recollects them – 'conscious of myself, / And of some other being' (1805: 2.32–3). This underlying doubt has a corrosive effect, disintegrating the story he has been telling himself about his own spiritual history, and breaking down his 'soul' into a set of discrete consciousnesses, each blinded in its own way. Wordsworth may use the word 'soul' here but the concept is not doing its work: for the moment, nothing seems to underlie the mutations of consciousness. Locke had set aside the word 'soul' altogether, replacing it with the notion of 'personal identity', which he defined as present consciousness plus the memories of having been 'the same' consciousness. Wordsworth has discovered a problem with that definition: that it is possible to have memories of past consciousness in which it is both the same and not the same. 'I' was 'I' but a different 'I'. In fact, quite a number of them. Though the poem does not end here, it maintains a complex representation of competing and overlapping selves, some recollected and some projected, in the present. Wordsworth is too honest to over-simplify the experience of consciousness. He shows how the sense of separation from nature leads to a sense of self-disintegration within the self, and how sadness and anxiety accompany this double loss.

Turning now to Blake, I shall be brief, since the terms of the argument have been established. Blake shares Wordsworth's intuition about the anxiety of selfhood; thus his many lamenting psyches and psychic portions lament their loneliness, their estrangement from others and from the world, and their own internal incoherence. One has only to think of the 'Shadowy Female', the malign projection of Nature, and the terror she induces, to recognise the role of existential alienation in Blake's analysis.

> ... the Sun is shrunk: the Heavens are shrunk
> Away into the far remote: and the Trees & Mountains withered
> Into indefinite cloudy shadows in darkness & separation.[16]

Think of this as an extravagant and universalised version of Wordsworth's complaint. The natural world, the outer world, ceases to be a home, and the subject is intimidated as a result, driven within to an awareness of frailty: 'every human soul [is] terrified / At the turning wheels of heaven shrunk away inward withring away'.[17] Blake's classically ambiguous syntax makes two readings of the sentence possible, and necessary: the wheels of heaven have shrunk away, withdrawn (as in the passage from *Jerusalem*, above) *and* the soul itself has shrunk inward, withering as a consequence. In Blake, loss of the world and loss of the self occur simultaneously: self-imposed subjection to an autonomous exterior world leads to a reduced sense of agency and self-control. Thus, when Urizen creates 'this abominable void / This soul-shudd'ring vacuum',[18] it is at once the 'void immense, wild dark & deep' of Nature's 'womb', and the abyss of solitary subjectivity. Again thanks to Blake's 'squinting' syntax, his own 'deep world within' is a 'void immense, wild dark & deep', mysterious and fearful to him.[19] Throughout Blake's prophetic books, the internal paranoia of the disarticulated self is rendered in the way that his characters or psychic portions lament their ambivalence – love and hate, jealousy and longing – toward one another. At bottom they crave reconciliation, as if to corroborate Melanie Klein's arresting claim that, in the psychic disintegration characteristic of loneliness, 'the lost parts, too, are felt to be lonely'.[20] Each psychic portion is also uneasy in itself, puzzled by its own nature, as if separation from the others had forced the question upon it. Those characters who are sufficiently self-conscious to bewail their state lament like Ahania that they have been 'cast' into 'the World of Loneliness',[21] or echo Tharmas when he says, 'I am like an atom / A Nothing left in darkness yet I am an identity'.[22] Selfhood is for characters such as Thel, Tharmas, Urizen, Eno and Ahania an intolerable paradox in which the subject feels lonely and displaced, and all the more so the more it fears that its subjectivity is superfluous. Blake does not believe this predicament is inevitable; in fact, he holds that this experience of subjectivity has been long promoted by the sacrificial religions of the West, and more recently further boosted by materialist and empiricist philosophy. He has a solution – an essentially metaphysical one, similar in spirit if not in language to Wordsworth's in the 'Intimations Ode' – that entails the subject's reinvention of itself as a higher agent. But he sees the temptation to despair of itself as a constitutive feature of subject-life – or if you like, a typical debut.

To become conscious of alienation from the material world is at the same time to become conscious of passivity and incoherence in the self. Existential alienation begins as a discovery (the Gnostic 'awakening'): it is not truly a state of alienation until it becomes self-conscious. But it only becomes self-conscious by recognising a pre-existing condition. World existed before self; the self existed before self-consciousness; alienation existed before being recognised as such. Knowledge of oneself trails after the fact of being. One was born late, in so far as the world existed before, and comes only belatedly to self-awareness. Thus, Blake represents Urizen's birth as the rising of 'a shadow of horror ... In Eternity'.[23] Jonas compares the Gnostic concept of a late awakening into a foreign world with Heidegger's concept of *Geworfenheit,* or 'thrownness'. Existential alienation means not simply 'I am not at home in the world' but 'I find myself in a world into which I was thrown; I am belated in this world'. In other words, there is a discovery not just about the world, but also about the belatedness of selfhood. As Jonas puts it, the concept of *Geworfenheit* 'expresses the original violence done to me in making me be where I am and what I am, the passivity of my choiceless emergence into an existing world I did not make and whose law is not mine'.[24] To discover that you do not belong in the world is at the same time to discover that you did not have the power to prevent yourself from being thrust into it, nor did you even recognise your predicament until now. Thus an internal 'violence' is done to me in the form of a blow to my self-conception: I am less than I thought myself, certainly much less than I wish to be. 'For the power of the star spirits, or of the cosmos in general, is not merely the external one of physical compulsion, but even more the internal one of self-estrangement. Becoming aware of itself, the self also discovers that it is not really its own, but is rather the involuntary executor of cosmic designs.'[25] Temporality is one of those 'cosmic designs' a psyche is compelled to 'execute', manifesting the passage of time in the form of its own mutations. In addition to its other obvious forms of power, material existence has the 'power' to estrange the self from itself by showing it that 'it is not really its own'. It did not make itself; it did not choose its nature, its origin or its destiny. The self does not belong to the world; but neither does it belong to itself. Its origin and its nature are not at its command; neither is its being.

And yet it is simultaneously culpable for existing in the existence it did not choose, as a solitary consciousness, 'A self-contemplating shadow',[26] which when it catches sight of its own reflection trembles like a guilty thing surprised. The notion of a primal, perhaps unmerited, guilt of being lies at the heart of the Platonic tradition. Socrates, as we have seen, says the Orphics called the body a prison 'with the idea that the soul is being punished for something'. The emphasis is affective: the soul *feels* as if it were being punished for something, without knowing what it has done wrong or whether its punishment is just. Gnosticism and Neoplatonism account for the soul's original descent as the result of a desire for individuation on the part of a lesser God or of a universal Soul. In both, following from Platonism, no individual human action on earth brought about the fall, as by contrast it does in the Christian myth of Original Sin. Yet individuation itself is a tautology for separate being (as also in *The Book of Urizen*). Thus instead of Original Sin there is only an elegant paradox of unmerited guilt: life is the punishment for the involuntary crime of entering upon it. This idea brings us all the way up to Schopenhauer, who also thought that in existence itself lies guilt ('each of us is here being punished for his existence')[27] and Beckett, who took Schopenhauer's view: 'The major sin is the sin of being born.'[28] It is not necessary to endorse any of these views to recognise that they hit upon a psychological truth: consciousness feels an obscure guilt about being, that is, about its being what it is: individual and separate, unbound and immaterial. We are so used to hearing these qualities celebrated that we neglect the other possibility. The Gnostic myth has proved durable because it addresses this psychological truth in emphasising the soul's exile and loneliness, which are bound up with its sense of guilt and its apprehension of punishment. To this complex of ideas Wordsworth and Blake add an intricate psychology of self-division which, in their view, both springs from and deepens the alienation of consciousness.

Notes

1 W. S. Merwin, 'Cold Spring Morning', *W. S. Merwin: Collected Poems 1996-2011*, ed. J. D. McClatchy (New York: Library of America, 2013), pp. 587–8.
2 Søren Kierkegaard, *The Sickness Unto Death*, trans. Howard V. Hong and Edna H. Hong (Princeton, NJ: Princeton University Press, 1980), p. 14.
3 Laura Quinney, 'Blake and His Contemporaries', in Robert DeMaria, Jr. et al. (eds), *The Blackwell Companion to British Literature*, vol. 3, *Long Eighteenth-Century Literature: 1660–1837* (Chichester and Malden, MA: Wiley-Blackwell, 2014), pp. 329–44.
4 Pierre Courcelle, 'Tradition platonicienne et Tradition chrétienne du corps-prison', *Revue des études latines* (1965), 406–43.
5 Plato, *Complete Works*, ed. John M. Cooper (Indianapolis and Cambridge, MA: Hackett Publishing Company, 1997), 400c, pp. 118–19.
6 Pierre Courcelle, 'Le Corps-Tombeau', *Revue des études anciennes* 68 (1966), 101–22.
7 *Protrepticus* B 107–8, in Aristotle, *The Complete Works of Aristotle*, ed. Jonathan Barnes, vol. 2 (Princeton, NJ: Princeton University Press, 1984), p. 2416.

8   Walter Burkert, *Ancient Mystery Cults* (Cambridge, MA: Harvard University Press, 1987), p. 87.
9   *Ibid.*, p. 114.
10 Plato, *Republic*, trans. Robin Waterfield (Oxford and New York: Oxford University Press, 1993), 592b, p. 343.
11 William Wordsworth, *Wordsworth's Poetry and Prose*, ed. Nicholas Halmi (New York: Norton, 2014), 'Tintern Abbey', p. 66.
12 William Wordsworth, *The Prelude: 1799, 1805, 1850*, eds Jonathan Wordsworth, M. H. Abrams and Stephen Gill (New York and London: Norton, 1979). References to this are given in the text, citing the date of the version, the book and line numbers.
13 Wallace Stevens, 'It Must Be Abstract', *Notes Toward a Supreme Fiction*, IV, lines 13–14, *Collected Poetry & Prose* (New York: The Library of America, 1997), p. 332.
14 Wordsworth, *Wordsworth's Poetry and Prose*, pp. 432–3.
15 See Søren Kierkegaard, *Concluding Unscientific Postscript*, vol. 1, trans. Howard V. Hong and Edna H. Hong (Princeton, NJ: Princeton University Press, 1992), especially 'Becoming Subjective', pp. 129–89.
16 William Blake, *The Complete Poetry & Prose of William Blake*, ed. David V. Erdman, 2nd edn (Berkeley, CA and London: University of California Press, 1982), p. 219. *Jerusalem*, plate 66, lines 50–2. The Blake references are given in endnotes to provide detail of the books and line numbers.
17 Blake, *Complete Poetry & Prose*, p. 350. *The Four Zoas*, p. 73, lines 22–3.
18 *Ibid.*, p. 70. *The Book of Urizen*, ch. 1, lines 4–5.
19 *Ibid.*, p. 72. *The Book of Urizen*, ch. 2, lines 15–17.
20 Melanie Klein, 'The Sense of Loneliness', *Envy and Gratitude* (New York: Simon and Schuster, 2009), p. 302.
21 Blake, *Complete Poetry & Prose*, p. 88. *The Book of Ahania*, ch. 5, line 64.
22 *Ibid.*, p. 302. *The Four Zoas*, p. 4, lines 43–4.
23 *Ibid.*, p. 70. *The Book of Urizen*, ch. 1, lines 1–2.
24 Hans Jonas, *The Gnostic Religion*, 2nd edn (Boston: Beacon Press, 1963), p. 335.
25 *Ibid.*, p. 329.
26 Blake, *Complete Poetry & Prose*, p. 71. *The Book of Urizen*, ch. 1, line 21.
27 Arthur Schopenhauer, 'On the Suffering of the World', *Essays and Aphorisms*, trans. R. J. Hollingdale (London: Penguin Books, 1970), p. 49.
28 Anthony Cronin, *Samuel Beckett: The Last Modernist* (New York: Harper-Collins, 1997), pp. 121–2.

11

Transgressing the boundaries of reason: Burke's poetic (Miltonic) reading of the sublime

Eva Antal

> 'many of the objects of our inquiry are in themselves obscure and intricate'
> Edmund Burke, 'Preface', *A Philosophical Enquiry*[1]
>
> 'as the saying is, *Homo solus aut deus, aut dæmon:* a man alone is either a saint or a devil'
> Robert Burton, *The Anatomy of Melancholy*[2]

The sublime experience in the Age of Reason

In his inspiring book, *'The Stranger Within Thee': Concepts of the Self in Late-Eighteenth-Century Literature*, Stephen D. Cox, while elaborating on the relations between self-knowledge, sensibility and intimacy, mentions the cult of the sublime in eighteenth-century art, where the sublime, the newly discovered and thoroughly analysed aesthetic quality, 'was considered simultaneously to dramatize and "absorb" the self'.[3] On the one hand, the experience of the overwhelming power of the sublime threatens to engulf the individual, on the other hand, the self is forced to enter the dramatic dynamism of the aroused emotions and, transgressing its boundaries, has to experience its own limitations. Although the outlined process is philosophically elaborated upon by Immanuel Kant, the thematisation of the sublime experience has its roots in eighteenth-century British aesthetics. As early as the 1710s, in accordance with the neoclassical hegemony of order and rationality, several writers – for instance, John Dennis, Alexander Pope and Joseph Addison – exhibited the greatness of the divine mind in the sublime quality of nature, referring to it as 'sublimity', 'the great', 'majestic' or 'magnificent' (to mention a few of the terms employed).[4] In *The Spectator*, in 1712, Addison dedicated several of his periodical essays to the topic, primarily discussing the possible effects of the natural sublime on the imagination, though in his analysis, 'the *great*, the *uncommon*, or *beautiful*' are not strictly differentiated. Rather, he pays attention to the delight they can ignite in the human mind:

> Everything that is *new* or *uncommon* raises a pleasure in the imagination, because it fills the soul with an agreeable surprise, gratifies its curiosity, and gives it an idea of which it was not before possessed.[5]

Jonathan Richardson, the elder, in his *An Essay on the Theory of Painting* (1725) simply equated the sublime with the best, the excellent: '*the greatest, and most noble thoughts, images, or sentiments, conveyed to us in the best chosen words*, [being taken] to be the perfect sublime in writing; the admirable, the marvellous'.[6]

On the other hand, focusing on the relation between the human and the divine, Shaftesbury and Addison (among others) emphasised the creative power of imagination in the *aisthesis* of the sublime experience. In *The Spectator*, Addison claims that in nature we can gain 'delight in the apprehension of what is great or unlimited', while poetry – for instance, Milton's words – 'are apt to raise a secret ferment in the mind of the reader, and to work, with violence, upon his passions'.[7] Besides emphasising the passionate quality of poetry, Addison also explains the psychological response of the reader:

> If we consider, therefore, the nature of this pleasure [reading Milton], we shall find that it does not arise so properly from the description of what is terrible, as from the reflection we make on our selves at the time of reading it.[8]

The eighteenth-century readings of the sublime have much to say about the sensible experience of the world; moreover, at the same time, the debates were also likely to be concerned about the questions of imagination, understanding, morality, cogitation, self-articulation, and power. Edmund Burke's early writing on the sublime, which dates from the 1750s, when he was in his late twenties, can be placed in his own *œuvre* as a preliminary study on the discourse of power. There is a consensus that his treatise, to quote Rodolphe Gasché, 'was the first to propose an uncompromising empiricist – that is, sensualist – account of aesthetic experience, and to have radically uncoupled this experience from other extrinsic considerations (particularly, moral and religious)'.[9]

In Edmund Burke's sensualist analysis, the greatness of the sublime ('the great') is a challenge as it is painful not only to the mind but also to the body. In his philosophical – or rather aesthetical – treatise, *A Philosophical Enquiry into the Origin of our Ideas of the Sublime and Beautiful* (1757), the main concern is the study of our emotions related to the beautiful and the sublime; however, right from the 'Preface', he consciously focuses on the sublimity of poetic language, which is elaborated upon in Part Five. In my interpretation, I rely principally on Patricia Meyer Spacks's ideas about the importance of intimacy featuring not only reading but also writing that requires a contextualised 'significant self' and displays the process of self-formation in interpretation.[10] She even introduces the term 'psychological privacy' to emphasise the relevance of 'intimacy as authenticity, as a space of self-discovery'.[11] While Spacks speaks of 'authenticity', Cox is concerned about 'the true self' that 'cannot be conceptualized simply by reference to innate dispositions; all the vagaries of its sensibility must be taken into account'.[12] The vagaries are abundant in philosophical and literary works of the period and Burke's reading (and writing) of the sublime can prove fruitful study to present the process of such an individual approach.

'Dark with excessive *light*': Miltonic obscurity in Edmund Burke's *Enquiry*

Burke's *A Philosophical Enquiry* owes a lot to John Locke and his highly influential sensualist-empiricist philosophy. Although the work, in its argumentation, is highly influenced by Lockean ideas, in some of his points Burke proves to be strikingly anti-Lockean. Although Locke's 'clear and distinct' ideas give the background (and the frame) to the philosophical treatise, in the development of his concept, Burke relies much more on his own readings; in particular, John Milton's impact is emphatically displayed in the 'dark and obscure' rhetoric of the work. On the one hand, Burke's main concern is the study of our emotions related to the beautiful and the sublime; on the other hand, right from the 'Preface', he consciously pays attention to the sublimity of poetic language, which is thematised in Part Five. The reader has the vague notion that throughout, besides the great quantity of classical (mis)quotations, Milton's 'strong expressions' overpower the argumentation. The concept of the Burkean sublime owes a lot to Miltonic obscurity, more exactly, to his own reading of Milton, the poet whom Addison introduced as a 'sublime genius'.[13] In this chapter, I collect the Miltonic quotations and (mis)quotations in *A Philosophical Enquiry* and try to interpret their importance in the formulation of the differences between the beautiful and the sublime with continual reference to the imagery of light/clarity v. darkness/obscurity – the dichotomy goes together with continual references to reason v. emotion in Burke's writing of the self.

John Locke's second edition of *An Essay Concerning Human Understanding* (1694) was the work that 'placed the whole question of perception, and of the mind's sensibility to what it perceives, at the heart of eighteenth-century attempts to determine the nature of the self'.[14] In his treatise, Locke radically questions the constancy of personal identity by stressing the variability of individual experience. He says that '*self* is not determined by Identity or Diversity of Substance, which it cannot be sure of, but only by Identity of consciousness'.[15] The Lockean theory of the rejection of innate – and commonly shared – ideas leads, for instance, to Berkeley's exaggeratedly self-centred, solipsistic philosophy ('*solus ipse*', 'only (one) self'), or to its criticism in the empiricist approach of the Common Sense School, members of which emphasised the balance between the actual existence of the self and its vague perceptions, while others – Hume and Shaftesbury, for instance – highlight the importance of empathy and the moral sense of the human selves.[16] Framing the cognitive dimensions of the *Enquiry*, Burke relies on Locke's 'simple ideas, which convey themselves into the Mind, by all the ways of Sensation and Reflection', which include pleasure and pain.[17] Locke calls all the elements of our thinking – sensations, external objects, operations of the mind – ideas, and claims their source to be experience.[18] Consequently, Burke's treatise has several references to Locke not only in the introductory parts on pleasure and pain and their connections with the beautiful and the sublime, but also in the last section, in Part Five dedicated to the effects of words.

Burke presents a simplified two-sided pattern, when he compares the beautiful and the sublime in the different sensations, objects and living beings capable of producing the pleasantness of beauty or the astonishment of the sublime. But actually, his system of sensory and bodily effects of external objects displays a five-part system of inner sensations: (positive) pleasure v. (positive) pain, in-between indifference, while the removal of pain gives relief (relative or negative pleasure, i.e. delight) and the diminution of pleasure gives grief (as relative or negative pain).[19] The sublime is introduced on the side of pain, while beauty is pleasurable.[20]

Besides the widely known parts on the definition of the sublime and its comparison with the beautiful,[21] the Preface 'On Taste' is also frequently quoted, in which Burke places special emphasis on man's own 'creative power', imagination. Although he follows Locke, stating that 'this power of the imagination is incapable of producing anything absolutely new; it can only vary the disposition of those ideas which it has received from the senses',[22] it rather makes us able to combine our sensory experiences, 'images in a new manner, and according to a different order',[23] somehow, in his theory, imagination 'mediates between and joins the inner self with the external world'.[24] Moreover, reflecting on the contemporary debate concerning the hierarchy of arts, he affords absolute prominence to words, to poetry over painting – not only in Part Five but throughout. With this claim, he 'follows the lead of Addison that it is imagination, with its ability to arouse passions and feelings and with its openness to the suggestions of words, that naturally forms the basis of all imitations'.[25] As he says in the *Enquiry*, combining the Lockean sensualist ideas with the Moral Philosophers' position:

> In reality poetry and rhetoric do not succeed in exact description so well as painting does; their business is to affect rather by sympathy than imitation; to display rather *the effect of things* on the mind of the speaker, or of others [the reader], than to present a *clear idea* of the things themselves.[26]

But rhetorically, in Burke's treatise, his own readings are taken as important sensory experiences. If I say that the cognitive hero is Locke, given the frame of the work, then those providing sensations to Burke's imagination are the poets and the classics. The method is borrowed from Longinus who, in his *On Sublimity*, did not intend to write a theoretical book on the concept: he was more concerned about the style of sublimity, providing an abundance of literary quotations as examples in the style of a handbook of rhetoric. Burke's major source of sublime poetry is Milton (misquoted), while in the Lockean references, classical, Greek or Latin, examples follow (usually misquoted as well). Citing Milton's *Paradise Lost* as an example of the sublime was a cliché in Burke's time; Dennis, Richardson, Addison and Dr Johnson valued the power of the 'passionate' (Richardson), or 'Paradisiacal' (Dennis), or 'dreadful', extravagant Miltonic verse.[27]

In Burke's treatise Milton first appears when the astonishing power of obscurity is exemplified: 'No person seems better to have understood the secret of heightening, or of setting terrible things, if I may use the expression, in their strongest light by the force of a judicious obscurity, than Milton.'[28] And he gives the early description of death, as 'the king of terrors':

> The other shape,
> *If shape it might be called* that shape had none
> Distinguishable, in member, joint, or limb;
> Or substance *might be called* that shadow seemed,
> For each seemed either; black he stood as night;
> Fierce as ten furies; terrible as hell;
> And shook a deadly dart. What seemed his head
> The likeness of a kingly crown had on.[29]

Burke emphasises its 'gloomy pomp'; 'significant and expressive uncertainty of strokes and colouring'; and that it is all 'dark, uncertain, confused, terrible, and sublime to the last degree'.[30] The vagueness of the Miltonic description is highlighted with the repeated uncertainty of the expression 'might be called' and the blurring of shapes and shadows.

In connection with clarity v. obscurity, while Locke declared that knowledge, understanding and argumentation are bound to clear ideas, Burke writes more for the heart than the head. When he first compares painting and poetry, he prefers the affective and emotive power of words to the clear ideas and pictures of the painted objects:

> It is one thing to make an idea clear, and another to make it *affecting* to the imagination. If I make a drawing of a palace, or a temple, or a landscape, I present a very clear idea of those objects; but then (allowing for the effect of imitation which is something) my picture

can at most affect only as the palace, temple, or landscape, would have affected in the reality. On the other hand, the most lively and spirited verbal description I can give, raises a very obscure and imperfect *idea* of such objects; but then it is in my power to raise a stronger *emotion* by the description than I could do by the best painting.[31]

This time the example is Milton's description of Satan, in which rhetorical confusion is again highlighted:

> He above the rest
> In shape and gesture proudly eminent
> Stood like a tower; his form had yet not lost
> All her original brightness, nor appeared
> Less than archangel ruin'd, and th' excess
> Of glory obscured: as when the sun new ris'n
> Looks through the horizontal misty air
> Shorn of his beams; or from behind the moon
> In dim eclipse disastrous twilight sheds
> On half the nations; and with fear of change
> Perplexes monarchs.[32]

As Burke explains, the human mind is tested and perplexed here 'by a croud of great and confused images'. If you, the reader, try to understand them separately, 'you lose much of the greatness'; if you 'join them', you lose clarity. And he concludes that poetic imagery is generally characterised by this kind of obscurity.[33]

Thus, being opposed to the eulogy on obscurity, light is rather related to the fine and pleasant (also relaxing) beautiful, the realm of clarity. Painting is obviously bound to light and Locke is obsessed about 'clear and distinct' ideas while, according to Burke, excess of light can be sublime, though 'darkness is more productive of sublime ideas than light'.[34] The most puzzling part is when he displays the torturing play of light and dark, quoting again from *Paradise Lost*, this time with a slight alteration (or lapse):

> — With the majesty of *darkness* round
> Circles his throne. ['Covers his throne' in the original]
> ...
> *Dark* with excessive *light* thy skirts appear. ['bright' instead of 'light'][35]

Burke tries to display how extreme light blinds you, how 'a light which by its very excess is converted into a species of darkness'[36] draws you into the realm of darkness, into the realm of obscure images. His misquotation is not falsification, or misreading; it is probable the slight changes are rather due to false recall and 'excessive familiarity with the text'.[37] We can wonder whether he knew these lines by heart, otherwise his hearing the words within speaks of another kind of reading/reception. However, it is striking that 'skirts' mentioned in the second short quotation is closely associated with 'circles' in the first one, which shows that these images are already built up in Burke's imagination of the Miltonic sublime.

Burke here highlights the essence of the Miltonic rhetoric since the eighteenth-century commentators of *Paradise Lost* stress that Milton favoured the usage of contradictions in his diction. In the 1730s, the Bentley-Pearce controversy debated whether those contradictions were paradoxes and oxymorons to provoke the reader, perhaps anomalies, or was Milton simply expressing the extremity of a sensual experience in 'strong and bold' wording. Interpreting the famous 'darkness visible' as 'a TRANSPICUOUS *Gloom*', Zachary Pearce claims that 'Absolute darkness is strictly speaking invisible; but where there is a Gloom only, there is so much Light remaining as serves to shew that there are Objects, and yet that those Objects cannot be distinctly seen'.[38] *Paradise Lost* is 'a field of opposing stresses and signals', displaying the struggles of creation *ex nihilo* in its sublime *discordia concors*, while the order of the universe is celebrated as a 'sublime *concordia discors*'.[39]

In Burke's writing, the power of the sublime is displayed in Milton's lines with one exception when Milton is quoted to present beauty. This exceptional Miltonic quotation from 'L'Allegro' is on music and exemplifies/explains the characteristic synaesthesia of the harmonious combinations of the sweet, light and soft sensations, how 'beautiful sounds agree with our descriptions of beauty in other senses':[40]

> And ever against eating cares,
> Lap me in *soft* Lydian airs; ...
> In notes with many a *winding* bout
> Of *linked sweetness long drawn* out;
> With wanton heed, and giddy cunning,
> The *melting* voice through *mazes* running;
> *Untwisting* all the chains that tie
> The hidden soul of harmony.[41]

This example shows that though Burke relied on his contemporaries' ideas on sensibility and consciousness, he was much more influenced by his own (private) reading experience, highlighting how Miltonic poetry could inspire him. Besides *Paradise Lost*, then, 'L'Allegro', a juvenile poem, is referred to and it does not seem to present the sublime. Although Burke omits two 'majestic' lines of the poem with reference to the soul and immortality so that the verse should only display the sweet 'melting' of mixed sensations, the quote still shows the strength of Milton's puzzling rhetoric.[42]

We should admit that Milton's poetry, if we disregard the beautiful harmony offered by his music in 'L'Allegro', displays the realm of gloomy (and painful) obscurity. Returning to (its) darkness, Burke disagrees with Locke[43] as the philosopher's opinion is that 'darkness is not naturally an idea of terror; and that, though an excessive light is painful to the sense, that the greatest excess of darkness is no ways troublesome'.[44] In contrast, Burke thinks that darkness has an associative terror and that 'an association of a more general nature, an association which takes in all mankind may make darkness terrible'.[45] It is interesting to note that when Locke's ideas are quoted or referred to, classical – Greek or Latin – examples follow (usually also misquoted) so that the reader should associate clarity with the classics in Burke's treatise.[46]

In Part Five of the *Enquiry*, Burke turns his attention to the effect of words. Following Locke, he differentiates three categories: the aggregate words (representing simple ideas naturally united, for example 'tree', 'castle', 'horse'), the simple abstract words (simple ideas such as 'red', 'circle' and so on, the relation for Locke) and compounded abstract words (which are the combinations of simple ideas and relations, for example, 'virtue', 'honour', 'persuasion'). He claims that all types of words raise three effects in the mind of *the hearer*: the sound, the picture (of the thing signified by the sound) and the affection of the soul.[47] After studying whether all words affect us in the same way, he concludes that quite often we do not have images when we hear and use words. In a long description it is impossible that the human mind is given enough time to picture the concepts evoked by the sounds:

> In short, it is not only of those ideas which are commonly called abstract, and of which no image at all *can* be formed, but even of particular real beings, that we converse without having any idea of them excited in the imagination .... Indeed so little does poetry

depend for its effect on the power of raising sensible images, that I am convinced it would lose a very considerable part of its energy, if this were the necessary result of all description.[48]

In comparison with painting, poetry is said to be not 'an imitative art', its energy derives from the effective power of words, the passions the words can arouse in us. It is partly due to our sympathy and the ability to share emotions, partly due to the 'affecting nature' of poetic descriptions of rarely occurring things (death, war, famine) and partly due to unusual word-combinations presenting us with unreal and supernatural things unfamiliar to us. 'These words affect the mind more than the sensible image did' and Burke speaks of clear and strong expressions, where 'the former regards the understanding; the latter belongs to the passions. The one describes a thing as it is; the other describes it as it is felt.'[49]

Reaching the final conclusion, or rather summary, Burke gives us, the readers, the absolute negative sublime described in Milton's words on hell:

— O'er many a dark and dreary vale
They pass'd, and many a region dolorous;
O'er many a frozen, many a fiery Alp;
Rocks, caves, lakes, fens, bogs, dens, and shades of death,
A universe of death.[50]

Burke is mesmerised by the terrible strength of these words and several times he repeats them in fragments. He selects the expression, 'a universe of death' as a strong combination 'of two ideas not presentible but by language', resulting in a great and amazing conception, where these ideas 'if they may properly be called ideas which present no distinct image to the mind; – but still it will be difficult to conceive how words can move the passions which belong to real objects, without representing these objects clearly'.[51] The striking rhetoric of 'a universe of death' is to shock the reader, as Burke earlier claims: it produces the astonishment that is 'that state of the soul, in which all its motions are suspended, with some degree of horror ... the effect of the sublime in its highest degree'.[52]

In this chapter I have focused on Burke's reading experience, although his *Enquiry* with its original 'emphasis upon the significance of the passions' opens up the way to psychological investigations. As Frances Ferguson states, 'Burke ... appears to be caught between a completely *nonsubjective (nonidealist) scientism* on the one hand

and a completely *subjective irrationalism* on the other ... between empiricism and irrationalism.'[53] In other words, Burke was caught between his philosophical and poetic inspirations in his psychological (and reader-response) speculation on the effect of the sublime. I wonder whether his later political ideas and his view of the French revolution owe a lot to the Miltonic sublime, but the political reading of the sublime is not within my remit here. However, focusing on the development of the sensible self, I will conclude by discussing the possibilities of self-transcending in Kant's moral theory of the sublime.

Coda: the Miltonic-Burkean moment of the Kantian sublime

While in his *Enquiry*, Burke was concerned with the passionate rhetorical sublime, in his conclusion, elaborating on the power of poetic language, he moves rather towards an understanding of man's ideal sublimity – as if he had started an imaginary dialogue with Shaftesbury. Shaftesbury highlights the importance of sympathy and *sensus communis* in social interactions, Burke quotes Milton's powerful words evoking strong emotions being shared by us all. Rather manipulatively, with the sensible reading of 'the universe of death' and experiencing the shocking power of the phrase, the Burkean sublime – in its negative way (*via negativa*) – leads us to the sublime of the Kantian moral imperative.

Kant was influenced by Burke's empiricist aesthetics, though in his *The Critique of Judgement* (1790) Burke's ideas are criticised (or built in). However, Kant's early, pre-critical work titled *Observations on the Feeling of the Beautiful and the Sublime* (1764) owes a lot to the Burkean differentiation of the pleasurable, feminine and amiable beautiful v. the painful, masculine and fearful sublime. In the first section of *Observations*, Kant discusses the two different dispositions (and also their subtypes) and he situates Milton's portrayal of hell among the examples of objects and works inciting 'enjoyment but with horror'.[54] This Miltonic moment can make us curious about the (hidden) connections between the Burkean and the Kantian sublime.[55]

I agree with Ferguson that while Burke, in his empiricism, blurred the differences or rather did not bother to make a distinction between responses and objects, 'the Kantian aesthetic made clear the need to talk less about the reality of objects and responses than about the place of the mental image'.[56] In his formalist idealism, Kant is concerned with the functioning of the human faculties, the imagination and reason, which is displayed in the subjective experience of the natural sublime. In *The Critique of Judgement* the immediate context of the sublime is provided by the argument on the beautiful. According to Kant, we like both the beautiful and the sublime for their own sake, but, in the case of the former, our liking is connected with the presentation of quality, while in the case of the latter with the presentation of quantity.[57] The other significant difference is that we find the beautiful charming and pleasant but the sublime simultaneously attracts and repels the mind. Although both of them give pleasure, the sublime is accompanied by 'a negative pleasure' that is produced by 'the feeling of a momentary inhibition of the vital forces' – or, 'blockage'[58] – followed immediately by their solemn and forceful outpouring. The ideas of 'negative pleasure' and blockage, or rather resistance, recall Burke, who, referring to the sight of large objects, finds that infinity has 'the most genuine effect' of 'delightful horror' on the mind.[59] Similarly, Addison, discussing the pleasures of imagination, claims that 'our imagination loves to be filled with an object, or to grasp at any thing that is too big for its capacity'.[60] However, besides these apparent similarities, there is a profound difference, to quote Kant: 'the sublime, in the strict sense of the word, cannot be contained in any sensuous form, but rather concerns ideas of reason'.[61] The concluding statement of the introductory paragraph of 'The Analytic of the Sublime' is followed by a powerful insight claiming that for the beautiful in nature we must seek the basis outside, while for the sublime merely within *ourselves*. Comparing it to the beautiful, the sublime is regarded as 'a monster or ghost' of the philosophical discourse being 'not a property of nature ... but a purely inward experience of consciousness'.[62]

Kant then introduces the distinction between the mathematically and the dynamically sublime; through the imagination the mathematical is referred to as the faculty of cognition and the dynamic to the faculty of desire. To quote the first definition from the end of paragraph 25: '*The sublime is that, the mere capacity of* [its] *thinking evidences a faculty of mind transcending every standard of sense.*'[63] Estimating the magnitude of the monstrous objects involves two operations: in the apprehension the imagination tries to understand or grasp the greatness (that is, its own greatness), while in the comprehension it tries to unite and totalise the apprehended sight. The perplexity aroused in the spectator is caused by the 'failure' of imagination since the spectator's imagination reaches its maximum and as it cannot expand on that maximum, it sinks back into itself. The sublime displays 'our imagination in all its boundlessness, and with it nature, as sinking into insignificance before the ideas of reason, once their adequate presentation is attempted'.[64] In the experience of the mathematical sublime, the mind tries to gain control, providing a unity to the 'infinite multiplicity', since, as Ferguson sums up, *'the self*, always wanting to be *a self*, gets to remedy its own sense of deficiency in setting a limit between the finite and the infinite'.[65]

In this section of the text – before 'the entering' of the dynamically sublime – the Kantian abyss does open up marking 'the point of excess for the imagination (towards which it is driven in the apprehension of the intuition) ... in which it fears to lose itself'.[66] In the same passage we can also find the metaphor of 'violence' though here imagination is violent to the internal sense. Kant introduces the conflicting (f)actors of the following 'dynamic' paragraphs, namely, the faculties of the mind: the imagination and reason, which are supposed to be in harmony in the theory of the beautiful. It seems that in 'The Analytic of the Sublime' the trope of the abyss and the trope of power/violence are interlinked – the seducing sublime of the abyss must be bridged over by the *word of power* (and law). The Kantian language *beautifully* describes the solitude man needs to sense the sublime in nature. However, under Burke's influence, Kant throughout emphasises that besides the narcissistic isolation all of us individually should experience, a position of safety should also be granted to each spectator. The last paragraph is followed by a long and illuminating comment in which, with the implicit limitation of its sensible representation and its sacrifice, the way is cleared for the sublime to refer to the supersensible or transcendental self. In an earlier section (§27) we read that the inadequacy of the imagination is aroused by an idea *'that is a law for us'* and at the same time it evokes the feeling of respect.[67] The comprehension of the infinite with regard to the imagination is – seemingly – a failure, while it is a law of reason that is forced upon the imagination so that it should accept its limitation. Thus, to quote the final definition: '[t]he *sublime* is what pleases immediately by reason of its own opposition to the interest of sense'; that is, 'an object (of nature) the *representation of which determines the mind to regard* [i.e. think] *the elevation of nature beyond our reach as equivalent to a presentation of ideas (als Darstellung von Ideen zu denken)*.'[68] For Kant from this definition only one step – a *salto mortale* – is needed to reach the moral law and the realm of the practical reason, which is now linked with the empirical in the aesthetics of the sublime.

In the third *Critique,* as Paul Crowther points out, 'the superiority of moral consciousness, and its feeling of respect, is explicitly made the basis of sublimity.'[69] Here Kant links the moral law with the 'law-ordained function' of the imagination, 'which is the genuine characteristic of human morality, where reason has to impose its dominion upon sensibility. ... in the aesthetic judgement upon the sublime this dominion is represented as exercised through the imagination itself as an instrument of reason'.[70] On the one hand, the ambiguity of imagination seems incongruous – it fails by being incapable of comprehending the infinite greatness and succeeds by functioning as the agent of reason for the moral law. On the other hand, in a forced way, the Kantian imagination functions as the agent of reason here and exercises power over itself for the sake of morality, for the sake of linking the moral law with the human world. Kant explains the functioning of 'the universality of a maxim as a law' in his *Groundwork of the Metaphysic of Morals* (1785):

> ... the law is not valid for us *because it interests us* (for this is heteronomy and makes practical reason depend on sensibility – that is to say, on an underlying feeling – in which case practical reason could never give us moral law); the law interests us because it is valid for us as men [human beings] in virtue of having sprung from our will as intelligence and so from our proper self; ....[71]

Our duty, namely, the acting out of respect for the law does not only mean respect for the law but also self-respect; respect for our own selves as moral beings. For Kant, the development of our moral feeling means a subjective interiorisation of the sublimity of the moral law that has its objective ground in reason. While Burke tried to provide his concept of the sublime with a sensible-emotional frame, Kant, moving beyond those boundaries, relies on the sublimity of our *own* sensible-moral existence.

Notes

1 Edmund Burke, *A Philosophical Enquiry into the Sublime and Beautiful and Other Pre-Revolutionary Writings*, ed. David Womersley (London: Penguin Books, 2004), p. 53.
2 Robert Burton, *The Anatomy of Melancholy*, ed. Holbrook Jackson with introductions by Holbrook Jackson and William H. Gass (New York: New York Review Books, 2001), p. 248.
3 Stephen D. Cox, '*The Stranger Within Thee*': *Concepts of the Self in Late-Eighteenth-Century Literature* (Pittsburgh: University of Pittsburgh Press, 1980), p. 7.
4 See Walter John Hipple Jr., *The Beautiful, the Sublime, and the Picturesque in Eighteenth-Century British Aesthetic Theory* (Carbondale, IL: The Southern Illinois University Press, 1957), pp. 16–17. See more in Andrew Ashfield and Peter de Bolla (eds), *The Sublime: a Reader in British Eighteenth-Century Aesthetic Theory* (Cambridge: Cambridge University Press, 1998).
5 See Joseph Addison in *The Spectator*, no. 412, 23 June 1712. Quoted in Ashfield and de Bolla (eds), *The Sublime*, pp. 62–3. Original emphasis. The other essays are from issues of no. 413, 24 June 1712; no. 414, 25 June 1712; no. 417, 28 June 1712; no. 418, 30 June 1712; and no. 489, 20 September 1712 (see *ibid.*, pp. 62–9).
6 Jonathan Richardson, the elder, from *An Essay on the Theory of Painting* (London, 1725). Quoted in Ashfield and de Bolla (eds), *The Sublime*, p. 45. Original emphasis.
7 Joseph Addison, *The Spectator*, no. 413, Tuesday 24 June 1712 and no. 418, Monday 30 June 1712. Quoted in Ashfield and de Bolla (eds), *The Sublime*, pp. 63 and 67.
8 Joseph Addison, *The Spectator*, no. 418, Monday 30 June 1712. Quoted in Ashfield and de Bolla (eds), *The Sublime*, pp. 67–8.
9 Rodolphe Gasché, '... And the Beautiful? Revisiting Edmund Burke's "Double Aesthetics"', in Timothy M. Costelloe (ed.), *The Sublime from Antiquity to the Present* (Cambridge: Cambridge University Press, 2012), p. 24.
10 Quoted in Cox, '*The Stranger Within Thee*', p. 12.
11 Patricia Meyer Spacks, *Privacy: Concealing the Eighteenth-Century Self* (Chicago: University of Chicago Press, 2003), p. 8.
12 Cox, '*The Stranger Within Thee*', p. 25.
13 Quoted in Leslie Moore, *Beautiful Sublime: The Making of Paradise Lost 1701–1734* (Stanford, CA: Stanford University Press, 1990), p. 5.
14 Cox, '*The Stranger Within Thee*', p. 13.
15 John Locke, *An Essay Concerning Human Understanding*, ed. Peter H. Nidditch (Oxford: Clarendon Press, 1979), bk II, ch. 27, §23,

p. 345. This concept is dealt with further in Christopher Fox's *Locke and the Scriblerians: Identity and Consciousness in Early Eighteenth-Century Britain* (Berkeley, CA: University of California Press, 1988).

16 Perhaps the most humorous presentation of the Lockean selves can be found in Sterne's *Tristram Shandy*, where only sympathy can connect the individuals, living in their own, closed monomania. See more in Spacks, *Privacy*, pp. 49–54. Opposed to the Sternean parody, Burke's socio-political reading rather reveals the criticism of the Lockean authority and dominance, supported by Milton's powerful words. The Latin epigraph of this chapter is quoted by Burke in his 'Thoughts on the Cause of the Present Discontents': 'the man who lives wholly detached from others, must be either an angel or a devil': Edmund Burke, *A Philosophical Enquiry into the Origin of our Ideas of the Sublime and the Beautiful, and Other Pre-Revolutionary Writings*, ed. David Womersley (London: Penguin Books, 2004), p. 274.
17 See Locke, *An Essay Concerning Human Understanding*, bk II, ch. 7, §1, p. 128.
18 *Ibid.*, bk II, ch. 1, §1, p. 104.
19 Burke, *A Philosophical Enquiry*, I. 2–3.
20 *Ibid.*, I.7.
21 *Ibid.*, I.7; II.1 and III.27.
22 *Ibid.*, p. 68, 'Preface'.
23 *Ibid.*, p. 68.
24 James Engell, *The Creative Imagination. Enlightenment to Romanticism* (Cambridge, MA: Harvard University Press, 1981), p. 71.
25 *Ibid.*, p. 148.
26 Burke, *A Philosophical Enquiry*, V.5, p. 195. Added emphasis.
27 Steven Knapp, *Personification and the Sublime, Milton to Coleridge* (Cambridge, MA: Harvard University Press, 1985), p. 52 and Richard A. Etlin, 'Architecture and the Sublime', in Costelloe, *The Sublime*, p. 270. See also Moore, *Beautiful Sublime*.
28 Burke, *A Philosophical Enquiry*, II.3, p. 103.
29 *Ibid.*; John Milton, *Paradise Lost*, ed. Christopher Ricks (Harmondsworth: Penguin Books, 1989), bk 2, lines 666–73. Added emphasis.
30 Burke, *A Philosophical Enquiry*, II.3, p. 103.
31 *Ibid.*, II.4, pp. 103–4. Original emphasis.
32 *Ibid.*, II.4, p. 105. Milton, *Paradise Lost*, bk 1, lines 589–99.
33 *Ibid.*, II.4, p. 106.
34 *Ibid.*, II.14, p. 121. See Locke, *An Essay Concerning Human Understanding*, bk II, ch. 19, §1, 'Of Clear and Obscure, Distinct and Confused Ideas', p. 326.
35 Burke, *A Philosophical Enquiry*, II.14, p. 121. Milton, *Paradise Lost*, bk 2, lines 266–7 and bk 3, line 380. The emphasis is Burke's own.
36 Burke, *A Philosophical Enquiry*, II.14, p. 121.

37 Frances Ferguson, *Solitude and the Sublime: Romanticism and the Aesthetics of Individuation* (New York and London: Routledge, 1992), p. 44.
38 Quoted in Peter C. Herman, *Destabilizing Milton:* Paradise Lost *and the Poetics of Incertitude* (Basingstoke: Palgrave Macmillan, 2005), p. 13.
39 Joseph Wittreich and David Norbrook quoted in Herman, *Destabilizing Milton*, p. 15. 'Getting lost' in *Paradise Lost* and its contradictions had proved fruitful not only for Burke. While Burke, conjuring up Milton's words in his mind, formulated a new interpretation of the sublime, William Blake, in his revolutionary engraving techniques, tried to make 'darkness visible'. Two different ways of self-expression are presented in their strikingly new reading of Milton.
40 Burke, *A Philosophical Enquiry*, III.25, p. 155.
41 Milton, 'L'Allegro', lines 135–44. The omitted lines are rather sublime: 'Married to immortal verse, / Such as the meeting soul may pierce' (lines 137–8). M. H. Abrams, E. Talbot Donaldson, Alfred David *et al.* (eds), *The Norton Anthology of English Literature*, vol. 1 (New York; London: Norton & Company, 1986), p. 1414. Original emphasis.
42 Samuel H. Monk remarks that Burke regarded 'Il Penseroso', the pair poem of 'L'Allegro', as 'the finest poem in the English language', and he imagined it to have been composed by Milton in a cloister or an abbey. See Monk, *The Sublime: A Study of Critical Theories in XVIII-Century England* (Ann Arbor, MI: The University of Michigan Press, 1960, originally published New York: The Modern Language Association of America, 1935), p. 91.
43 Locke, *An Essay Concerning Human Understanding*, bk II, ch. 7, §4, p. 130. 'For though great light be insufferable to our Eyes, yet the highest degree of darkness does not at all disease them ...'.
44 Burke, *A Philosophical Enquiry*, IV.14, pp. 171–2.
45 *Ibid.*, p. 172.
46 According to Ferguson, twenty-four passages out of forty-three are misquoted. Ferguson, *Solitude and the Sublime*, p. 44.
47 Burke, *A Philosophical Enquiry*, V.4, p. 190.
48 *Ibid.*, V.5, p. 193. Original emphasis.
49 *Ibid.*, V.7, p. 198.
50 Burke, *A Philosophical Enquiry*, V.7, p. 197. Milton, *Paradise Lost*, bk 2, lines 618–22. And it continues: 'A Universe of death, which God by curse / Created evil, for evil only good, / Where all life dies, death lives, and Nature breeds, / Perverse, all monstrous, all prodigious things, / Abominable, inutterable, and worse / Than Fables yet have feign'd, or fear conceiv'd, / Gorgons and Hydras and Chimeras dire.' (lines 622–8).

51 Burke, *A Philosophical Enquiry*, V.7, p. 198.
52 *Ibid.*, II.1, p. 101.
53 Ferguson, *Solitude and the Sublime*, p. 40. Added emphasis.
54 Immanuel Kant, *Observations on the Feeling of the Beautiful and the Sublime*, trans. J. Goldthwait (Berkeley, CA: University of California Press, 1960), p. 46, and Paul Crowther, *The Kantian Sublime* (Oxford: Clarendon Press, 1989), p. 9.
55 Leslie E. Moore in his *Beautiful Sublime* elaborates on the connections between Kant and Milton and calls attention to §49 in *The Critique of Judgement*, where Kant discusses the question of the *genius* (pp. 253–300).
56 Ferguson, *Solitude and the Sublime*, p. 3.
57 See more in Crowther's *The Kantian Sublime*; Engell's *The Creative Imagination*, and Thomas Weiskel, *The Romantic Sublime* (Baltimore, MD: Johns Hopkins University Press, 1976).
58 I borrow the concept of 'blockage' from Neil Hertz, *The End of the Line. Essays on Psychoanalysis and the Sublime* (New York: Columbia University Press, 1985).
59 Burke, *A Philosophical Enquiry*, II.8, p. 115.
60 Joseph Addison, *The Spectator*, no. 412, Monday 23 June 1712. Quoted in Ashfield and de Bolla, (eds), *The Sublime*, p. 62. Here Addison also mentions 'the speculations of eternity or finitude' that are pleasing to the understanding.
61 Immanuel Kant, *The Critique of Judgement*, trans. James Creed Meredith (Oxford: Clarendon Press, 1991), p. 92.
62 Paul de Man, *Aesthetic Ideology* (Minneapolis: University of Minnesota Press, 1996), p. 74.
63 Kant, *Critique of Judgement*, p. 98. Original italics.
64 *Ibid.*, p. 105.
65 Ferguson, p. 86. Added emphasis.
66 Kant, *Critique*, p. 107.
67 *Ibid.*, p. 105. Original emphasis.
68 Kant, *Critique*, pp. 118–19, and Immanuel Kant, *Kritik der Ästhetischen Urtheilskraft, Werke in sechs Bänden*, vol. 4 (Köln: Könemann, 1995), p. 139. Original emphasis.
69 Crowther, *The Kantian Sublime*, p. 27.
70 Kant, *Critique*, p. 120.
71 Immanuel Kant, *Groundwork of the Metaphysic of Morals*, trans. H. J. Paton (New York: Harper & Row, 1956), p. 129. Original emphasis.

12

Self and community in radical defence in the French revolutionary era: the example of *Oppression!!! The Appeal of Captain Perry to the People of England* (1795)

Rachel Rogers

In the years following the American and French revolutions, the British reform movement gained momentum, sometimes galvanised by these events but equally drawing upon an understanding of a tradition of radical opposition to illegitimate authority which had a very particular national heritage stretching back to the era before the Norman Conquest. In the 1790s, there was a proliferation of political writing, often in the form of pamphleteering, and the establishment or revival of clubs and societies dedicated primarily to achieving some form of political or constitutional reform. The London Corresponding Society (LCS) was founded in 1792 and sought to contribute to the political education of its members, many of whom included, for the first time, artisans and craftsmen. Furthermore, from early 1792 onwards, the Society for Constitutional Information began to lose its gentleman-reformer reputation, attracting a more socially diverse membership. Through its backing of Part Two of Thomas Paine's *Rights of Man*, published in February 1792, it began to take a much more radical departure from its earlier moderate Whig platform.[1]

This revived, and in some ways, increasingly democratised culture of radical reform, in the context of the events taking place in France, provoked the anxiety of the British authorities. Prime Minister and loyal servant of George III, William Pitt, and his inner circle of ministers, feared the upsurge of revolutionary activity on the British mainland. Their alarm was fuelled by the colourful reports of the network of informers who infiltrated organisations such as the LCS, reporting that 'the minds of the People are constantly kept in a state of fermentation, by the most seditious and treasonable writings, which are read to the different divisions every evening'.[2] Such reports of treason being disseminated were denounced by reformers insisting that 'there was a time when SPIES and INFORMERS were held infamous in England, and when an honest government disdained to employ such vile instruments of treachery and despotism'.[3] The Pitt Government's reliance on espionage led them to believe that reformers were intent on undermining the legitimacy of the British constitution, precipitating a concerted effort to suppress the movement and silence its principal advocates. This 'system of terror and imposition'[4] went some way to eradicating the culture of reform in Britain, assisted in large part by the widespread support given to loyalist associations set up around the country to pledge allegiance to the King and constitution and prevent gatherings from being held. One such 'Society of Loyal Britons', gathered at the New Crown Inn in Southwark in October 1793, pledged its entire service to the Government 'to discountenance, deter, and prevent, to the utmost of our Power, the circulation of Inflammatory Pamphlets, Papers, or Conversation; and finally, to lend our united assistance to hand down to the latest Posterity, our inestimable CONSTITUTION.'[5] Reform action was perceived as undermining the constitutional legitimacy of the country.

Yet such denunciations did not go unchallenged and one of the many reactions to this loyalist backlash against calls for reform, both within society at large and from within the ranks of the Government, was the growing tendency of individuals who had been victim of governmental repression to publish or proclaim their own defence. Such defences were one form of political participation that was open to them and allowed radicals to foreground the injustices of the existing system while also highlighting how individual persecution was of relevance to the broader community. As Charles Pigott put it,

> The case of an individual becomes a matter of public appeal, and deserves to excite universal anxiety and alarm, whenever it is marked by injustice and oppression. The people are loudly called on to oppose every act of individual tyranny, exercised against the common rights

and liberties of the subject; otherwise, they may be assured, it will be eagerly seized as a precedent by those in power, and, once established, may eventually terminate in the total annihilation of every thing most dear which our ancestors bequeathed us.[6]

Persecution of reformers was not only an assault on the liberty of individuals, but it was a slight on the tradition of constitutional liberty that Britain prided itself on having established and preserved. Through such claims, reformers saw individual suffering as inseparable from the fate of the body politic more widely.

This chapter will attempt to fit one particular self-defence tract, that of the editor Sampson Perry, into the wider picture of the 1790s reform movement, exploring how such writing was in many ways an attempt to reassert individual agency in the face of ministerial determination to prosecute reformers. Yet such tracts can also be seen as an alternative form of political participation, using individual cases of persecution to emphasise the inseparability of the self and the community and illustrate even more firmly the need for parliamentary and judicial reform. Finally, it will be important to emphasise how Perry's tract in many ways *enacted* those changes that were being called for within reform circles. Self-defences bypassed both Parliament and established legal authority, taking the form of direct appeals to the community of citizens or, in other cases, unmediated exchanges with the jury in a court of law. Such pleas to a broad community of 'fellow citizens' could in many ways be taken as demonstrating, and in some senses, *performing*, radicals' preference for a much more democratic form of political decision-making, to replace the flawed apparatus of representation seen as responsible for corruption in the highest echelons of power. It also illustrates the influence of ideas circulating in France on British radical activists, many of whom, like Perry, had visited France in the wake of the establishment of the National Convention in September 1792 and had witnessed ongoing debates on the shape of the new constitution in the making.

The ministerial backlash against the reform movement, 1792–95

Toleration of reform sentiment in 1795, when Sampson Perry wrote his self-defence from within one of London's most notorious prisons, Newgate, was much reduced in comparison with the early years of the decade. In the years immediately after the fall of the Bastille, many of those with a desire to see some sort of structural change within government or society expressed their own blueprints for reform with relative freedom. By late 1792, however, such openness incurred heightened risk. The narrowing scope for the articulation of reformist ideas was in part due to developments in France where, after the arrest of the King and his family in August, the Revolution took a more radical direction. A republic was established and a committee of the recently inaugurated National Convention set about devising a new constitution. Yet, the reactions of the British Government were also in part a response to the alarm provoked by the widespread circulation of the second part of Thomas Paine's pamphlet, *Rights of Man*, following its publication in February 1792. This pamphlet, endorsed by the Society for Constitutional Information, made its way around the country in cheap form, and appeared to be accessible to those who had hitherto had very little direct contact with political debate. As Thomas Paine himself judged, writing from exile in France, once the work began to reach a wider readership 'this once harmless, insignificant book, without undergoing the alteration of a single letter, became a most wicked and dangerous libel'.[7] It was its accessibility to a larger reading public rather than the ideas it contained which alarmed the ruling authorities.

The Government reacted by passing the Royal Proclamation Against Seditious Writings in May 1792, a measure which led to the prosecution of Paine for seditious libel and also prompted the indictment of radical publishers and booksellers. Thomas Spence, for example, recounts how he was threatened by 'Church and King' vigilantes, being 'repeatedly surrounded, insulted, and even threatened with his life, and the destruction of his little all, if he did not give up part of his bread, and decline selling the *Rights of Man*, and other political tracts'.[8] Paine's own publishers, James Ridgway and Daniel Isaac Eaton were also targeted as a result of their association with the work. Sampson Perry was consistently detained behind bars in the months before his escape to France in late 1792, after his newspaper *The Argus* began to adopt an increasingly radical stance. As editor, Perry had made sure the paper alerted its readers to the publication of Part Two of *Rights of Man* and the paper became increasingly irreverent towards figures of authority and followed developments in France closely.

After the calling out of the militia in December 1792, again by Royal Proclamation, in defence of the Tower of London against a potential invasion attempt and simultaneous local uprising, further ministerial actions followed in late 1793. Most notably, the leading Scottish reformer Thomas Muir was arrested on sedition charges after his involvement in the first Convention of the People in Edinburgh in December 1792. Muir, who chose to defend himself at trial rather than rely on the advocacy skills of lawyer Henry Erskine, was sentenced to transportation after being convicted by the Scottish court. Further indictments followed, with William Skirving and Maurice Margarot being convicted of sedition in January 1794, while Joseph Gerrald, who also defended himself at trial, was sentenced to transportation after his sedition charge was meted out in March of the same year.[9] The English trials for high treason, brought about by the involvement of leading figures of the London Corresponding Society in the British Convention of late 1793, were held in late 1794. The accused were ultimately acquitted by the jury, something which Thelwall heralded as the triumph of the public-minded spirit of the people of England. His self-defence, prepared to be read out at his trial but eventually only published and read out *a posteriori* in political gatherings, celebrated the verdict, not as bearing out his faith in the British constitution, but as vindicating the innate virtue of the British people:

> if under all these circumstances, the accumulated weight and pressure laid upon me was not sufficient to bear down and crush so insulated and unprotected a man, there must be something in the dispositions of the people of Great Britain – something eminently virtuous in this country, which every Briton must reflect upon with pride, and which must render every individual still more anxious to promote its happiness and prosperity.[10]

Yet despite the high-profile acquittals of leading radicals in late 1794, other lesser-known activists languished in prison, sometimes on outstanding libel charges, others for debts incurred while pursuing dissident forms of print journalism. In 1795, the year of the infamous 'Gagging' Acts, when Perry wrote his own defence tract from 'the felon side of Newgate',[11] many radical publishers, editors and writers were still behind bars, purging sentences which, for Perry, would outlive the century itself.[12] What has been shown by Iain McCalman is that Newgate was a micro radical community, and that, far from having a purely repressive impact on the radical movement, joint incarceration could be a motor for creative partnerships.[13] Perry's tract *Oppression!!!*, as well as his more substantial history of the events in France, *An Historical Sketch of the French Revolution*, were published by Newgate inmate H. D. Symonds, who was also involved in the publication of John Thelwall's self-defence tract. Fellow prisoners could therefore be not only sources of inspiration but could provide material outlets for publication projects which in themselves drew substantially upon the experience of incarceration, the common ground of many radical activists at the time.

This concerted effort to stem the tide of opinion in favour of radical reform was perceived by many as a form of oppression which jarred with claims that Britain was a model of constitutional liberty. John Thelwall was not alone in seeing ministerial reactions as a form of persecution which was unbefitting to a country which prided itself on being a bastion of free speech.[14] Take for example Thomas Spence's account of his own arrest in 1792 by Bow-Street Runners: 'Well, indeed might Mr. Spence exclaim, What country am I in! Nature shudders at such instances of the depravity in the human race; and those despicable characters scarcely deserve the epithet of *human*, much less the animating title of Britons!'[15]

For Spence, the loyalist assault on those selling political pamphlets was something that stained the British reputation for toleration. Charles Pigott, in his tract *Persecution*, a written version of the defence statement he had prepared awaiting news on his trial for sedition in 1793, also lamented the degeneration of the age-old principles of British liberty, stating, 'It would appear from the late extraordinary and desperate measures that we have witnessed in this country, as if the old system of Versailles was engrafted on the political system of Britain.'[16] Britain was no better than *Ancien Régime* France, struggling under the weight of despotism. John Thelwall also suggested that the repressive measures instituted by George III's ministers were unbecoming of a free country, suggesting that it was 'a phenomenon unparalleled in British History',[17] prompting him to conjure up the memory of Britain's tradition of resistance to unlawful authority: 'Immortal memory of our brave and simple ancestors! do I stand here to defend my life, upon a charge of High Treason, against this monstrous train of possibilities, constructions and improbable contingencies? – Am I still in Britain?'[18] Sampson Perry joined his fellow radical writers in lamenting the 'multiplied persecution'[19] of the official reaction to radical reform literature and its dissemination, which resulted in his own individual prosecution and outlawry from the community.

Sampson Perry and the quest for individual agency

Sampson Perry considered himself a particular victim of ministerial persecution, signing off all post-1793 writings and letters as 'persecuted editor' or 'late editor of *The Argus*', epithets which came to define his political self and drive his subsequent publication enterprises. This sentiment was not without just cause, since, as he details in most of his major works of the period, he was pursued relentlessly by the British authorities for his radical editorship of *The Argus*. The newspaper was eventually closed down and his printing press taken over by the ministerial publication the *True Briton* while Perry was in exile in Paris in early 1793. Perry had already been detained in prison on successive charges of seditious libel in 1791 and 1792 and was indicted again on his release from prison in July 1792 for stating that the Commons was not composed of the people's representatives and that the people were to be condemned for their docility in submitting to its laws. He suggested that a Convention was necessary because the people had played no part in electing their representatives. Perry, aware that he would be arrested imminently, agreed to leave the country after two years of open conflict with the ruling administration. He incurred a charge of outlawry and was 'proscribed that community of which I was a member, without a trial, or hearing, or even a specification of a crime'.[20] Outlawry, as Mary Bunch has noted, 'operated as a kind of social and civic death through banishment from the community' and the individual could not claim protection by the same framework of laws as the recognised citizen.[21] It was this charge that he sought help in overturning in his defence tract having been jailed once again on his return from France in the spring of 1795.

In many ways therefore, Perry's tract, like those of other radicals who advanced their own cases in oral testimony or pamphlets, was an attempt to assert his own agency in the face of what was perceived as an arbitrary campaign to sully the reputation of those whose opinions did not chime with those of the establishment. Rather than accept the views peddled in the government-backed press that he was the author of 'scandalous and atrocious libels',[22] intent on undermining the constitutional fabric of the country, Perry chose to state his own case, countering the accusations levelled at him. He details what he sees as his unchanging views, which had, he claims, been consistently expressed in newspaper columns and should constitute the true basis for judgement of his opinions. These were, firstly, the need for a reform of the system of parliamentary representation and the eradication of governmental abuses and, secondly, a criticism of the Government's ill-advised policy of intervening in the internal affairs of France.[23] His primary areas of interests are stated simply and justified by reference to the fact that 'every disinterested man'[24] would have come to the same conclusions from an informed enquiry into public affairs. He portrays himself as a rational, enquiring man, desirous of outing the truth and with 'pure' principles.[25]

Set in direct contrast with his irreproachable conduct is the whimsical behaviour of government representatives. They are accused of hounding him into exile, interpreting the law in a 'partial' way and giving in to 'an accelerated movement to gratify the resentment, or indulge the vengeance of any persons, however distinguished in rank, or elevated by office'.[26] While Perry highlights the 'purity' of his own intentions,[27] he contrasts this with the immoral abuses of the government and the basing of libel indictments on '*innuendoes*' rather than legitimate facts.[28] Like Pigott who condemned the 'unlawful idea of being governed by *individual conjecture*, in opposition to *positive fact*',[29] Perry cast into doubt the entire basis of the apparatus of justice under the ruling government. In both portraits, there is a reversal of the stereotypes that had been constructed by loyalist propaganda, namely, the opposition between the upstanding British establishment and the anarchic and fickle revolutionaries to which British reformers were assimilated. Yet, in the climate of repression that reigned, Perry argued, for the frank and virtuous reformer to contest the underhand behaviour of the authorities was inconceivable. Perry suggests that 'to complain of the Government is to be seditious',[30] a view put forward by many of his fellow radicals who had been accused of political crimes. Sedition or treason charges were levelled at those who simply sought to advance a new vision of society. Thelwall considered that under current conditions, any 'individual of active mind' could be accused of engaging in thinking which could be 'tortured into a charge of treason'.[31] To think was to grapple with ideas and therefore provide alternative readings of matters of public interest. For Thelwall, this type of speculation did not automatically lead to tangible attempts to undermine the system under which people were governed and could therefore not be considered treasonable. In Pigott's view, to conclude that because a man toasts the French Republic he 'harbours treason in his breast' is 'to torture a man's thoughts and words'.[32] The image of language being 'tortured to a sense' was one which a number of radical activists and their legal representatives used to describe the behaviour of the authorities towards those who articulated their opposition to the British political system.[33] In many ways, as John Barrell has noted, the confrontation between radical ideas and loyalist movement was as much about language as ideas. Radicals concluded that simply to express an opinion that diverged from that propounded in official circles was to court the charge of libel or worse.

To defend oneself from the witness box or in print from charges of seditious libel or treason was also to differentiate oneself in the face of a blanket judgment against radicals of all persuasions. Radicals were often termed 'Jacobins' or 'Democrats' and caricatures by artists such as James Gillray and Thomas Rowlandson were often composed in two-compartmental designs, pitting British 'liberty' against French 'slavery', or the virtuous Britannica against the bloodthirsty French, in a binary way which erased all potential for a spectrum of opinions. In a similar way, writers such as William Playfair dismissed the radical activist as a deluded democrat who 'is a despot when in Office and a rebel when out and in private life oppressive to inferiors and insolent to superiors'.[34] Hannah More, the popular writer of chapbooks and loyalist propaganda set out her idea of what reformers were seeking in one of the fictional conversations in her *Village Politics*:

Tom: And what dost thou take a democrat to be?

Jack: One who likes to be governed by a thousand tyrants and yet can't bear a king.

Tom: What is Equality?

Jack: For every man to pull down every one that is above him till they're all as low as the lowest.

Tom: What is the new Rights of Man?

Jack: Battle murder and sudden death.[35]

Radical writers aimed at defending their own individual reputations, and putting forward their case, attempting to show the personal nature of political sentiment within the reform movement. John Thelwall's tract was a 'vindication' of his 'motives and political conduct', and Sampson Perry's appeal was a 'justification of his principles and conduct' to counter the misrepresentation they believed they had been victims of.

Yet defending oneself could also lead to accusations of immodesty and self-promotion, or at least the fear of such accusations on the part of radical activists. Perry begins his own tract by stating, 'It was my intention to have said nothing of myself for fear of being accused of vanity, or a desire to be distinguished from the rest of my Fellow Sufferers.'[36] He insists that to be 'conspicuous' and to 'rush into public notice' is something to be 'dreaded' rather than coveted.[37] His decision to state his own case was 'forced' upon him by the circumstances of his persecution rather than chosen. As Michael Davies has outlined, according to historian E. P. Thompson, 'self-dramatisation' was 'the so-called characteristic vice of the English Jacobins'[38] and one could see in the self-defensive literature published by radicals in the wake of targeted prosecutions if not a form of self-dramatisation, at least a need for self-justification. In a context where radicals were penning utopias named after themselves or claimed to have devised novel and grandiose plans to remedy the ills of society and improve the lot of humanity at large, critics saw in the outspoken work of radical reformers the characteristics of the 'egotist deeply persuaded of his mission'.[39]

Nevertheless, to a substantial extent, radicals did shun notoriety, partly because they saw it as incompatible with the achievement of 'lasting popular esteem'[40] accrued over time and through consistent devotion to truth among one's fellow men, but also because for many militant reformers the substantial strides made towards overhauling social inequity in France remained an example to be followed. The practice of referring to fellow men and women as 'citizen', rather than 'Sir', though derided by loyalist commentators, was praised and employed by members of the LCS. Many members of the international community visiting Paris during the early years of the French Revolution adopted the custom of dropping their own titles and used the term 'citizen' in their correspondence and discussions. There was a residual admiration therefore for these levelling aspects of language that could be used to erase social distinctions.

Such attentiveness to trends apparent in France prompted a considerable sense of discomfort with distinguishing oneself from the rest of the community. Although Perry's tract is clearly penned as a defence of his own person, a testimony forced upon him by the actions of his prosecutors and a truthful statement of his own oppression, the tract also hints at the necessity of reform of the political community more widely. The very injustice of Perry's treatment at the hands of the Government is the clearest demonstration of the inseparability of the individual from the community and the need for reform of the body politic.

The individual cause wedded to the public good

Perry, like Thelwall, wedded personal testimony with a call for wider reform. While the former added to his own personal case a defence of the reputation of French citizens, the latter presented his account as 'the natural and constitutional right of Britons to annual parliaments, universal suffrage, and the freedom of popular association' as well as being a vindication of his own course of action. For Thelwall, his decision not to conduct his own defence in court was because 'the stake was not individual',[41] as he had to take into account the fate of his co-accused, but also 'the national in general'.[42] The outcome of the trials was as important for the whole country as for the indicted himself and, as Michael Scrivener has argued, 'Thelwall wanted both an acquittal and a vindication of the political movement of which he was a part'.[43] Perry also saw his own case in terms of the more general concept of 'the public good'.[44] He argued that if laws of the land were being 'perverted by arbitrary Magistrates', then it would be 'necessary that the jealousy of each citizen should be awakened to repress the dangerous encroachment, since no one member of Society can be said to be secure from the undue exercise of so dangerous a power'.[45] Perry exhorts his fellow citizens to draw upon their own sense of public duty to ensure that governments do not overstep their powers and to stifle the current ministry's tendency to wield despotic power. He highlights the way in which his case has brought to public attention the abuses within the exercise of government duties, referring to the 'unwarrantable stretch of authority'[46] demonstrated in his case, and he insists that such abusive governments will not last 'without the desired reform be [*sic*] complied with'.[47]

Not only does Perry use his own self-defence to depict the current abuses at the heart of the ruling authorities, but he also seizes upon the opportunity to defend the changes under way in France. At the time of publication, the Thermidorian Government was in the process of consolidation, and, although the sanguinary actions of the *Comité de Salut Public* had come to an end, the memory of the purge of those depicted as internal and external enemies of the Republic was still alive in Britain. The radicalisation of the revolution and the executions of the Terror had been portrayed in lively fashion in contemporary newspaper reports. In such a context, Perry's decision to vindicate the ongoing revolution in France was a bold one. He insists that his incarceration in French jails 'excited no disgust or reproach in me' and he, like others, has 'suffered unavoidably' in the 'ephemeral tyranny of men who are now no more'. As for the French people themselves, 'they are conciliating and kind, and it is no over-strained metaphor, to add that if the flame, the terrible flame which has raged with so much violence, has consumed much, it has not failed to purify that which it has left behind'.[48] In defending himself from sedition charges, Perry also attempts to revise what he saw as a popular misconception about the progress and impact of changes in France. He uses his account to vindicate the French Revolution, and even puts forward the surprisingly candid view, rare even among radical reformers of the time, that the Terror had 'purified' the nation. A defence of the French, in 1795, at a time when Britain had been engaged in war for two years and when anti-war sentiments were being voiced not only within the country at large, but also in parliamentary debate, was a subversive condemnation of the ruling ministry. It was also a stance that Charles Pigott adopted when he chose to 'boldly declare, in the presence of my country, that my fervent wishes shall be daily offered up for the success and final establishment of the FRENCH REPUBLIC'.[49] Not only does Perry, like Pigott, outline his own case and the injustice of his treatment, to illustrate the need for reform in Britain, but he brings his own country into direct comparison with France, a comparison from which Britain emerges unfavourably.

Perry goes as far as suggesting that the treatment he received at the hands of the authorities was a direct violation of the British constitutional tradition, encapsulated in the settlement concluded at the time of the Glorious Revolution. He states that his arrest 'without any Warrant whatever' was 'in defiance of the Bill of

Rights, and of the Constitution'.[50] Such an accusation would have resonated in the light of the debate over Britain's constitutional heritage which raged in the early 1790s. While Edmund Burke had lauded the settlement of 1689 as 'the cornerstone of our constitution as reinforced, explained, improved, and in its fundamental principles for ever settled',[51] Thomas Paine had denounced it as a 'bill of wrongs, and of insult',[52] arguing that it constituted no more than an elite bargain in which privilege had been shared out among those in power, with the people being given the simple right to petition but no say in matters which would have conferred on them a genuine degree of sovereignty. Perry does not enter into a discussion of the merits of the Bill of Rights, but simply shows how his own treatment was in direct violation of the principles inscribed in it. He thus calls less for an overhaul in the constitutional arrangement itself than for a reform of the abuses which undermined Britain's claims to be a nation of liberty.

Perry's stated audience is his fellow countrymen and in his tract he bypasses established legal, parliamentary and constitutional channels, penning an 'appeal' to 'the people of England'.[53] What such an appeal illustrates is firstly Perry's mistrust of ordinary processes of representation, through the existing legal apparatus, but also his reliance on the community for recognition, exoneration and financial aid. Such leapfrogging of time-honoured institutions also reveals the sympathy that Perry, like other radical reformers, harboured for more direct forms of popular involvement in the political process.

A direct appeal to the community: performing radical change

Like many radical reformers tried for political crimes, Perry had little faith in the ability of government to effectuate reform from the inside. This was partly why the form of a convention was so enticing. Perry himself made such a point in his *Historical Sketch of the French Revolution*,[54] echoing Paine who had argued that 'no government has the right to alter itself, either in whole or in part. The right, and the exercise of that right, appertains to the nation only, and the proper means is by a national convention, elected for the purpose, by all the people.'[55] Although Thelwall argued that the form of a convention did not necessarily imply that its organisers were bent on undermining the existing government, the word itself did conjure up the examples not only of the continental conventions established in revolutionary America, but of the National Convention of France. These were revolutionary councils, set up to confer on the reform of existing institutions and examine what could be set up to replace them. Despite Thelwall's contention, therefore, that to consider 'fifty or sixty such men assembled in convention' as bent on overturning the established government of Britain was 'an absurdity so monstrous' that those who thought it should be detained in Bedlam,[56] there was no denying that the choice of the term for the gatherings of reformers in Edinburgh in 1792 and 1793 was provocative. It is clear to see why such bodies fuelled the Pitt ministry's fears of tumult in Britain. Even if there was no revolutionary intent underpinning such political forums, the form of a convention appealed to radicals militating for greater involvement of the people in determining the government under which they lived.

This mistrust of the existing governmental apparatus can be detected in Perry's self-defence where he declines to appeal to his persecutors, but instead hopes to 'be restored by my Fellow Citizens to my lost rank as a freeman'.[57] Perry may have been writing his defence in preparation for an upcoming retrial after having been incarcerated on his return to Britain in 1795, and therefore had potential jury members in mind as readers. As James Epstein has pointed out, 'reformers looked to the jury to counterbalance the advantages of the legal establishment': unlike other institutions, the jury system was not seen as corrupted by the exercise of power, despite the practical reality that many juries were selectively chosen, or 'packed', by the prosecution. Epstein continues, 'Radicals inherited a pro-jury tradition of opinion dating from the seventeenth century in which the jury was seen as a representative institution whose origins were coeval with the ancient law itself.'[58] Charles Pigott expressed his faith that the members of his jury would 'judge independently for yourselves'[59] rather than be guided by the prejudices of his prosecutors. This faith is mirrored by Thomas Muir who declined to 'trouble the Court with any observations whatever, but reserve myself entirely till I come to address the jury, whom in this country I hold to be judges both of the law and the fact'.[60]

Self-defence tracts were thus designed to appeal directly to the people, whether as real or potential members of a jury in a political trial or as fellow citizens whose civic education required refining.

John Thelwall published his *Vindication* 'before the tribunal of the public' so as to ensure 'that the investigation of the principles upon which we have acted may prepare them to apprehend with greater justice the practices by which our persecutors have aimed at our destruction'.[61] There was a sense that political tracts or addresses also aimed at educating countrymen in their civic duties or at least prompting them to be more critical of the actions of their government. Perry suggests that he returned to Britain 'in the hope that my countrymen were now become qualified to judge between their real and their pretended patriots'[62] and he highlights the need for his fellow countrymen to awaken from their civic slumber and take an active role in matters directly affecting them. Radicals were quick to call upon their countrymen to renounce their apathy and take on the habits of active questioning, redefining, as they did so, the very notion of what a citizen was.[63]

Radicals also addressed their fellow countrymen as possible donors to the radical cause. Perry outlines how he was initially due to be tried before the Privy Council, but before the trial could go ahead the King's Bench had to remove the charge of outlawry he had incurred after going into exile in France. Perry was seeking financial assistance from the community to help him to overturn the verdict and uses the language of collective resistance to generate support for his cause: 'if a Member of the community loses his liberty in struggling for the common cause, he may be allowed to call upon that community to assist him in its recovery'.[64] Perry's appeal to the community to help erase his status as an outlaw was not unusual. There were frequent collections made for radical reformers and their families labouring under the weight of legal prosecutions within the LCS. This was particularly the case after the arrests of the leading delegates to the British Convention in May 1794. An informer who monitored LCS activities, known as 'Spy Metcalfe', reported in July 1794 that 'Citizen Hodgson reported that the Committee of Correspondence had paid nine guineas from the Subscription for Wives & Children &c as follows'.[65] This announcement of the contributions provided by LCS membership fees to the victims of the treason indictments is followed by the breakdown of the sums handed out to the families of the imprisoned men. Collective sums, generated from within the reform community, were often distributed to those suffering from political persecution. In a similar way, following the assault on the Tuileries and the death of those fighting in the Paris militia against the National Guard, core members of the British contingent in Paris, many of them members of the Society for Constitutional Information, led a campaign to raise funds for the families of those that had been involved in the assault. Robert Rayment and Thomas Marshall claimed to have been amongst the four instigators of the initiative to provide financial relief for the families of the killed and injured, an action which showed the depth of their affinity with the direction of the Revolution.[66] Perry was therefore not alone in expecting some pecuniary help from those who sympathised with his actions.

Yet, such direct appeals to collective aid and action were not simply pragmatic attempts to procure financial resources. Such addresses reflected the sympathy that radicals harboured for some of the more far-reaching changes being discussed and implemented across the Channel. Perry's close acquaintance from the SCI, Robert Merry, and Scottish radical and Paris resident John Oswald, both published pamphlets in late 1792 and early 1793 which set out the merits of a political system where representation would be replaced by a more direct system of democratic control, in which people gathered together in primary assemblies would take an active role in deliberating upon but also deciding on new laws.[67] Appeals to the 'tribunal of the public' in Thelwall's terms, could also be the very enactment therefore of a type of political relationship which radicals believed would correct some of the iniquities of existing structures through a heightened degree of popular consultation and decision-making.

Self-defence speeches and tracts are a useful lens through which to understand some of the departures in the British reform movement in the wake of the attempt to clamp down on expressions of criticism of the existing political and constitutional framework in the years after 1792. While some reformers withdrew from engagement in political activity, others were drawn to ultra-radical underground organisations such as the United Britons or, like John Thelwall and Sampson Perry, used the form of the historical account to suggest the need for reform. Self-defences were another medium which was employed, not only to show the iniquity of official reactions to individual reformers, but to highlight how individual cases of persecution could not be divorced from the well-being of the community at large. In their form – direct appeals to the people of England – they can also be seen as a performance of the very changes that reformers hoped to see enacted within society. These included universal suffrage, direct forms of democratic decision-making and an end to the injustice inscribed in the legal system. In wedding cases of individual injustice to the fate of the national community, self-defences could act therefore as one way of perpetuating a culture of opposition at a time when the reform agenda had been severely curtailed by the repressive actions of both the ruling authorities and the loyalist associational movement.

Notes

1 For more on the development of club culture see Peter Clark, *British Clubs and Societies 1580–1800: The Origins of an Associational World* (Oxford: Oxford University Press, 2000) and Valérie Capdeville, *L'Âge d'or des clubs londoniens (1730–1784)* (Paris: Honoré Champion, 2008).
2 Mary Thale (ed.), *Selections from the Papers of the London Corresponding Society, 1792–1799* (Cambridge: Cambridge University Press, 1983), p. 23.
3 Charles Pigott, *Persecution: The Case of Charles Pigott* (London: Eaton, 1793), p. 9.
4 John Thelwall, *The Natural and Constitutional Right of Britons to Annual Parliaments, Universal Suffrage, and the Freedom of Popular Association: Being an indication of the Motives and Political Conduct of John Thelwall, and of the London Corresponding Society* (London: Printed for the Author, 1795), p. 19.
5 The National Archive, HO 42/26, no. 701.
6 Pigott, *Persecution*, pp. 51–2.
7 Thomas Paine, 'A Letter Addressed to the Addressers', *The Complete Writings of Thomas Paine*, ed. Philip S. Foner (New York: Citadel, 1945), vol. 2, p. 477.
8 Thomas Spence, *The Case of Thomas Spence, Bookseller* (London: T. Spence, 1792), p. 4.
9 For further details on Muir's trial and the case of the Scottish Jacobins, see J. Epstein, '"Our Real Constitution": Trial Defence and Radical Memory in the Age of Revolution', in James Vernon (ed.), *Re-reading the Constitution: New Narratives in the Political History of England's Long Nineteenth Century* (Cambridge: Cambridge University Press, 1996). See in particular pages 32–3 for an account of Muir's case.
10 Thelwall, *The Natural and Constitutional Right of Britons*, p. 93.
11 Sampson Perry, *Oppression!!!: The Appeal of Captain Perry, Late Editor of the Argus, to the People of England* (London: Citizen Lee, 1795), p. 13.

12 The 'Two Acts' banned political lecturing (Treasonable and Seditious Practices Act) and public meetings attended by more than fifty people, unless they had been authorised by a local magistrate (Seditious Meetings Act). Such legislation was effectively an attempt to repress the public and open nature of the radical reform movement in the 1790s yet in reality very few actual prosecutions were brought against radical leaders. For more on the impact of the Two Acts see John Barrell, *Imagining the King's Death: Figurative Treason, Fantasies of Regicide, 1793–1796* (Oxford: Oxford University Press, 2000).

13 See Ian McCalman, 'Newgate in Revolution: Radical Enthusiasm and Romantic Counterculture', *Eighteenth-Century Life*, 99 (Feb. 1998), 95–110. Perry's work is, in my view, an example of what historian Ian McCalman has termed 'the paradoxical outcome of the unfreedom of Newgate'.

14 The Society of Loyal Britons agreed that 'The English Government hath for ages been the admiration of all Europe, its Constitution being so happily founded in Wisdom, Justice, Equity, and Humanity, that from the Influence, Purity, and Mildness of its Laws, the Prince and the Peasant enjoy equally the Protection of this invaluable Blessing. The French Nation in particular, hath, from time immemorial, looked upon England, as the only Nation that enjoys pure and genuine Liberty, with envy and disgust.' The National Archive, HO 42/26, no. 701.

15 Spence, *The Case of Thomas Spence*, p. 7.
16 Pigott, *Persecution*, p. 2.
17 Thelwall, *The Natural and Constitutional Right of Britons*, p. 17.
18 *Ibid.*, p. 13.
19 Perry, *Oppression*, p. 9.
20 *Ibid.*
21 Mary Bunch, 'Outlawry and the Experience of the (Im)possible: Deconstructing Biopolitics', Unpublished Ph.D. dissertation (University of Western Ontario, Canada, 2010), p. 1. Outlawry was officially eradicated as a legal category in England in 1879. Early pronouncements of outlawry were accompanied by the Latin phrase, *caput gerat lupinum* ('may he bear a wolf's head'). Not only was the recipient of the writ of outlawry formally proscribed by law, but he was also considered inhuman, literally an animal who could be hounded to death.
22 *The Evening Mail*, 15–17 June 1791.
23 Perry, *Oppression*, p. 6.
24 *Ibid.*, p. 7.
25 *Ibid.*, p. 11.
26 *Ibid.*, pp. 4–5.
27 *Ibid.*, p. 5.
28 *Ibid.*, p. 7.

29 Pigott, *Persecution*, p. 23. Original emphasis.
30 Perry, *Oppression*, p. 7.
31 Thelwall, *The Natural and Constitutional Right of Britons*, p. 12.
32 Pigott, *Persecution*, p. 15.
33 This expression was used by the defence attorney, Sergeant Adair, in the trial of William Stone, brother of British national and Paris resident John Hurford Stone in his trial in 1796. See the trial proceedings in T. B. Howell and T. J. Howell, *A Complete Collection of State Trials* (London: Longman, Hurst, Rees, Orme and Brown, 1816–28), vol. 25, p. 1339.
34 William Playfair, *The History of Jacobinism: Its Crimes, Cruelties and Perfidies* (Philadelphia: Cobbett, 1796), vol. 1, p. 320.
35 Hannah More, *Village Politics: Addressed to all the Mechanics, Journeymen, and Day-Labourers, in Great Britain* (York: Walker, 1793), p. 15.
36 Perry, *Oppression*, p. 3.
37 *Ibid.*, p. 4.
38 Michael Davies, '"Meet, Sing, and Your Chains Will Drop Off Like Burnt Thread": The Political Songs of Thomas Spence', in Alastair Bonnet and Keith Armstrong (eds), *Thomas Spence: The Poor Man's Revolutionary* (London: Breviary Stuff, 2014), p. 117.
39 *Dictionary of National Biography* (London: Smith, Elder and Co), vol. 17 (1885–1900), p. 118. Thomas Spence named his vision of a utopian society after himself in *The Constitution of Spensonia* (London, 1803).
40 Perry, *Oppression*, p. 4.
41 Thelwall, *The Natural and Constitutional Right of Britons*, p. iv.
42 *Ibid.*, p. iii.
43 Michael Scrivener, *Seditious Allegories: John Thelwall & Jacobin Writing* (University Park, PA: Pennsylvania State University Press, 2001), p. 173.
44 Perry, *Oppression*, p. 4.
45 *Ibid.*, p. 5.
46 *Ibid.*, p. 5
47 *Ibid.*, p. 7.
48 *Ibid.*, p. 10.
49 Pigott, *Persecution*, p. 26.
50 Perry, *Oppression*, p. 12.
51 Edmund Burke, *Reflections on the Revolution in France*, ed. L. G. Mitchell (Oxford: Oxford University Press, 2003), pp. 16–17.
52 Thomas Paine, *Rights of Man* [1791; 1792], ed. Eric Foner (Harmondsworth: Penguin, 1984), p. 193.
53 Perry, *Oppression*, p. 1.

54 Sampson Perry, *An Historical Sketch of the French Revolution: Commencing with Its Predisposing Causes, and Carried on to the Acceptation of the Constitution, in 1795* (London: Symonds, 1796), vol. 1, p. 20.
55 Paine, 'Letter Addressed to the Addressers', *The Complete Writings of Thomas Paine*, ed. Foner, vol. 2, p. 477.
56 Thelwall, *The Natural and Constitutional Right of Britons*, p. 17.
57 Perry, *Oppression*, p. 5.
58 James Epstein, *Radical Expression: Political Language, Ritual, and Symbol in England, 1790–1850* (Oxford: Oxford University Press, 1994), p. 33.
59 Pigott, *Persecution*, p. 24.
60 Howell *et al.*, *A Complete Collection of State Trials*, vol. 23, p. 129.
61 Thelwall, *The Natural and Constitutional Right of Britons*, p. iii.
62 Perry, *Oppression*, p. 10.
63 I spoke at length on British radicals' definitions of citizenship at the conference on 'British Conceptions of Citizenship' in Toulouse, organised jointly by the CAS research centre and CRECIB in April 2014. The papers have since been published in the *Revue Française de Civilisation Britannique*. See Rachel Rogers, '"The definition of a virtuous man": British Radicals' Views of Citizens and Citizenship in the French Revolutionary Era', *Revue Française de Civilisation Britannique* [Online], XXI-1 2016, OpenEdition, doi: 10.4000/rfcb.921, accessed 4 April 2017.
64 Perry, *Oppression*, p. 12.
65 Cited in Thale, *Papers of the London Corresponding Society*, p. 199.
66 See the prison file of Robert Rayment in the Archives Nationales, Paris, F7 4774 88.
67 See Robert Merry, *Réflexions politiques sur la nouvelle Constitution qui se prépare en France, adressées à la République* (Paris: Reyner, 1792) and John Oswald, *The Government of the People, or a Sketch of a Constitution for the Universal Commonwealth* (Paris: The English Press, 1792).

Bibliography

Primary sources

Addison, Joseph and Richard Steele. *The Spectator*. Donald F. Bond (ed.), 5 vols. Oxford: Clarendon Press, 1965; 1987.

Aristotle. *The Complete Works of Aristotle*. Jonathan Barnes (ed.), vol. 2. Princeton, NJ: Princeton University Press, 1984.

Barrow, Isaac. *The Theological Works Of Isaac Barrow, D.D., Master Of Trinity College, Cambridge*. The Rev. Alexander Napier, M.A., Trinity College, Cambridge, Vicar of Holkham, Norfolk (ed.), 9 vols. Cambridge: Cambridge University Press, 1859.

Blake, William. *The Complete Poetry and Prose of William Blake*. David Erdman (ed.), 2nd edn. Berkeley, CA: University of California Press, 1982.

Boswell, James. *Boswell Laird of Auchinleck 1778-1782*. Joseph W. Reed and Frederick Pottle (eds). Edinburgh: Edinburgh University Press, 1993.

— *Boswell on the Grand Tour, Germany and Switzerland, 1764*. F. A. Pottle (ed.). London: Heinemann, 1953.

— *Boswell on the Grand Tour, Italy, Corsica and France, 1765-1766*. Frank Brady and F. A. Pottle (eds). London: Heinemann, 1955.

— *Boswell's Column 1777-1783*. Margery Bailey (ed.). London: William Kimber, 1951.

— *Boswell's London Journal 1762-1763*. F. A. Pottle (ed.). Harmondsworth: Penguin, 1966.

— *Boswell: The Ominous Years, 1774-1776*. Charles Ryskamp and F. A. Pottle (eds). New York: Heinemann, 1963.

— *Life of Johnson*. R. W. Chapman and Pat Rogers (eds). Oxford: Oxford University Press, 1953, 1980 edn.

Burke, Edmund. *A Philosophical Enquiry into the Origin of our Ideas of the Sublime and the Beautiful, and Other Pre-Revolutionary Writings*. David Womersley (ed.). London: Penguin Books, 2004.

— *Reflections on the Revolution in France*. L. G. Mitchell (ed.). Oxford: Oxford University Press, 2003.

Butler, Joseph. *The Analogy of Religion Natural and Revealed to the Constitution and Course of Nature*. W. E. Gladstone (ed.). Oxford: Clarendon Press, 1896. Facsimile edition, *The Works of Joseph Butler*, vol. 1. Bristol: Thoemmes Press, 1995.

Descartes, René. *Les passions de l'âme*. François d'Arcy (ed.). Paris: Garnier Flammarion, 1998.

— *Œuvres philosophiques*, tome III: 1643–1650. Ferdinand Alquié and Denis Moreau (eds). Paris: Classiques Garnier, 2010.

Du Plaisir. *Sentiments sur les lettres et sur l'histoire avec des scrupules sur le style*. Philippe Hourcade (ed.). Genève: Droz, 1975.

Evelyn, John. *Memoirs of John Evelyn …: comprising his diary, from 1641–1705-6, and a selection of his familiar letters, to which is subjoined, the private correspondence between King Charles I and Sir Edward Nicholas; also between Sir Edward Hyde, afterwards Earl of Clarendon, and Sir Richard Browne, ambassador to the Court of France, in the time of King Charles I and the usurpation*. H. Colburn (ed.), vol. 3. London, 1827.

— *The Diary of John Evelyn*. E. S. De Beer (ed.), vol. 3. Oxford: Clarendon Press, 1955.

Fielding, Henry. *An Apology for the Life of Mrs. Shamela Andrews in The journal of a voyage to Lisbon, Shamela, and Occasional Writings*. Martin C. Battestin (ed.). Oxford: Clarendon Press, 2008.

Haywood, Eliza Fowler. *Love in Excess, Or, The Fatal Enquiry*. David Oakleaf (ed.). Peterborough, Ontario: Broadview Press, 2000.

— *Reflections on the Various Effects of Love* […]. London: Printed for N. Dobb, 1726.

Howell, Thomas B. and T. J. Howell. *A Complete Collection of State Trials*, vols 23 & 25. London: Longman, Hurst, Rees, Orme and Brown, 1816–28.

Hume, David. *An Enquiry Concerning Human Understanding*. Peter Millican (ed.). Oxford: Oxford University Press, 2007.

— *An Enquiry Concerning the Principles of Morals: A Critical Edition*. Tom L. Beauchamp (ed.). Oxford; New York: Oxford University Press, 2006.

— *A Treatise of Human Nature*. David Fate Norton and Mary J. Norton (eds). Oxford: Oxford University Press, 2009.

— *A Treatise of Human Nature*. L. A. Selby-Bigge (ed.); 2nd edn, P. H. Nidditch (ed.). Oxford: Clarendon Press, 1978.
Hutcheson, Francis. *An Essay on the Nature and Conduct of the Passions and Affections*. London: John Darby and Thomas Browne, 1728.
— *An Inquiry into the Original of our Ideas of Beauty and Virtue*. London: John Darby, 1725.
Johnson, Samuel. *A Dictionary of the English Language*. London: Johnson, Dilly et al., 1755, 1799 edn.
— 'Diaries and Prayers', in Allan Ingram (ed.), *Patterns of Madness in the Eighteenth Century: A Reader*. Liverpool: Liverpool University Press, 1998, pp. 107–11.
— *Dr Johnson on Shakespeare*. W. K. Wimsatt (ed.). Harmondsworth: Penguin, 1969.
— *Johnson on Shakespeare*. Arthur Sherbo (ed.), *The Yale Edition of the Works of Samuel Johnson*, vols 7 and 8. New Haven, CT and London: Yale University Press, 1968.
— *Rasselas, Prince of Abissinia*. J. P. Hardy (ed.). Oxford: Oxford University Press, 1968.
— *The Rambler*. 3 vols. London: C. & J. Rivington et al., 1823.
Kant, Immanuel. *Kritik der Ästhetischen Urtheilskraft: Werke in sechs Bänden*. Vol. 4. Köln: Könemann, 1995.
— *Observations on the Feeling of the Beautiful and the Sublime*. Trans. J. Goldthwait. Berkeley, CA: University of California Press, 1960.
— *The Critique of Judgement*. Trans. James Creed Meredith. Oxford: Clarendon Press, 1991.
Keats, John. *The Letters of John Keats, 1814–1821*. Hyder Edward Rollins (ed.), 2 vols. Cambridge, MA: Harvard University Press, 1958.
Kierkegaard, Søren. *Concluding Unscientific Postscript to Philosophical Fragments*. Trans. Howard V. Hong and Edna H. Hong. Princeton, NJ: Princeton University Press, 1992.
— *The Sickness Unto Death*. Trans. Howard V. Hong and Edna H. Hong. Princeton, NJ: Princeton University Press, 1980.
Killigrew, Anne. *'My Rare Wit Killing Sin': Poems of a Restoration Courtier*. Margaret J. M. Ezell (ed.). Toronto: Iter and Centre for Reformation and Renaissance Studies, 2013.
— *Poems*. Richard Morton (ed.). Gainesville, FL: Scholars' Facsimiles and Reprints, 1967.
La Fayette, Marie-Madeleine Pioche de La Vergne. *Romans et nouvelles*. Alain Niderst (ed.). Paris: Bordas, 1990.
Locke, John. *An Essay Concerning Human Understanding*. Peter H. Nidditch (ed.). Oxford: Clarendon Press, 1979.
Malebranche, Nicolas. *De la recherche de la vérité*. Jean-Christophe Bardout (ed.), 3 vols. Paris: Vrin, 2006.

— *Œuvres*. Geneviève Rodis-Lewis and Germain Malbreil (eds), vol 1. Paris: Gallimard, 1979.
Mandeville, Bernard. *The Fable of the Bees*. Phillip Harth (ed.). Harmondsworth: Penguin Books, 1970.
Marivaux, Pierre Carlet de Chamblain de. *Journaux et œuvres diverses*. Frédéric Deloffre and Michel Gilot (eds). Paris: Garnier frères, 1969.
Milton, John. *Paradise Lost*. Christopher Ricks (ed.). London: Penguin Books, 1989.
More, Hannah. *Village Politics: Addressed to all the Mechanics, Journeymen, and Day-Labourers, in Great Britain*. York: Walker, 1793.
Paine, Thomas. *Rights of Man* [1791; 1792]. Eric Foner (ed.). Harmondsworth: Penguin Books, 1984.
Pepys, Samuel. *The Diary of Samuel Pepys*. R. Latham and W. Matthews (eds), vol. 7. Oxford: Oxford University Press, 2000.
Perry, Sampson. *Oppression!!!: The Appeal of Captain Perry, Late Editor of the Argus, to the People of England*. London: Citizen Lee, 1795.
Pigott, Charles. *Persecution: The Case of Charles Pigott*. London: Eaton, 1793.
Plato. *Complete Works*. John Cooper (ed.). Indianapolis, IN and Cambridge, MA: Hackett, 1997.
— *Republic*. Trans. Robin Waterfield. Oxford and New York: Oxford University Press, 1993.
Playfair, William. *The History of Jacobinism: Its Crimes, Cruelties and Perfidies*. Philadelphia: Cobbett, 1796.
Pope, Alexander. *An Essay on Man*. Maynard Mack (ed.), Twickenham edition, vol. III, 1. London: Routledge, 1993.
— *An Essay on Man*. Tom Jones (ed.). Princeton, NJ: Princeton University Press, 2016.
— *The Art of Sinking in Poetry: Martinus Scriblerus' Peri Bathous: A Critical Edition*. Edna Leake Steeves (ed.). New York: Russell and Russell, 1952.
— *The Correspondence of Alexander Pope*. George Sherburn (ed.), 5 vols. Oxford: Clarendon Press, 1956.
— *The Dunciad*. James Sutherland (ed.), Twickenham edition, vol. V. London: Methuen, 1943.
— *The Dunciad in Four Books*. Valerie Rumbold (ed.), rev. edn. Harlow: Longman, 2009.
— *The Prose Works of Alexander Pope*. Norman Ault and Rosemary Cowler (eds), 2 vols. Oxford: Basil Blackwell, 1936–68.
Reid, Thomas. *Essays on the Intellectual Powers of Man* [1785]. Derek R. Brookes (ed.), intro. Knud Haakonssen. Edinburgh: Edinburgh University Press, 2002.

Richardson, Samuel. *Pamela; or, Virtue Rewarded*. Peter Sabor (ed.). Harmondsworth: Penguin Books, 1980.

— *Pamela; or, Virtue Rewarded*. Thomas Keymer and Alice Wakely (eds). Oxford: Oxford University Press, 2001.

Schopenhauer, Arthur. *Essays and Aphorisms*. Trans. R. J. Hollingdale. London: Penguin Books, 1970.

Shaftesbury, Anthony Ashley Cooper (the Third Earl of). *Characteristics of Men, Manners, Opinions, Times*. Lawrence E. Klein (ed.). Cambridge: Cambridge University Press, 1999.

Smith, Adam. *An Inquiry into the Nature and Causes of the Wealth of Nations*. Edwin Cannan (ed.), 5th edn. London: Methuen & Co., 1904.

— *The Theory of Moral Sentiments*. Knud Haakonssen (ed.). Cambridge: Cambridge University Press, 2002.

— *The Theory of Moral Sentiments*. Ryan Patrick Hanley (ed.). London: Penguin Books, 2009.

Spence, Thomas. *The Case of Thomas Spence, Bookseller*. London, 1792.

Sterne, Laurence. *The Life and Opinions of Tristram Shandy, Gentleman*. Melvyn New and Joan New (eds). Gainesville, FL: University Presses of Florida, 1978.

— *The Sermons of Laurence Sterne*. Melvyn New (ed.). Gainesville, FL: University Presses of Florida, 1996.

Thale, Mary (ed.). *Selections from the Papers of the London Corresponding Society, 1792–1799*. Cambridge: Cambridge University Press, 1983.

Thelwall, John. *The Natural and Constitutional Right of Britons to Annual Parliaments, Universal Suffrage, and the Freedom of Popular Association: Being a Vindication of the Motives and Political Conduct of John Thelwall, and of the London Corresponding Society*. London: Printed for the author, 1795.

Tillotson, John. Lord Archbishop of Canterbury. *The Works of the Most Reverend John Tillotson ... In Twelve Volumes: Containing Two Hundred And Fifty Four Sermons And Discourses On Several Occasions*, etc. London: Printed for R. Ware, A. Ward, J. and P. Knapton *et al*. London: 1743.

Villedieu, Madame de, Marie-Catherine Desjardins, *Annales galantes de Grece*. La Haye: Chez Adrian Moetjens, 1688.

Ward, Ned. *The London Spy*. Arthur Hayward (ed.). London: Cassell, 1927.

Wordsworth, William. *Wordsworth's Poetry and Prose*. Nicholas Halmi (ed.). New York: Norton, 2014.

— *The Prelude: 1799, 1805, 1850*. Jonathan Wordsworth, M. H. Abrams and Stephen Gill (eds). New York and London: Norton, 1979.

Secondary sources

Abrams, M. H. *Natural Supernaturalism: Tradition and Revolution in Romantic Literature*. London: Oxford University Press; New York: W. W. Norton & Company, 1971.

— and E. Talbot Donaldson *et al.* (eds). *The Norton Anthology of English Literature*. Vol. 1. New York and London: Norton & Company, 1986.

Aers, David (ed.). *Culture and History 1350–1600*. New York; London; Toronto: Harvester Wheatsheaf, 1992.

Ainslie, George. *Breakdown of Will*. Cambridge: Cambridge University Press, 2001.

Allison, Henry E. 'Locke's Theory of Personal Identity: A Re-Examination', *Journal of the History of Ideas*, 27:1 (Jan.–March 1966), 41–58.

Andreadis, Harriette. *Early Modern England, Female Same-Sex Literary Erotics 1550–1714*. Chicago and London: University of Chicago Press, 2001.

Ashfield, Andrew and Peter de Bolla (eds). *The Sublime: A Reader in British Eighteenth-Century Aesthetic Theory*. Cambridge: Cambridge University Press, 1998.

Atherton, Margaret. 'Locke's Theory of Personal Identity', *Midwest Studies in Philosophy*, 8:1 (Sept. 1983), 273–93.

Babb, Lawrence. 'The Cave of Spleen', *The Review of English Studies*, 12 (1936), 165–76.

Bachelard, Gaston. *The Poetics of Space* [1957]. Trans. Maria Jolas. Boston, MA: Beacon Press, 1994.

Bakhtin, Mikhail M. *The Dialogic Imagination: Four Essays*. Austin, TX: University of Texas Press, 1981.

Balibar, Étienne (ed.). *John Locke: Identité et différence. L'invention de la conscience*. Paris: Seuil, 1998.

Ballaster, Ros. 'Performing *Roxane*: The Oriental Woman as the Sign of Luxury in Eighteenth-Century Fictions', in Maxine Berg and Elizabeth Eger (eds), *Luxury in the Eighteenth Century: Debates, Desires and Delectable Goods*. Basingstoke: Palgrave, 2002, pp. 165–77.

— *Seductive Forms: Women's Amatory Fiction from 1684 to 1740*. Oxford: Oxford University Press, 1992.

Barash, Carol. *English Women's Poetry, 1649–1714: Politics, Community, and Linguistic Authority*. Oxford: Clarendon Press, 1996.

Barrell, John. *Imagining the King's Death: Figurative Treason, Fantasies of Regicide, 1793–1796*. Oxford: Oxford University Press, 2000.

Beauclerk, Charles. *Nell Gwyn: Mistress to a King*. New York: Grove Press, 2006.

Beer, Gillian. '*Pamela*: Rethinking *Arcadia*', in Margaret Anne Doody and Peter Sabor (eds), *Samuel Richardson: Tercentenary Essays*. Cambridge: Cambridge University Press, 1989, pp. 23–39.

Bony, Alain. 'Philosophie et discours littéraire: identité personnelle et conscience de soi chez Hume et dans l'essai périodique', in Robert Ellrodt (ed.), *Genèse de la Conscience Moderne: Études sur le développement de la conscience de soi dans les littératures du monde occidental*. Paris: Presse Universitaires de France, 1983, pp. 182–92.

Brewer, John. *The Pleasures of the Imagination: English Culture in the Eighteenth Century*. London: Harper Collins, 1997.

Bronson, Bertrand H. 'Johnson Agonistes', in *Johnson Agonistes and Other Essays*. Cambridge: Cambridge University Press, 1946, repr. 2012.

Brooks-Davies, Douglas. *Pope's* Dunciad *and the Queen of Night: A Study in Emotional Jacobitism*. Manchester: Manchester University Press, 1985.

Brower, Reuben Arthur. *Alexander Pope: The Poetry of Allusion*. Oxford: Clarendon Press, 1959.

Burkert, Walter. *Ancient Mystery Cults*. Cambridge, MA: Harvard University Press, 1987.

Butler, Janet. 'The Garden: Early Symbol of Clarissa's Complicity', *Studies in English Literature*, 24 (1984), 527–44.

Carraud, Vincent. *L'invention du moi*. Paris, Presses Universitaires de France, 2010.

Castle, Terry J. 'P/B: *Pamela* as Sexual Fiction'. *Studies in English Literature*, 22 (1982), 469–89.

Cazzato, Luigi. '*Tristram Shandy* and the Epistemology of the Hobby-Horse', *Textus*, 16:2 (2003), 213–32.

Clark, Peter. *British Clubs and Societies 1580–1800: The Origins of an Associational World*. Oxford: Oxford University Press, 2000.

Clingham, Greg (ed.). *New Light on Boswell: Critical and Historical Essays on the Occasion of the Bicentenary of* The Life of Johnson. Cambridge: Cambridge University Press, 1991.

Courcelle, Pierre. 'Le Corps-Tombeau', *Revue des études anciennes*, 68 (1966), 101–22.

—— 'Tradition platonicienne et tradition chrétienne du corps-prison', *Revue des études latines* (1965), 406–43.

Cox, Stephen D. *'The Stranger Within Thee': Concepts of the Self in Late-Eighteenth-Century Literature*. Pittsburgh: University of Pittsburgh Press, 1980.

Crane, R. S. 'Suggestions Toward A Genealogy of the "Man of Feeling"', *English Literary History*, 1:3 (Dec. 1934), 205–30.

Crowther, Paul. *The Kantian Sublime*. Oxford: Clarendon Press, 1989.

Davidoff, Leonore and Catherine Hall. *Family Fortunes: Men and Women of the English Middle-Class, 1780–1850*. London; Melbourne; Sydney: Hutchinson, 1987.

Davis, Michael. '"Meet, Sing, and Your Chains Will Drop Off Like Burnt Thread": The Political Songs of Thomas Spence', in Alastair Bonnet and Keith Armstrong (eds), *Thomas Spence: The Poor Man's Revolutionary*. London: Breviary Stuff, 2014, pp. 109–25.

de Man, Paul. *Aesthetic Ideology*. Minneapolis: University of Minnesota Press, 1996.

Deutsch, Helen. *Resemblance and Disgrace: Alexander Pope and the Deformation of Culture*. Cambridge, MA: Harvard University Press, 1996.

Doody, Margaret A. *A Natural Passion: A Study of the Novels of Samuel Richardson*. Oxford: Clarendon, 1974.

— 'Introduction', in Samuel Richardson, *Pamela; or, Virtue Rewarded*. Peter Sabor (ed.). London: Penguin, 1980; 1985 (repr.), pp. 7–22.

Douglas, Mary. *Purity and Danger: An Analysis of Concepts of Pollution and Taboo*. London: Routledge & Kegan Paul, 1966.

Drury, Joseph. 'Haywood's Thinking Machines', *Eighteenth Century Fiction*, 21:2 (Winter 2009), 201–28.

Edwards, Thomas R., Jr. *This Dark Estate: A Reading of Pope*. Berkeley, CA: University of California Press, 1963.

Ellrodt, Robert (ed.). *Genèse de la conscience moderne. Études sur le développement de la conscience de soi dans les littératures du monde occidental*. Paris: Presses Universitaires de France, 1983.

— *Montaigne et Shakespeare: L'émergence de la conscience moderne*. Paris: José Corti, 2011.

— *Montaigne and Shakespeare: The Emergence of Modern Self-Consciousness*. Manchester: Manchester University Press, 2015.

— *Seven Metaphysical Poets: A Structural Study of the Unchanging Self*. Oxford: Oxford University Press, 2000.

Engell, James. *The Creative Imagination: Enlightenment to Romanticism*. Cambridge, MA: Harvard University Press, 1981.

Epstein, James. '"Our Real Constitution": Trial Defence and Radical Memory in the Age of Revolution', in James Vernon (ed.). *Re-reading the Constitution: New Narratives in the Political History of England's Long Nineteenth Century*. Cambridge: Cambridge University Press, 1996, pp. 22–51.

— *Radical Expression: Political Language, Ritual, and Symbol in England, 1790–1850*. Oxford: Oxford University Press, 1994.

Etlin, Richard A. 'Architecture and the Sublime', in Timothy M. Costelloe (ed.), *The Sublime from Antiquity to the Present*. Cambridge: Cambridge University Press, 2012, pp. 230–73.

Evans, James E. '"The Splendour of Our Golden Age": The Duchess of Mazarin and Epicurean Voluptuousness in Late Stuart England', *1650–1850 Ideas, Aesthetics, and Inquiries in the Early Modern Era*, 19 (2012), 45–62.
Faulkner, Thomas C. and Rhonda S. Blair. 'The Classical and Mythographic Sources of Pope's Dulness', *Huntington Library Quarterly*, 43:3 (1979–80), 213–46.
Ferguson, Frances. *Solitude and the Sublime: Romanticism and the Aesthetics of Individuation*. New York and London: Routledge, 1992.
Ferraro, Julian D. 'Crowds and Power and Pope', *The Review of English Studies*, 63:262 (2012), 779–96.
Fisher, Philip. *The Vehement Passions*. Princeton, NJ: Princeton University Press, 2002.
Flesch, William. *Comeuppance: Costly Signaling, Altruistic Punishment, and Other Biological Components of Fiction*. Cambridge, MA: Harvard University Press, 2008.
— 'Hyperbolic Discounting and Intertemporal Bargaining', in Jason Potts and Daniel Stout (eds), *Theory Aside*. Durham, NC: Duke University Press, 2014, pp. 199–217.
Fox, Christopher (ed.). *Locke and the Scriblerians: Identity and Consciousness in Early Eighteenth-Century Britain*. Berkeley, CA; London: University of California Press, 1988.
Francus, Marilyn. 'The Monstrous Mother: Reproductive Anxiety in Swift and Pope', *English Literary History*, 61:4 (Winter 1994), 829–51.
Gasché, Rodolphe. '... And the Beautiful? Revisiting Edmund Burke's "Double Aesthetics"', in Timothy M. Costelloe (ed.), *The Sublime from Antiquity to the Present*. Cambridge: Cambridge University Press, 2012, pp. 24–36.
Gee, Sophie. *Making Waste: Leftovers and the Eighteenth-Century Imagination*. Princeton, NJ: Princeton University Press, 2010.
Giles, Heidi. 'Resolving the Institution of Marriage in Eighteenth-Century Courtship Novels', *Rocky Mountain Review*, 66.1 (2012), 76–82.
Goldberg, Rita. 'Charity Sermons and The Poor: A Rhetoric of Compassion', *The Age of Johnson*, 4 (1991), pp. 171–216.
Golden, Morris. 'Public Context and Imagining Self in *Pamela* and *Shamela*', *English Literary Studies*, 53.2 (1986), 311–29.
Gregori, Flavio. *Il wit nel* Tristram Shandy: *totalità e dialogo*. Rome: Edizioni dell'Ateneo, 1987.
Gregory, Jeremy. 'Religion: Faith in the Age of Reason', *Journal for Eighteenth-Century Studies*, 34:4 (Dec. 2011), 435–44.
Griffin, Martin I. J. *Latitudinarianism in the Seventeenth-Century Church of England*. Leiden; New York; Köln: Brill, 1992.

Gubar, Susan. 'The Female Monster in Augustan Satire', *Signs*, 3 (1977), 380–94.
Gustafsson, Johan E. 'Did Locke Defend the Memory Continuity Criterion of Personal Identity?', *Locke Studies*, 10 (2010), 113–29.
Gutiérrez Sumillera, Rocío. 'Tristram's Identity Revisited', *Babel-Afial*, 17 (2008), 77–98.
Harris, Tim. 'Scott [formerly Crofts], James, duke of Monmouth and first duke of Buccleuch (1649–1685)'. *Oxford Dictionary of National Biography*. Oxford: Oxford University Press. Online edn www.oxforddnb.com, accessed 25 April 2013.
Harvey, David. *A Brief History of Neoliberalism*. Oxford: Oxford University Press, 2005.
Herman, Peter C. *Destabilizing Milton: Paradise Lost and the Poetics of Incertitude*. Basingstoke: Palgrave Macmillan, 2005.
Hertz, Neil. *The End of the Line: Essays on Psychoanalysis and the Sublime*. New York: Columbia University Press, 1985.
Hess, Scott. *Authoring the Self: Self-Representation, Authorship, and the Print Market in British Poetry from Pope through Wordsworth*. New York and London: Routledge, 2005.
Hill, Christopher. *The Century of Revolution*. Walton-on-Thames: Nelson, 1961; 1980.
Hipple, Walter John, Jr. *The Beautiful, the Sublime, and the Picturesque in Eighteenth-Century British Aesthetic Theory*. Carbondale, IL: Southern Illinois University Press, 1957.
Hirschman, Albert O. *The Passions and the Interests: Political Arguments for Capitalism before Its Triumph*. Princeton, NJ: Princeton University Press, 1977.
Hundert, E. J. 'The European Enlightenment and the History of the Self', in Roy Porter (ed.), *Rewriting the Self: Histories from the Renaissance to the Present*. London: Routledge, 1997, pp. 72–83.
Ingram, Allan (ed.). *Patterns of Madness in the Eighteenth Century: A Reader*. Liverpool: Liverpool University Press, 1998.
Ingrassia, Catherine. 'Women Writing/Writing Women: Pope, Dulness and 'Feminization' in *The Dunciad*', *Eighteenth Century Life*, 14:3 (1990), 40–58.
James, Susan. *Passion and Action: The Emotions in Seventeenth-Century Philosophy*. Oxford: Oxford University Press, 2003.
James, William. *The Principles of Psychology*. New York: Henry Holt, 1908.
Jonas, Hans. *The Gnostic Religion*. 2nd edn. Boston, MA: Beacon Press, 1963.
Kettering, Sharon. 'Brokerage in the Court of Louis XIV', *The Historical Journal*, 36 (1993), 69–87.

Keymer, Thomas. 'Assorted Versions of Assaulted Virgins; or: Textual Instability and Teaching', in Lisa Zunshine and Jocelyn Harris (eds), *Approaches to Teaching the Novels of Samuel Richardson*. New York: Modern Language Association, 2006, pp. 24–31.
— *Richardson's Clarissa and the Eighteenth-Century Reader*. Cambridge: Cambridge University Press, 1992.
— and Peter Sabor. Pamela *in the Marketplace: Literary Controversy and Print Culture in Eighteenth-Century Britain and Ireland*. Cambridge: Cambridge University Press, 2005.
King, Kathryn R. *A Political Biography of Eliza Haywood*. London: Pickering & Chatto Publishers, 2012.
Klein, Lawrence E. *Shaftesbury and the Culture of Politeness: Moral Discourse and Cultural Politics in Early Eighteenth-Century England*. Cambridge: Cambridge University Press, 1994.
Klein, Melanie. 'The Sense of Loneliness', *Envy and Gratitude*. New York: Simon and Schuster, 2009, pp. 300–13.
Knapp, Steven. *Personification and the Sublime, Milton to Coleridge*. Cambridge, MA: Harvard University Press, 1985.
Kramnick, Jonathan Brody. 'Locke, Haywood, and Consent', *English Literary History*, 72:2 (2005), 453–70.
Kristeva, Julia. *Powers of Horror: An Essay on Abjection*. Trans. Leon S. Roudiez. New York: Columbia University Press, 1982.
Latimer, Bonnie. *Making Gender, Culture, and the Self in the Fiction of Samuel Richardson: The Novel Individual*. Farnham: Ashgate, 2013.
Lawlor, Clark. 'Poetry and Science', in Christine Gerrard (ed.), *Blackwell Companion to Eighteenth-Century Poetry*. Oxford: Blackwell, 2006, pp. 38–52.
Le Tellier, Robert Ignatius. *The English Novel, 1660–1700: An Annotated Bibliography*. Westport, CT: Greenwood Press, 1997.
Linker, Laura. *Dangerous Women, Libertine Epicures, and the Rise of Sensibility, 1670–1730*. Burlington, VT: Ashgate. 2011.
Lipsedge, Karen. 'A Place of Refuge, Seduction or Danger?: The Representation of the Ivy Summer-House in Samuel Richardson's *Clarissa*', *Journal of Design History*, 19.3 (2006), 185–96.
— *Domestic Space in Eighteenth-Century British Novels*. Basingstoke: Palgrave Macmillan, 2012.
— '"Enter into thy closet": Women, Closet Culture, and the Eighteenth-Century English Novel', in John Styles and Amanda Vickery (eds), *Gender, Taste, and Material Culture in Britain and North America: 1700–1830*. New Haven, CT: Yale University Press, 2006, pp. 107–22.
— '"I was also absent at my dairy-house": The Representation and Symbolic Function of the Dairy House in Samuel Richardson's Clarissa', *Eighteenth-Century Fiction*, 22.1 (2009), 29–48.

Lubey, Kathleen. 'Eliza Haywood's Amatory Aesthetic', *Eighteenth-Century Studies*, 39:3 (Spring 2006), 309–22.

Luhmann, Niklas. *Love as Passion: The Codification of Intimacy*. Cambridge, MA: Harvard University Press, 1986.

Macguire, Nancy Klein. 'The Duchess of Portsmouth: English Royal Consort and French Politician, 1670–85', in R. Malcolm Smuts (ed.), *The Stuart Court and Europe: Essays in Politics and Political Culture*. Cambridge: Cambridge University Press, 1996, pp. 247–73.

Manning, Susan. '"This Philosophical Melancholy": Style and Self in Boswell and Hume', in Greg Clingham (ed.), *New Light on Boswell: Critical and Historical Essays on the Occasion of the Bicentenary of* The Life of Johnson. Cambridge: Cambridge University Press, 1991, pp. 126–40.

Martin, Raymond and John Barresi. *Naturalization of the Soul: Self and Personal Identity in the Eighteenth Century*. London and New York: Routledge, 2000.

— *The Rise and Fall of Soul and Self: An Intellectual History of Personal Identity*. New York: Columbia University Press, 2006.

McCalman, Iain. 'Newgate in Revolution: Radical Enthusiasm and Romantic Counterculture', *Eighteenth Century Life*, 22 (1998), 95–110.

McKee, Patricia. 'Corresponding Freedoms: Language and the Self in *Pamela*', *English Literary History*, 52.3 (1985), 621–48.

McKeon, Michael. 'Richardson's *Pamela* and Political Allegory', in Lisa Zunshine and Jocelyn Harris (eds), *Approaches to Teaching the Novels of Samuel Richardson*. New York: Modern Language Association, 2006, pp. 100–5.

Monk, Samuel H. *The Sublime: A Study of Critical Theories in XVIII-Century England*. University of Michigan Press, 1960.

Moore, Leslie. *Beautiful Sublime: The Making of* Paradise Lost, *1701–1734*. Stanford, CA: Stanford University Press, 1990.

Müller, Patrick. *Latitudinarianism and Didacticism in Eighteenth-Century Literature: Moral Theology in Fielding, Sterne, and Goldsmith*. Frankfurt: Peter Lang, 2009.

Passmann, Dirk F. and Hermann J. Real. 'The Intellectual History of "Self-Love" and *Verses on the Death of Dr. Swift, D.S.P.D*', in Hermann J. Real (ed.), *Reading Swift: Papers from the Fifth Münster Symposium on Jonathan Swift*. Munich: Wilheim Fink, 2008, pp. 343–62.

Pontalis, J.-B. *Avant*. Paris: Gallimard, 2013.

Pope, Stephen. 'Expressive Individualism and True Self-Love: A Thomistic Perspective', *The Journal of Religion*, 71:3 (July 1991), 384–99.

Porter, Roy (ed.). *English Society in the Eighteenth Century*. Rev. edn. London: Penguin Books, 1990.

— *Rewriting the Self: Histories from the Renaissance to the Present*. London: Routledge, 1997.

Prince, Michael. *Philosophical Dialogue in the British Enlightenment: Theology, Aesthetics, and the Novel*. Cambridge: Cambridge University Press, 1996.

Quinney, Laura. 'Blake and His Contemporaries', in Robert DeMaria, Jr., Heesok Chang and Samantha Zacher (eds), *The Blackwell Companion to British Literature*, vol. 3. *Long Eighteenth Century Literature: 1650–1837*. Chichester and Malden, MA: Wiley-Blackwell, 2014, pp. 329–44.

Ricoeur, Paul. 'Narrative Identity', *Philosophy Today*, 35:1 (Spring 1991), 73–81.

— *Oneself as Another*. Chicago: University of Chicago Press, 1995.

— *The Course of Recognition*. Cambridge, MA: Harvard University Press, 2007.

Rivers, Isabel. 'Shaftesbury and the Defence of Natural Affection', *Reason, Grace and Sentiment. A Study of the Language of Religion and Ethics in England, 1660–1780*, vol. 2, *Shaftesbury to Hume*. Cambridge: Cambridge University Press, 2000, pp. 85–152.

Rodis-Lewis, Geneviève. *Le problème de l'inconscient et le cartésianisme*. Paris: Presses Universitaires de France, 1950.

Rogers, Pat. *Grub Street: Studies in a Subculture*. London: Methuen, 1972.

— *Literature and Popular Culture in Eighteenth-Century England*. Brighton: Harvester Wheatsheaf, 1985.

Røstvig, Maren-Sofie. *The Happy Man: 1700–1760*. Oslo: Norwegian University Press, 1962.

Roussel, Roy. 'Reflections on the Letter: The Reconciliation of Distance and Presence in *Pamela*', *English Literary History*, 41:3 (1974), 375–99.

Rumbold, Valerie. 'Cut the Caterwauling: Women Writers (Not) in Pope's *Dunciads*', *The Review of English Studies*, New Series, 52:208 (Nov. 2001), 524–39.

Sams, Henry W. 'Anti-Stoicism in Seventeenth- and Early Eighteenth-Century England', *Studies in Philology*, 41:1 (Jan. 1944), 65–78.

— 'Self-Love and the Doctrine of Work', *Journal of the History of Ideas*, 4:3 (June 1943), 320–32.

Schechtman, Marya. 'Memory and Identity', *Philosophical Studies*, 153:1 (2010), 65–79.

Scholtz, Gregory F. 'Anglicanism in the Age of Johnson: The Doctrine of Conditional Salvation', *Eighteenth-Century Studies*, 22:2 (1988–89), 182–207.

Scrivener, Michael. *Seditious Allegories: John Thelwall & Jacobin Writing*. University Park, PA: Pennsylvania State University Press, 2001.

Shifrin, Susan. '"At the end of the Walk by Madam Mazarines Lodgings": Si(gh)ting the Transgressive Woman in Accounts of the Restoration Court', in Susan Shifrin (ed.), *Women as Sites of Culture: Women's Roles in Cultural Formation from the Renaissance to the Twentieth Century*. Burlington, VT: Ashgate, 2002, pp. 195–205.

Shuger, Deborah. 'The "I" of the Beholder: Renaissance Mirrors and the Reflexive Mind', in Patricia Fumerton and Simon Hunt (eds), *Renaissance Culture and the Everyday*. Philadelphia: University of Philadelphia Press, 1999, pp. 21–41.

Sitter, John E. *The Poetry of Pope's* Dunciad. Minneapolis: University of Minnesota Press, 1971.

Smith, Philip A. 'Bishop Hall, "Our English Seneca"', *PMLA*, 63:4 (Dec. 1948), 1191–204.

Spacks, Patricia Meyer. *Imagining a Self: Autobiography and Novel in Eighteenth-Century England*. Cambridge, MA: Harvard University Press, 1976.

— *Privacy: Concealing the Eighteenth-Century Self*. Chicago: University of Chicago Press, 2003.

Spellman, W. M. 'Archbishop John Tillotson and the Meaning of Moralism', *Anglican and Episcopal History*, 56 (1987), 404–22.

— *The Latitudinarians and the Church of England*. Athens, GA; London: University of Georgia Press, 1993.

Spurr, John. *England in the 1670s: 'This Masquerading Age'*. Oxford: Blackwell, 2000.

Stallybrass, Peter, and Allon White, *The Politics and Poetics of Transgression*. London: Methuen, 1986.

Tancke, Ulrike. *'Bethinke Thy Selfe' in Early England. Writing Women's Identities*. Amsterdam; New York: Rodopi, 2010.

Taylor, Charles. *Sources of the Self: The Making of the Modern Identity*. Cambridge, MA: Harvard University Press, 1989.

Thiel, Udo. *The Early Modern Subject: Self-Consciousness and Personal Identity from Descartes to Hume*. Oxford: Oxford University Press, 2011.

Tierney-Hynes, Rebecca. 'Fictional Mechanics: Haywood, Reading, and the Passions', *The Eighteenth Century*, 51:1–2 (Spring/Summer 2010), 153–72.

Turner, James Grantham. *Libertines and Radicals in Early Modern London: Sexuality, Politics, and Literary Culture, 1630–1685*. Cambridge: Cambridge University Press, 2002.

Varey, Simon. *Space and the Eighteenth-Century Novel*. Cambridge: Cambridge University Press, 1990.

Weinberg, Shelley. 'Locke on Personal Identity'. *Philosophy Compass*, 6:6 (2011), 398–407.

Weiskel, Thomas. *The Romantic Sublime*. Baltimore, MD: Johns Hopkins University Press, 1976.
Williams, Carolyn D. 'Breaking Decorums: Belinda, Bays and Epic Effeminacy', in David Fairer (ed.), *Pope: New Contexts*. London; New York: Harvester Wheatsheaf, 1990, pp. 59–79.
Williamson, Marilyn L. *Raising Their Voices: British Women Writers, 1650–1750*. Detroit: Wayne State University Press, 1990.
Wynne, Sonya. 'The Mistresses of Charles II and Restoration Court Politics', in Eveline Cruickshanks (ed.), *The Stuart Courts*. Stroud: Sutton Publishing, 2000, pp. 171–90.
Zahavi, Amotz and Avishag Zahavi. *The Handicap Principle: A Missing Piece of Darwin's Puzzle*. New York: Oxford University Press, 1997.

Index

Abrams, M. H. 10–11
Adams, William 139–40
Addison, Joseph 104–7, 111, 147, 211, 213–15, 221
Aers, David 6
Ainslie, George 110
alienation 4, 18, 191–6, 201, 204, 206, 208
  see also existential alienation
altruism 17, 68, 70, 75, 80, 95, 101, 111
ambition 75–81 passim
Aquinas, Thomas 46–7
Argus, The 231, 234
Aristotle 50, 105, 192
Astell, Mary 29, 38
Augustine of Hippo 6, 11, 85, 90

Bakhtin, Mikhail 117, 182
Balibar, Étienne 8, 23n.31
Ballaster, Ros 73, 75, 78
Barbara Palmer, Countess of Castlemaine, Duchess of Cleveland 33
Barrell, John 236, 245n.12
Barresi, John *see* Martin, Raymond and John Barresi
Barrow, Isaac 3, 17, 46–54, 58n.56
Beale, Mary 30

Behn, Aphra 29, 37–9, 41
Bénichou, Paul 75–6
Blair, Rhonda 121–2, 126
Blake, William 3, 191–2, 205–8
  [First] Book of Urizen, The 205–6, 208
  Four Zoas, The 205–6
  Jerusalem 205
Blount, Martha 130
Bony, Alain 163–4
Book of Common Prayer 146
Boswell, James 18, 135–6, 138–48
  'Hypochondriack, The' 145–7
  journal 135–6, 141–7
  Life of Samuel Johnson, The 136, 139–40, 148
  No Abolition of Slavery 148
British Convention 232, 242
Bronson, Bertrand H. 138–9
Brooks-Davies, Douglas 122
Brower, Reuben 117
Bunyan, John
  Pilgrim's Progress, The 156
Burke, Edmund 210–23, 240
  Philosophical Enquiry, A 210, 212–23, 225n.16
Burkert, Walter 193
Butler, Joseph
  Analogy of Religion, The 4

263

INDEX

Calvinism 33, 45, 63
Campbell, Archibald
   Enquiry into the Original of Moral Virtue, An 70
capitalism 1, 7, 70, 118, 120, 129–30, 132
Carmichael, Gershom 66
carnivalesque 120, 122–4, 129–32
Carraud, Vincent 8
Castiglione, Baldassare 75
   Il libro del Cortegiano 75
Castle, Terry 168n.47
castration 126–8, 131
Catherine of Braganza 33
charity 2, 17, 46–7, 49–54
Charles II 17, 33–4, 37–40, 44
Chudleigh, Lady Mary 31
Cibber, Colley 118–19, 122, 124–8, 131
clarity 213–18
classical ideals 118–21, 124–6, 129–32
common sense 5, 13, 213, 220
Condillac, Étienne Bonnot de 62
confinement 153, 155, 157
consciousness 4, 6–7, 13, 60, 74, 107, 135, 146, 148, 155, 157, 159–61, 196–208 *passim*, 213, 218, 221, 223
   continuity of consciousness 170–2, 183
   labyrinth of consciousness 173
   see also self-consciousness
conversation 136, 139–40, 157, 174–5, 177–82
   inner conversation 174–7
Corneille, Pierre 76
costly signalling 17, 96, 103–4, 109, 111
Courcelle, Pierre 192
Cox, Stephen D. 210, 212
Crowther, Paul 223

Darwin, Charles 95, 100, 102
Defoe, Daniel
   Roxana 38

deformity 117–18, 127, 129, 131–2
DeMaria, Robert, Jr 149n.11
Dempster, George 144
Denham, John 147
Descartes, René 6
   Discours de la méthode 6
   Passions de l'âme, Les 62–3, 76–7, 92n.6
despair 40, 111, 136–9, 145–6, 156, 161, 193, 197, 206
Deutsch, Helen 117–18, 131–2
Diego, Hannah 143
Douglas, Mary 124
Dryden, John 27, 34, 36–7, 39, 41, 139
Du Plaisir, René
   Duchesse d'Estramène, La 84–5
   Sentiments sur les lettres et sur l'histoire avec des scrupules sur le style 85

Eaton, Daniel Isaac 231
Edinburgh 147, 232, 241
Eglinton, Alexander Montgomerie, 10th Earl of 144
Ellrodt, Robert 6, 20n.8
epistolary novel 151–64
Epstein, James 241
Erskine, Andrew 144
Erskine, Henry 232
Evelyn, John 38
evolution of cooperation 103–4, 109
evolutionary psychology 97, 100, 111
executions 143–4
existential alienation 192–207 *passim*
Ezell, Margaret J. M. 27–8, 32

Faulkner, Thomas 121–2, 126
fear 136–9, 144, 147
female self 151–64
Ferguson, Frances 217–22
Fielding, Henry 153
   Shamela 158

Finch, Anne 31
Fisher, Philip 103
Fox, Christopher 20n.7
Francus, Marilyn 121

'Gagging' Acts, or Two Acts (1795) 232, 245n.12
Gay, John *Beggar's Opera, The* 143
Gentileschi, Artemisia 30
George III 228, 233
Gerrald, Joseph 232
Glorious Revolution 7, 33, 239
Gnosticism 191–3, 197, 200–3, 206–8
Gregori, Flavio 186n.23
Gregory, Jeremy 149n.16
grotesque
　body 117–18, 125, 127–31
　female 117–18, 121–32
　goddesses 121–32
　male 125–8
　mothers 121–2, 125–32
　politics 118–20, 129
　topography 123–5
Gubar, Susan 121
Gwyn, Nell 34, 38–9

happiness 44–54, 77
Hartley, David 191
　Observations on Man 135
Harvey, William 120
Hawkins, John 140
Haywood, Eliza 17, 29, 130–1, 153
　Love in Excess 78–90
　Reflections on the Various Effects of Love 80
Heidegger, Martin 207
Herod Antipas of Judea 35, 37
Herodias 29, 35
Hess, Scott 120, 133n.8
Hill, Christopher 7
Hirschman, Albert O. 95
Hobbes, Thomas 61, 108–9
hope 138, 140
Hortense Mancini, Duchess of Mazarin 37–8

Hume, David 4, 13–14, 17, 61, 95, 101, 103, 109, 143, 146, 191, 213
　Treatise of Human Nature, A 13–14, 163–4
Hutcheson, Francis 17, 61–70
　Inquiry into the Original of our Ideas of Beauty and Virtue, An 61, 65
hyperbolic discounting 110

identity 170–85
idleness 139–40, 148
imagination 138, 141–3, 145–6, 156, 174–6, 179–80
Ingrassia, Catherine 128–30
inside/outside 152–64
introversion 152–3, 157, 164
Iser, Wolfgang 186n.20

James II 30, 38
James, William 98, 109
Jansenism 75–6, 90
John the Baptist 27–9, 32, 35–7
Johnson, Samuel 11, 18, 104–8, 111, 135–41, 143–8
　Dictionary 136, 147–8
　Rambler 137
　Rasselas 138
Johnstone, John 147
Jonas, Hans 192, 206–7
judgement 136, 139–40, 147–8, 174–6

Kant, Immanuel
　Critique of Judgement, The 220–3
　Groundwork of the Metaphysic of Morals, The 223
　moral law 223
Keats, John 14
Keroualle, Louise de, Duchess of Portsmouth 34, 37
Kierkegaard, Søren 191, 201
Killigrew, Anne 3, 16
　'My Rare Wit Killing Sin': *Poems of a Restoration Courtier* 27–43

King's Bench 242
Klein, Melanie 206
Kristeva, Julia 4, 117

La Fayette, Madame de
  Princesse de Clèves, La 84, 89–90
Latimer, Bonnie 165n.7
Latitudinarianism 2, 46–9, 54, 55n.6, 66
Le Vasseur, Thérèse 142–3
Lee, Nathaniel 36–7
Lely, Sir Peter 30, 34
Lewis, Paul 143–4
Libertinism 28, 32–4, 38–41
Locke, John 1–10, 16, 60–1, 63, 65, 74–5, 98, 191, 205, 212–16, 218, 224n.15
  Essay Concerning Human Understanding, An 3–4, 6, 60, 65, 74, 148, 170–3, 213
London 119–20, 123–5, 129–30, 143, 147
London Corresponding Society (LCS) 228–9, 232, 237, 242
London Magazine 145
Longinus
  On Sublimity 214–15
Louis XIV 34

Mack, Maynard 117
madness 4, 36–7, 122, 125, 138, 140
Malebranche, Nicolas
  De la recherche de la vérité 62, 85, 90
Mancini, Hortense, Duchess of Mazarin 37–8
Mandeville, Bernard
  Fable of the Bees, The 17, 60–70, 95–111
Manley, Delariviere 29, 38
Manning, Susan 146
Marcus Aurelius
  Meditations 174
Marivaux 85–8
  Réflexions sur l'esprit humain 87

Martin, Raymond and John Barresi 5, 11
  Naturalization of the Soul 11
  Rise and Fall of the Soul and Self, The 5
Marx, Karl 98
Mary of Modena 28, 30
maternity 121, 125–32
McKee, Patricia 152, 156, 167n.35, 167n.44
McKeon, Michael 165n.14
medicine 118, 120, 123–4, 127, 132
melancholy 122–3, 140–8
memory 170–4, 183
Merry, Robert 243
Milton, John 147, 211–13, 215, 220
  'L'Allegro' 217–18
  Paradise Lost 215–19
Montaigne, Michel de
  Essais 6
moral sense 2, 17, 65–9, 213
morality 152–3, 160, 162–4, 173–4, 178, 181
More, Hannah 236
Muir, Thomas 232, 241

National Convention, France 230–1, 241
Neoplatonism 18, 191, 207
Newgate 143, 230, 232–3

obscurity 212–18
Oppression!!! The Appeal of Captain Perry to the People of England (1795) 230, 232–42
Orphic religion 192–3, 207
Oswald, John 243
other (the) 179–80, 182–3

Paine, Thomas 228, 231, 240
  Rights of Man 228, 231
Pascal, Blaise
  Pensées 8–10
passion(s) 44–54, 62–70, 76–89, 95, 100, 153, 160, 174

pastoral comedy 151–2
Pepys, Samuel 38–9
Perry, Sampson 230–43
  Historical Sketch of the French Revolution, An 233, 240
personal identity 1, 3–7, 10–11, 16–17, 74, 146, 148, 163–4, 170–3, 178, 183, 205, 213
Philips, Katherine 27, 33, 38, 40
Pigott, Charles 229–30, 233, 235–6, 239, 241
Pirandello, Luigi 15
Pitt, William, the Younger 228–9, 241
place 151–64
Plato and Platonism 6, 76, 192–3, 201, 207
  Cratylus 192
  Phaedo 193
  Phaedrus 193
  Republic 193
Playfair, William 236
Pontalis, Jean-Bertrand 14–15
Pope, Alexander 9–10, 18, 117–32, 147
  alternative selves 118, 128, 130–2
  anti-self 121, 131–2
  Dunciad, The 18, 118, 120–32
  Essay on Man, An 9–10
  heroic self 131
  Rape of the Lock, The 123
  Windsor Forest 118, 125, 129
Porter, Roy 33
Priestley, Joseph
  Letters to a Philosophical Unbeliever 135
Prince, Michael 187n.25
Pufendorf, Samuel von 66
Pythagoras; Pythagoreanism 192–3

reason 6, 9, 22n.28, 37, 44–51, 55n.6, 66–7, 76–7, 80–1, 125, 137–8, 146–8, 171–2, 213, 221–3
Reid, Thomas 5

Richardson, Samuel 18, 151–64
  Clarissa 153
  Pamela 151–64
Ricoeur, Paul 181–3
Ridgway, James 231
Rodis-Lewis, Geneviève 77
Rogers, Pat 120, 124
Romanticism 2, 10–11, 16, 18, 148, 191–208
Rome 136
Rousseau, Jean-Jacques 142–3, 145
Royal Proclamation Against Seditious Writings (1792) 231–2
Rumbold, Valerie 133n.5, 134n.37

Salome 28–9, 34–8, 40
Schopenhauer, Arthur 208
Scrivener, Michael 238
Scudéry, Madeleine de
  Artamène ou le grand Cyrus 76, 86
  Mathilde d'Aguilar 76
self
  dialogical self 174–6, 178–9, 182–4
  divided self 172, 174–6, 185
  self-approbation 17, 69, 102
  self-assessment 140–1, 156
  self-awareness 2, 11, 117, 135, 137–9, 143, 146–8, 152, 157, 164, 184
  self-consciousness 4–5, 7–8, 170–85
  self-defence 19, 230–44 *passim*
  self-examination 141, 173–6, 182–3
  self-fashioning 117, 127, 155, 157
  selfhood 6–7, 21n.13, 151–64, 167n.35, 170–85, 191–4, 197, 205–7
  self-interest 17, 49, 51–3, 55n.15, 58n.56, 60, 64, 66–70, 75, 77, 80, 100–2
  self-knowledge 9, 173–6, 178, 181, 183–5, 210

INDEX

self-love 2, 8, 17, 22n.28, 44–54, 55n.11, 55n.15, 60–70, 75, 80–1, 101, 103
sensualism 212, 214, 217
sermons 44–54
sexuality 6, 28, 31, 33, 36–9, 79, 83, 95, 99, 104, 109, 121, 123–4, 126, 128, 131–2, 134n.37, 152–3, 159, 168n.47
Shaftesbury, Anthony Ashley Cooper, 3rd Earl of 61, 63–6, 69, 173–9
  Characteristics of Men, Manners, Opinions, Times 173–7
  Moralists, The 179
  Soliloquy, or Advice to an Author 174–6, 178
Shakespeare, William 3–4, 12, 124, 136, 139, 147
  Hamlet 4, 156
  King Lear 105–8, 111
  Macbeth 139
Sitter, John 123–7
Smith, Adam 2, 17, 70, 95–8, 101–4, 107–9, 111
Society for Constitutional Information (SCI) 228, 231, 243
Socrates 173–4, 192–3, 207
  Socratic dialogue 174, 178–9
space 151–64
Spacks, Patricia Meyer 163–4, 212
Spence, Thomas 231, 233
Stallybrass, Peter 117, 119
Sterne, Laurence 18, 170–85
  History of Jacob, The 172
  Life and Opinions of Tristram Shandy, Gentleman, The 18, 170–85
Stevens, Wallace 195
Stoicism 46, 55n.6, 61, 173–4
sublime
  astonishment and 214, 219
  beautiful and 211–14, 216, 220–2
  concepts of 212–15, 223

moral sublime 211–12, 220–3
reading and 211, 213–15, 218–19
rhetorical 212–20
sensual experience of 217
Swift, Jonathan 119, 121
Switzerland 142
Symonds, H. D. 233

Taine, Hippolyte 138–9
Tancke, Ulrike 20n.8
Tate, Nahum 105–7, 111
Taylor, Charles 6, 11, 61
Temple, William 144
Thelwall, John 232–3, 235–43
Thiel, Udo 20n.7
Thompson, E. P. 21n.25, 237
Tillotson, John 3, 17, 44–54
True Briton, The 234
Tyburn 144

United Britons 243
Utrecht 143
  Treaty of 118

Villedieu, Madame de 88
Voltaire (François-Marie Arouet) 142

Walker, Robert 147
Walpole, Robert 118–19
Ward, Ned
  London Spy, The 120
White, Allon 117, 119
Williams, Carolyn 127
Wilmot, John, Earl of Rochester
  Satyr Against Reason and Mankind 40
Wodehouse, Edmund 28
Wordsworth, William 3, 10–11, 14, 18, 191–208
  'Ode: Intimations of Immortality' 193–4, 197, 199–203, 206
  Prelude, The 195–9
  'Resolution and Independence' 197
  'Tintern Abbey' 194–6, 203–4